SPORTING JUSTICE

The Sta

WINDSOR, WEDNESDAY, SE

Chatham's Colorful Co

Sports

ER 4, 1935

ders for O.B.A.A. Honor

Ontario Baseball Association--Championships

League WESTERN COUNTIES BASEBALL ASSN. Series Intermediate "A"

Championship Team Chatham All Stars - Chatham, Ont. 1935

Player	Age	Players' Personal Signature
Gordon Milburn		
Bill Henson		
Marvin Wrightman		
Jas. L. Harding		Jas L. Harding
Wm. Crosby		
Lyle Johnson		Lyle Johnson
R.L.Talbot		R L Talbot
Earl Chase		Earl Chase
Wilfred Harding		Wilfred Harding
Jack Scott		Jack Scott
Geo. Benson		
Ferg Jenkins		Fergie Jenkins
Chas. Scott		Charles Scott
Stanton Robbins		
W. Shaugnosh		W. Shaugnosh
H. Murphy,		Harry Murphy
Gerald Browning		Gerald Browning
Wm Land		William La[illegible]
Lloyd Jenkins		Lloyd Jenkins
E. Ladd		[illegible]
Andrew Harding		Andrew Harding
K. Terrell		[illegible]
Ben Talbot		Ben Talbot

I certify that the above players signed O.B.A. Certificates on or before July 15th of this year and ha[ve] taken part in at least three league games as members of this team.

Certified Correct

WESTERN COUNTIES BASEBALL ASS[N.]

L. Prescott

SEC.-TR.

O.B.A. Secretary

League Secret[ary]

NOTE—To be made in Triplicate.
Minor Series fill in Player's Age.

Birth Certificates for Players of Minor Championship Clubs must accompany this form. One copy will be [re]turned after inspection.

Championship Clubs must produce a copy of this form "properly certified" at all O.B.A. Play-Down games [in] which they take part.

SPORTING JUSTICE

The Chatham Coloured All-Stars and Black Baseball in Southwestern Ontario, 1915–1958

MIRIAM WRIGHT

WLU PRESS
WILFRID LAURIER UNIVERSITY PRESS

LAURIER
Inspiring Lives.

This book has been published with the help of a grant from the Canadian Federation for the Humanities and Social Sciences, through the Awards to Scholarly Publications Program, using funds provided by the Social Sciences and Humanities Research Council of Canada. Wilfrid Laurier University Press acknowledges the support of the Canada Council for the Arts for our publishing program. We acknowledge the financial support of the Government of Canada through the Canada Book Fund for our publishing activities. Funding provided by the Government of Ontario and the Ontario Arts Council. This work was supported by the Research Support Fund.

Canada | Canada Council for the Arts / Conseil des arts du Canada | Ontario | Ontario Arts Council / Conseil des arts de l'Ontario

LIBRARY AND ARCHIVES CANADA CATALOGUING IN PUBLICATION DATA

Title: Sporting justice : the Chatham Coloured All-Stars and Black baseball in southwestern Ontario, 1915–1958 / Miriam Wright.
Names: Wright, Miriam Carol, 1964– author.
Description: Includes bibliographical references and index.
Identifiers: Canadiana (print) 20230168302 | Canadiana (ebook) 2023016899X
ISBN 9781771125840 (softcover) | ISBN 9781771125864 (PDF) | ISBN 9781771125857 (EPUB)
Subjects: LCSH: Chatham Coloured All-Stars (Baseball team) | LCSH: Baseball players, Black—Ontario—Chatham—History—20th century. | LCSH: Baseball—Ontario—Chatham—History—20th century.
Classification: LCC GV875.C43 W75 2023 | DDC 796.357/640971333—dc23

Cover and interior design by Lara Minja. Front cover image: Leddy Library Archives and Special Collections, F1033 (Wilfred "Boomer" Harding Collection), Scrapbook 1. This photograph is also in a scrapbook owned by the family of Earl "Flat" Chase.

Waterloo, Ontario, Canada
www.wlupress.wlu.ca

This book is printed on FSC® certified paper. It contains recycled materials and other controlled sources, is processed chlorine-free, and is manufactured using biogas energy.

Printed in Canada

FSC www.fsc.org MIX Paper from responsible sources FSC® C103567

Wilfrid Laurier University Press is located on the Haldimand Tract, part of the traditional territories of the Haudenosaunee, Anishnaabe, and Neutral Peoples. This land is part of the Dish with One Spoon Treaty between the Haudenosaunee and Anishnaabe Peoples and symbolizes the agreement to share, to protect our resources, and not to engage in conflict. We are grateful to the Indigenous Peoples who continue to care for and remain interconnected with this land. Through the work we publish in partnership with our authors, we seek to honour our local and larger community relationships, and to engage with the diversity of collective knowledge integral to responsible scholarly and cultural exchange.

CONTENTS

ACKNOWLEDGEMENTS

The idea for this book began while co-directing the public history project and website "Breaking the Colour Barrier: Wilfred 'Boomer' Harding and the Chatham Coloured All-Stars." That project would never have happened without the trust and generosity of Pat and Blake Harding, who were willing to share their carefully preserved scrapbooks on the Chatham Coloured All-Stars and sports career of their father and father-in-law, Wilfred "Boomer" Harding, as well as their time and commitment to see the project through. I never would have imagined a chance meeting at a history event I attended in Chatham in 2015 would lead to such a journey, but I am so grateful for it. I am privileged to have co-directed the project with colleagues in Leddy Library, University of Windsor, Heidi Jacobs and Dave Johnston, whose vision and expertise helped grow the project in ways I could not have done on my own. The support of the Chatham Sports Hall of Fame, the Chatham-Kent Black Historical Society and Black Mecca Museum, the Ontario Trillium Foundation, and the University of Windsor was instrumental, along with the many University of Windsor students and others who worked on it. A special thank you to all the families of the Chatham Coloured All-Stars who were willing to share their stories to make the history and memories of this team come to life once again.

As I turned to the book, I was grateful to have the help of Ron Leary, whose research assistance went far beyond what I might have expected or imagined. His keen eye and research instincts (along with his tolerance for reading newspapers on microfilm) helped me move the story backward and forward in time, tracking clues and finding answers. As well, his help getting the manuscript ready for publication was also invaluable. I had several great student research assistants including Joshua Deehan, Julienne Rousseau, and Willow Key. I also had other research help from Linda Bunn, who kindly volunteered to search early newspapers in Windsor and Essex County for reports on Black baseball teams. I received assistance from librarians and staff at the Chatham-Kent Black Historical Society and Black Mecca Museum (particularly Dorothy Wright Wallace and Samantha Meredith), the Chatham-Kent Public Library, the London Public Library's London Room, the Strathroy Public Library, the Chatham-Kent Museum, and the Canadian Baseball Hall of Fame and Museum. My sister Lisa Wright also retrieved a few sources for me in London, and helped me make connections to new avenues. Thanks also to Stacie Amo for the map of the East End. I am indebted to those who read earlier versions of my manuscript, including Pat and Blake Harding, Dorothy Wright Wallace and Samantha Meredith of the Chatham-Kent Black Historical Society and Black Mecca Museum, Ron Leary, my mother, Patricia Wright, and my partner, Robert Hong, whose historical eye and judgment were helpful at the right time. The anonymous reviewers for Wilfrid Laurier University Press provided valuable insights and suggestions, pointing me to new ideas, sources, and directions. I have appreciated the ongoing support and encouragement of Wilfrid Laurier University Press Senior Editor Siobhan McMenemy, as well as advice from Murray Tong, Alicia Chantal, and others from the production team. As always, Robert (Bob) Hong, my parents, Glen and Patricia Wright, and the rest of my family provided interest and encouragement as I moved through this project.

Finally, I wanted to say how gratifying it has been over the past few years to see so many people engage with the history of the Chatham Coloured All-Stars and the history of sport in Chatham's Black community. These are important stories, revealing much about the people who turned to sport to find joy in a difficult world, and sometimes, to change it.

ONTARIO
BASEBALL
AMATEUR
ASSOCIATION
CHAMPIONS

1

Introduction

On a late August day in 1947, ten former members of the Chatham Coloured All-Stars,[1] a Black men's baseball team, reunited in Chatham, Ontario's Stirling Park.[2] The All-Stars team, which had played in local and regional amateur baseball leagues in the 1930s, was playing again for the first time in seven years. Baseball and community recreation had long been a part of the history and culture of Black communities in southwestern Ontario. Wilfred Harding, one of the former members of the Chatham Coloured All-Stars, claimed years later that growing up in the 1920s and 1930s, baseball "was our life from morning pretty well to night."[3] As Harding explained, times were hard for young Black people, and playing baseball was "a release from it all for most of us. Gosh, what a great time we had we had."[4]

More than just providing welcome recreation, however, baseball, and sports, also became a path that led Black athletes into white spaces, pushing the boundaries of racial lines that were embedded in the society of interwar southwestern Ontario. Black baseball teams had been playing in the Chatham area for decades, but in 1933 the Chatham Coloured All-Stars were the first in the community to move into the primarily white world of organized amateur baseball. Joining a local city league affiliated with the provincial Ontario Baseball Amateur Association (OBAA), the All-Stars gained a profile and presence not obtained by earlier Black teams.[5] In 1934, they surprised many baseball observers when they won the OBAA Intermediate B title, the first and only known Black team to do so.[6] In the following years, the All-Stars moved into a more competitive circuit, and made the OBAA playoffs twice more before they disbanded.

During the 1947 reunion in Stirling Park, the All-Stars defeated their opponents, the Chatham Shermans, a white team that had won the 1946 provincial championship, by a score of 8–6.[7] According to the *Chatham Daily News*, the game, which attracted 3,500 fans, was a "crowd-pleasing affair with a little touch of everything but the 'Old Champions' had the edge on the play and deserved their win."[8] Starting pitcher for the All-Stars was Earl "Flat" Chase,[9] a North Buxton-born, Windsor, Ontario-raised player who had become a legend in regional baseball, remembered for his fastball pitches and fence-clearing home runs.[10] Catching for Chase was Donise Washington, one of two players from Detroit who moved to Chatham in 1934 for room and board, and a chance to play baseball. Washington, the *Chatham Daily News* assured its readers, "caught a good game." Playing shortstop was Washington's friend, fellow Detroiter Donald Tabron. According to the *Daily News,* Tabron got one run, two hits, and he "pulled a perfect double steal." Washington and Tabron had long since returned to the United States, but they both came back to play with the All-Stars one last time. On first base was Wilfred Harding, widely known in the community as "Boomer."[11] Harding was a multi-sport athlete, excelling in hockey, soccer, and track, and he would soon begin a long career in officiating.[12] He and his older brother, Leonard (Len), had carried the All-Stars through some challenging times in the years following their OBAA championship win. Their younger brother, Andrew (Andy), who joined the All-Stars later in the 1930s, was also on the field that day in 1947, taking a spot at centre field. On second base was another former teammate, Ross Talbot. He and his older brother Ben had been with the All-Stars from the team's first days in the Chatham City Baseball League in 1933. Likewise, Gouy Ladd, playing at right field, had been a reliable member of the team for as long as the All-Stars were together. Providing support on the field were three others who had played on both the All-Stars and another Black team from the 1940s, the Taylor Athletic Club (Taylor AC): Albert (Abie) Scott, Ken Milburn, and William (Bill) Crosby.[13]

That so many of the former Chatham Coloured All-Stars returned for the reunion game suggests the ties among the men ran deep. Hints of that camaraderie can be seen in a team photograph taken in the fall of 1934. Unlike many team portraits of that era, the men in the All-Stars photograph look relaxed, some with their hands resting on each others' shoulders. Their easy smiles and casual poses, however, belie the more complicated and contradictory experiences of this baseball team in a racialized world. As Black men in 1930s southwestern Ontario, their lives were shaped by race and class, which affected where they lived, the jobs they could get, the public places they could visit, and which sports teams they could join.[14] The very existence of all-Black baseball teams like the All-Stars reveals the segregated nature of sports in that era. As sports historian Colin Howell has argued, the sports history of non-white peoples "reflects their marginalization and segregation in a society that regarded separation on the basis of colour as a natural part of the internationally accepted moral order."[15]

Black baseball teams existed in southwestern Ontario since the late nineteenth century, and they had long been a central part of community life. Howell notes, "Baseball clubs were part of a network of sociopolitical institutions in black communities, including the church and various mutual-improvement societies, that promoted the community potential for creativity and self-improvement."[16] Rob Ruck, author of *Sandlot Seasons: Sport in Black Pittsburgh*, claims that sports helped unite diverse Black populations in the northern US in the early twentieth century.[17] Sport also "provided black Pittsburgh with a pleasant cultural counterpoint to the often grim experiences encountered at work and in the neighborhood."[18] He explained that on the sports field, Black Pittsburgh residents could "revel in their athletic grace and prowess."[19] Ornella Nzindukiyimana and Kevin Wamsley, bringing a much-needed emphasis on Black women's experiences of sport in interwar southern Ontario, remind us that male athletes had sisters, wives, and mothers who were also part of their world.[20] Sports were important in Black families and communities as it was "an institution upon which the community had a measure of control, was a source of strength and positivity."[21] Sports were part of community-building as family and friends supported each other in the parks and on the playing fields.

This book will explore that complex history, the connections between baseball, family and community, and baseball and social justice, all in the context of a capitalist, racialized, and racist society. While much of the public history and commemoration of the Chatham Coloured All-Stars has focused on the team's 1934 championship win,[22] this book will present a longer history of the team and its connection to Black baseball in southwestern Ontario and Michigan from 1915 to the 1950s. It begins with an earlier exhibition team, the Chatham Colored Giants, that laid a foundation

Fig. 1.1 (overleaf) ▪ Chatham Coloured All-Stars, taken in 1934. Back row, from left: Louis Pryor (coach), Gouy Ladd, Sagasta Harding, Wilfred "Boomer" Harding, Percy Parker (coach). Second row, from left: Hyle Robbins, Earl "Flat" Chase, Kingsley Terrell, Donise Washington, Donald Tabron, Ross Talbot, Clifford Olbey. Front row (seated on the floor), from left: Stanton Robbins, Jack Robinson (batboy), Len Harding. Photo credit: Leddy Library Archives and Special Collections, F1033 (Wilfred "Boomer" Harding Collection), Scrapbook 1.

Polish
HOME

for Black baseball in Chatham in the 1920s. The Chatham Coloured All-Stars, emerging in 1933, built on that legacy and were guided and supported in its first years by members of the older team. The book then follows the All-Stars, from their entry into the Chatham City Baseball League in 1933 to their run to the OBAA championship in 1934. After 1934, the All-Stars continued to advance, moving into a more competitive regional Western Counties Baseball Association (WCBA) league in the "Intermediate A" OBAA circuit, and reaching the provincial playoffs twice more before they disbanded after the 1940 season. By the end of the 1930s, the team had also become more independent and willing to speak about racist and unfair treatment they experienced. Even after the All-Stars stopped playing, former members were influential in local baseball. Several of the players were among the first Black men to play on white teams in Chatham, effectively beginning racial integration in baseball. They also supported and guided a new generation of Black baseball players through new Black teams, the Taylor AC (later renamed the Chatham Panthers), in the 1940s and 1950s.

In exploring this intergenerational baseball history, this book develops several themes, including the way racism manifested in the players' experiences on and off the field, the connection between sports and social justice, the Black diaspora and its impact on regional baseball, the economics and politics of amateur baseball, models of Black masculinity, and the way the players themselves, and their family members, remembered and made sense of that time in their lives. In developing both the narrative and themes, contemporary newspaper sources, as well as oral histories and newspaper interviews conducted with some of the former Chatham Coloured All-Stars players in the period from 1967 to 2001 are drawn on, as well as interviews conducted from 2016 to 2019 with friends and family members of the team.

While a more detailed discussion of those sources will be provided later in this chapter, I wanted to begin by noting the ways the history of race and racism is approached. As Victoria Paraschak has explained, "racist sporting spaces," exist where either participants or spectators "experience treatment as a racialized 'other' in sport."[23] With inequality on display, she explains, "sport becomes a space where the unequal race relations in the broader society are reinforced."[24] Playing in these primarily white leagues made the All-Stars, and their Black fans, vulnerable to racial conflict. Both oral history and contemporary newspaper sources suggest that racist insults, as well as physical altercations on the diamond and in the stands, were part of this team's everyday experiences. These sources, along with the socio-economic-political context of the time, are used to identify and reflect on the way race and racism affected them. In many cases, I can directly corroborate newspaper accounts with oral histories. Other times, however, the evidence requires speculation on the way race may have directly affected baseball games, drawing on newspaper accounts (themselves highly racialized, as they were written through the lens of white reporters) and supported through layering of what is known about the racial politics and conditions of the era.

Apart from providing insights into the everyday racial conflicts experienced by the Chatham Coloured All-Stars, the book will explore the specific ways that the Black members of the team, and the wider Black community of Chatham, were linked to a larger network of Black people in southwestern Ontario and across the border into the United States. As descendants of Black people who had arrived in southern Ontario under various circumstances, as enslaved people, as self-emancipated refugees from American slavery, or as free people migrating from the northern United States, the people of Chatham of the 1920s and 1930s continued to have strong cross-border ties, both economic and familial. These ties also had an impact on baseball, as Black teams from the United States interacted with Black players and teams in Chatham in their foundational years. Scholars of African-descended peoples of the Americas, including Paul Gilroy and Rinaldo Walcott have used the concept of "Black diaspora" or "Black Atlantic" to explore the ways that migration, movement, and crossing borders have been integral to Black identities, cultures, and experiences.[25] Walcott explains that in the Canadian context, the history of the "back and forth movements" of Black people across the Canada-US border in the nineteenth and twentieth centuries is particularly important. Other scholars, including Gamal Abdel-Shehid and Janelle Joseph, have explored sports and the Black diasporas in Canada.[26] Although focusing primarily on African Caribbean athletes and communities in Canada, their work suggests the significance of considering the fluidity of borders in the context of Black people and sport.

Thinking about Black diasporas in a Canadian context also leads to tracing the specific webs of connections of family and community that formed the heart of Black baseball in southwestern Ontario in the 1920s through the 1950s. The constellations of players who made up the Chatham Colored Giants, the Chatham Coloured All-Stars, and the Taylor AC/Panthers were linked to each other through family and community. Brothers, brothers-in law, uncles and nephews, and cousins were the foundations of these teams. These families in turn had ties to Black families and players in Detroit, and communities in southern Ontario including Windsor, North Buxton, Chatham, and London. These "genealogies of baseball" allow us to see not only how Black baseball teams grew and developed in southern Ontario, but also the ways that these familial and social networks were integral to the histories of Black communities. Baseball, as a social and cultural expression, allows us to see how those networks shaped the lives of Black people in the region.

Another theme explored in this book is the confluence of race and economics, and how a Black baseball team operated in a racialized, capitalistic environment. As Colin Howell has argued, sports, even amateur sports, are deeply embedded in capitalism.[27] Teams had to operate their clubs as businesses, raising money to pay for uniforms, diamond fees, and travel. Amateur clubs relied on the largesse of local business sponsors (if they could get them), as well as the admission fees they collected from spectators, to stay afloat. During the Great Depression, when competition for people's diminishing pocket change was fierce, attracting business sponsors and fans was a constant concern. As Black men in a racialized labour market, the Chatham Coloured All-Stars faced greater barriers in financing their own ball clubs, or in asking for business sponsors in the community. The worries and obstacles the All-Stars encountered in running their ball club were a constant feature throughout their eight years together.

At the same time, the racialized, capitalistic context of organized amateur baseball also led to the "commodification" of the Chatham Coloured All-Stars themselves. As a Black team in a largely white environment, they began attracting large crowds, particularly when they played out-of-town exhibition games. At a time when local baseball struggled to stay afloat financially, the team's ability to attract paying customers made them a valuable commodity in regional baseball circles. After winning their 1934 OBAA championship, the All-Stars were invited to join a newly-expanded WCBA in the southwestern Ontario baseball circuit. Organizers at the time identified them as a "money team" that could be counted on to bring needed cash into the league. Indeed, the team's "labour" was in demand, and white baseball organizers were aware of the financial benefits of allowing a Black team into their midst.[28]

Although the Chatham Coloured All-Stars encountered significant barriers, economic and social, as they took part in primarily white amateur baseball of southwestern Ontario, they grew increasingly confident over time. Indeed, by the later 1930s, the All-Stars became more vocal about unfairness and racism they experienced both on and off the field. They openly challenged local and provincial amateur baseball leadership. Their resistance in a white-dominated baseball environment suggests the links between sport and social justice. Sports scholars have drawn a clear line between the community-building aspects of sports in racialized communities and the fight for social justice. According to Ruck, that same sense of pride and identity also contributed to sports acting as a springboard for a growing political consciousness in Black communities. Sports provided a space for Black players to interact with and compete with white athletes, providing "a forum for symbolic political assertion and an arena for real political struggle."[29] Sport fostered a sense of self-esteem, and "energized black consciousness during the 1930s and 1940s in ways that went unmatched by other aspects of black life."[30] Like Ruck, Howell links emerging community identity and self-esteem through sports, and social and political struggles for social justice. Howell argues that sports contributed to community-building for both Black and Indigenous Peoples in early twentieth-century Atlantic Canada, but it was also "a focal point for cultural and political struggles involving human rights and racial equality."[31] Developing sports in Black and Indigenous communities propelled some athletes into white-dominated sports environments, "drawn inexorably into a large world of sport that at once valued their skills and required them to bear the reputations of their people."[32] Similarly, Nzindukiyimana and Wamsley, looking at young Black women athletes in early twentieth-century Ontario, argue that sports provided a space to interact with white schoolmates, providing opportunities for cross-racial interactions not possible in segregated recreational and social spaces.[33] As well, sportswriter Shakeia Taylor, exploring the history of post-American Civil War Black baseball clubs, asserts these enterprises were "a simple but clear request to be included. To be thought of as a full people, on a green field, with belief that baseball might mean something more. That we might all be entitled to something more."[34] The request for inclusion and the search for something more is at the heart of the history of the Chatham Coloured All-Stars.

Finally, this book explores the ways that the former Chatham Coloured All-Stars, as well as their families, have remembered and memorialized the history of this team. As Katharine Hodgkin and Susannah Radstone explain in *Contested Pasts*, memory is about shaping and making sense of the past in the present, with all its political and strategic and ethical consequences.[35] Moreover, individual memory is not just private but draws on "scraps and bits of knowledge and information from the surrounding culture, and is inserted into larger cultural narratives."[36] In the context of Black North Americans who are part of the Black diaspora, memory and oral history have been particularly significant. In *Remembering Jim Crow: African Americans Talk About Life in the Segregated South*, the editors William H. Chafe, Raymond Gavins, and Robert Korstad explore the vital role that oral history has played in the lives of Black people over the generations during and after enslavement.[37] With little recognition or validation of their history in mainstream society, oral tradition was a way to instill a sense of identity and value of being Black and part of the Black diaspora in the younger generations. Oral history and tradition also offered lessons on navigating a racist and sometimes dangerous environment, as well as celebrating and modelling resistance to it.

In various oral histories and newspaper interviews conducted with former Chatham Coloured All-Stars and their family members, they reflected on and gave meaning to their experiences over time. By remembering and talking about baseball players and baseball teams, the narrators revealed something of themselves, of how they processed racism and economic inequality. In the interviews, the former players, and their family members gave insights into the qualities and characteristics that they valued, that were part of the culture in which they were raised, and that still resonated with them decades later. The oral histories also allow us to explore the way people constructed the All-Stars and other Black baseball players as "heroes," and their meaning in the Black community. These depictions reflect models of Black, heterosexual masculinity which, as Janelle Joseph argues, sometimes serve as a counter to racist and racialized stereotypes found in white society.[38] Nearly eighty years after he had last seen them play, John Olbey, younger brother of Chatham Coloured All-Stars member Cliff Olbey, could still name and describe the players. He said, "I knew the team and they're very well etched in my memory."[39]

Sources and Methodology

This book draws its source material from contemporary newspapers and oral histories. Both were the central features of a public history project, "Breaking the Colour Barrier: Wilfred 'Boomer' Harding and the Chatham Coloured All-Stars" that I co-directed, along with my colleagues at University of Windsor's Leddy Library, Heidi Jacobs and Dave Johnston, in partnership with the Harding family, the Chatham Sports Hall of Fame, and the Chatham-Kent Black Historical Society.[40] We were first alerted to the richness of newspaper coverage of the Chatham Coloured All-Stars through the family scrapbooks of All-Stars player Wilfred "Boomer" Harding. Compiled by his daughter-in-law Patricia Harding, the scrapbook contained dozens of newspaper articles from the *Chatham Daily News* detailing the team's eight-year history and beyond. Many of the articles were originally clipped and saved by Sarah Harding, mother of Len, Boomer, and Andy, supplemented with other articles carefully researched and collected by Patricia. Through our work on the public history project, the families of Earl "Flat" Chase, Donald Tabron, and Ken and Wanda Milburn also graciously allowed us access to their own family scrapbooks.

These scrapbook collections revealed the care with which subsequent generations of the families held the history of the Chatham Coloured All-Stars. It also alerted us to the potential of using contemporary newspapers to gain perspectives on the team. The scrapbooks were an important starting point, and those of us working on the public history project subsequently turned to microfilm to collect the full newspaper coverage of the 1934 baseball season. In researching this book, the scope of newspaper analysis has expanded, not only focussing on the full length of the Chatham Coloured All-Stars' existence from 1933 to 1940, but also reaching back to the 1910s to look at earlier baseball in the community and forward into the 1950s to study later teams.

In analyzing the newspapers, I have been mindful of what they can and cannot reveal about the history of the Chatham Coloured All-Stars. At a basic level, they document the comings and goings of the team, their schedules, the baseball statistics, and details about the evolving roster of players. These accounts also offer insights into the way that the white press viewed, described, presented, and promoted the team. As Colin Howell notes, sports journalism expanded in the interwar years as sports became more commercialized.[41] Journalists, needing to engage audiences and sell newspapers, told stories and created narratives as they documented the games. Don Morrow and Kevin Wamsley also describe the rise of 1930s newspaper sports columnists who crafted distinct styles and identities, and sometimes drew on racist and racialized language in describing non-white athletes.[42] White sportswriters with the *Chatham Daily News* and other regional newspapers of the 1930s used those devices, as well as drawing on racialized, and sometimes overtly racist language to describe the Chatham Coloured All-Stars. The articles and columns they produced reveal much about white stereotypes and perceptions of Black masculinity, a topic examined by other sports scholars including Gamal Abdel-Shehid and Janelle Joseph, among others. Although the newspaper writers acknowledged the race of the athletes, they tended to downplay or ignore the historic nature of the All-Stars' story as the first Black team to win a provincial championship, along with other achievements. Sports historians looking at the ways newspapers in the 1930s and 1940s covered Black athletic achievements have also noticed this ignorance to race by white journalists.[43]

Although contemporary newspapers provide insights into the history of the Chatham Coloured All-Stars, the oral histories from the players and their family members illuminate their own experiences and memories of the team. This book draws on oral histories conducted in the early 1980s with former members of the All-Stars as well as other members of Chatham's Black community. In that same period, the former All-Stars spoke to newspaper reporters, providing more insights on their time with the team. The book also uses a few oral history interviews we conducted for the "Breaking the Colour Barrier" project, along with a related project Heidi Jacobs and I co-directed, "Telling the Stories of Race and Sport in Canada," co-sponsored by the University of Windsor, the Chatham-Kent Black Historical Society, and the Essex County Black Historical Research Society.[44] The way the memory of the All-Stars has been recalled and expressed by the second and third generations of the original team members is deserving of a fuller analysis, but it is outside the scope of this book.

The oral history interviews conducted in the early 1980s with the former All-Stars players were part of a larger project done in conjunction with the Ontario Black Historical Society (OBHS) and the Multicultural History Society of Ontario (MHSO). Over the course of the project, which spanned from the late 1970s to the early 1980s, several dozen interviews with Black narrators were conducted, with a number featuring residents of the Chatham area. These included former members of the Chatham Coloured

All-Stars Kingsley "King" Terrell, Wilfred "Boomer" Harding, and Ferguson Jenkins Sr. (father of former Major League Baseball pitcher and National Hall of Famer Ferguson "Fergie" Jenkins Jr.). Another Chatham resident, Ken Milburn, who played with the Taylor AC in the 1940s, was part of that project. Others interviewed included Beulah (Harding) Cuzzens and Wanda (Harding) Milburn, who were sisters of the All-Stars players Len, Boomer, and Andy. Wanda Milburn was married to Ken Milburn (noted above). Wanda Milburn and Vivian Chavis, who was from North Buxton, Raleigh Township, just a few miles from Chatham, conducted the interviews with the former Chatham Coloured All-Stars players. The MHSO project was one of many oral histories conducted throughout North America that sought to bring new voices into the historical record, including women, working-class people, and people from historically-marginalized ethnic or cultural groups.[45] The Chatham area project coincided with a growing interest in Black history in southwestern Ontario. Led largely by members of Black communities, the region saw several museums and historical societies founded in the 1960s and 1970s.[46] This group of interviews conducted with the former members of the Chatham Coloured All-Stars reflected this attempt to build and reclaim the Black history of the region.

In interpreting these interviews, I am mindful of Joan Sangster's essay on working-class oral histories where she discusses two distinct, yet often overlapping methodological approaches.[47] Historians of the working class and other groups often use oral history to get a sense of the experiences of the people they interview, and to get glimpses into the material conditions of their lives. Since the 1980s, historians inspired by postmodernist perspectives have turned to questions about memory, subjectivity, and identity, and have used that framework to interpret oral history sources. From this perspective, the emphasis was less on the content and more on how people told the stories of their lives. They looked at what they remembered, what they omitted, how they identified, and how they made sense of what had happened to them. Sangster argues that portraying these two approaches as exclusive to each other is misleading, as many historians incorporate both into their analyses. She notes, "Attentiveness to language and narrativity need not obscure the importance of 'the social' in the lives of our interviewees, for subjectivity is always embedded in social life: material context, coercion and consent, and power and ideology profoundly shape our lives, as well as the way we understand and recount them."[48] In exploring these MHSO oral history interviews, as well as the others, both the ways that people told their stories, and what they revealed about the very real context of life for Black people in mid-twentieth-century Ontario, are considered. Speaking in the wake of the 1960s civil rights era, the former players recalled their own experiences with racism and connected them to the broader discussions about race in North America during that period.

Particularly important in contextualizing the MHSO interviews is the role of Vivian Chavis and Wanda Milburn in conducting them. Both were open about why they thought the history of the Chatham Coloured All-Stars was important. At the end of their interview with Boomer Harding, Chavis turned to him and said:

> I think the Chatham All-Stars and Boomer Harding should be heard of all over Ontario because I think for too long the accomplishments of coloured people have not been made known. This is one of the aims of this group that I belong to, and your sister, Wanda, has willingly worked to help bring this story to light.[49]

Her politics laid bare, Chavis explained she aimed to share previously ignored histories of Black people. Likewise, Milburn, who had been an athlete herself in her youth,[50] summarized the history in this way: "The All-Stars were a coloured baseball team who played in the Depression years, and who made history, who had a lot of fun together, a lot of trouble together too."[51] The team's accomplishments were deserving of historical recognition, she insisted, and she also wanted to remind people of the young men who made that history, who loved to play ball, but also had to deal with the challenges of being Black in a racist world. As the editors of *Remembering Jim Crow* note, "The efforts of black elders to preserve community history and family heritage became powerful tools for maintaining dignity and hope in the grim presence of racial segregation. By talking about the past, African Americans used oral traditions to convey knowledge to the younger generations much as their slave forebears did."[52] Both Chavis and Milburn felt the story of the All-Stars, and the larger Black community in southwestern Ontario needed to be remembered and shared, and these interviews reflected this larger pattern among the North American Black diaspora.

In conducting their interviews, Chavis and Milburn made no pretense of being "objective" or "neutral" observers (as was once advised in older oral history methodologies). They knew their participants well, and they actively

Fig. 1.2 ▪ Wanda (Harding) Milburn (far left), with her fellow Senior Track Team members at the Kent Field Meet in 1940. Wanda Milburn said that playing sports was a way to connect with her white classmates. In 1980, she worked on the Multicultural History Society of Ontario's oral history project. She and Vivian Chavis interviewed several former members of the Chatham Coloured All-Stars. Photo courtesy of Frances Dungey.

engaged in conversation with them. They had witnessed many of the events the men were describing and they contributed their own memories and experiences. They were also forthcoming when asking questions about racism (although they used the term "prejudice" rather than "racism"). While someone not from the local Black community may have avoided asking questions about race so directly, these oral history interviewers did not, often prompting the men to describe their experiences in more detail. Chavis and Milburn were clearly actively involved in shaping these interviews and telling these stories. In fact, in Milburn's own interview, she described her experiences with challenging racist hiring policies that denied her a job in Chatham during World War II.[53] The former All-Stars players' willingness to speak about both their fondly-remembered experiences, as well as some of the more difficult or painful ones, can be attributed in part, to Chavis and Milburn's approach to the interviews.

Finally, the former players who spoke at length in various interviews offered similar, yet distinctive recollections of their years with the All-Stars. All the players involved with the MHSO project, Wilfred Harding, Kingsley Terrell, and Ferguson Jenkins Sr., spoke most warmly about their fellow players, suggesting the lingering significance of the camaraderie and bonds among them decades later.[54] Of all the players, Harding was the most forthcoming about the racial politics of sport, perhaps reflecting his experiences playing in other white-dominated games like hockey and soccer. Hockey as a sport has been notoriously resistant to accepting non-white players, and perhaps his time with the game gave him broader perspectives. Jenkins also spoke freely about racism, and through travels for work he had seen first-hand the stark segregation in the US South in the 1940s and 1950s. Kingsley Terrell's interview suggests he was less interested in speaking about racism, although he did discuss it when asked. What came across most strongly in his interview was his love of baseball itself. He spoke in great detail about his favourite baseball moments, and about the skills and traits of his fellow players.

The Chatham Coloured All-Stars emerged out of a racialized, class-based environment. Pushed to the margins in employment, discouraged from participating in many areas of public life, many Black people found an outlet through sports. Traditions of playing baseball in the Black community date to the late nineteenth century, and the Chatham Coloured All-Stars drew on this older history. In forming a team and joining the Chatham City Baseball League, however, the Chatham Coloured All-Stars were moving into "white" spaces, which also made them vulnerable to racist conflict. They also had to navigate a capitalist environment, to raise money and attract paying spectators. As they developed a fan base, local and regional baseball organizers came to rely on the All-Stars to revive the sport that had fallen on hard times during the Depression. Despite the pressures, the All-Stars became more confident over time, and comfortable demanding equitable treatment from baseball organizations. By the late 1930s, they were speaking directly to the local press, mirroring actions of other Black groups in the region seeking civil rights, and social and economic justice. After the team disbanded following the 1940 season, the former members of the All-Stars continued to influence and support Black baseball in Chatham. Indeed, decades after they last played together, former members of the team and their family members, continued to reflect on the significance and meaning of those All-Stars' years.

This book spans three generations of Black baseball in the Chatham area, with a primary focus on the Chatham Coloured All-Stars in the 1930s. The book begins (in Chapter 2) with a brief history and profile of the Black population of Chatham's East End in the 1920s and 1930s. It explores life in the working-class neighbourhood, how people earned a living and supported families, and the role of baseball and recreation in their lives. Chapter 3 then turns to the larger history of Black baseball in North America, and the emergence of a Black baseball team, the Chatham Colored Giants, that modelled itself, in part, on Black baseball traditions. Appearing first in 1915, and then regrouping in the mid-1920s, the Colored Giants were part of a network of Black baseball that included teams and players from North Buxton, London, and Detroit. The team is important to the Chatham Coloured All-Stars' history in that it established a presence and visibility for Black baseball in Chatham in the 1920s which revived when the newer team emerged in the 1930s. The older team also provided leadership and experience to the All-Stars. Chapter 4 turns to the origins of the Chatham Coloured All-Stars and its connections to the older Black baseball teams. Unlike the Colored Giants, however, the Chatham Coloured All-Stars were invited into the white amateur city baseball league. This chapter looks at how and why that happened, and examines the overall context of baseball in the city. By the early 1930s, organized baseball was declining, and including a Black team was part of an attempt to revive the sport in the city. The chapter also introduces the players and their connections with other baseball families and teams in the region. Chapter 5 continues the history into the 1934 season, as the team added more players and developed an identity. As the All-Stars gained the spotlight, winning all but one of their regular season games, they also attracted the attention of white sportswriters who both celebrated their talents and portrayed them in racialized and racist ways. In Chapter 6, the team's experiences in the 1934 OBAA playoffs leading to their final championship win are explored. Contemporary newspaper accounts as well as oral histories provide insights into the controversies, racial conflicts, and politics of competing in the OBAA. Chapter 7 looks at the year following the All-Stars' OBAA championship win, as the team was invited into a more competitive baseball circuit in the WCBA with teams from London, Sarnia, Strathroy, and Wallaceburg. While regional baseball organizers wanted the All-Stars to attract audiences and help bring money to the league, the team continued to face racism and financial challenges. Chapter 8 follows the All-Stars in the later 1930s, focussing on the increased confidence they showed, and their willingness to challenge both the city league and Ontario Baseball Association (the OBAA became the OBA in 1939) officials when they experienced inequitable and racist treatment. Significant about this period was the way the team took their complaints to the public, using the media to garner support. In the late 1930s, other southern Ontario Black organizations made claims for equity and fairness in other areas of life. In this way, the team's growing outspokenness reflected a wider movement for change. Although the team disbanded after the 1940 season, the former members of the All-Stars continued to influence baseball in Chatham. Chapter 9 looks at the role that the All-Stars played in both integrating community baseball in the 1940s, and their creation and support of a new Black baseball team, the Taylor AC/ Panthers. The concluding chapter reflects on memory, and how some of the former Chatham Coloured All-Stars themselves spoke about each other, and their experiences, decades after they had last played together. It pays attention to the evolution of memory—the ways that the players and their families reflected on, and gave meaning to, their experiences over time in the context of a changing awareness of Black history and social justice.

2

Living in a Racialized World

Chatham's East End and the Black Community in the 1920s and 1930s

The history of Chatham's Black baseball teams (and women's softball teams) is tied to the larger history of the Black community in Chatham's "East End" neighbourhood. Located just east of the main downtown area, bounded by McGregor Creek (a Thames River tributary) to the north, and the Canadian National Railway tracks to the south, the neighbourhood was home to almost all the city's Black population. In 1921, just over 400 Black people lived in Chatham, a city of 13,256.[1] A mixed residential, commercial, and industrial neighbourhood, the East End's modest frame houses contrasted starkly with the grand brick homes in the city's middle-class districts. As Carmen Poole writes in her doctoral thesis, "the East End was 'experienced;' its aesthetic was and is distinct, you 'knew' when you were 'crossing the tracks.' It was as physical a boundary as it was metaphorical."[2]

Besides being physically and aesthetically distinct from the rest of Chatham, the East End was also a racialized space, a result of decades of discrimination in this southwestern Ontario community. Barrington Walker, in his study of Black people and the legal system in nineteenth and early twentieth-century Ontario, describes the East End as a "'hot spot,' a site of intraclass and interracial conflict."[3] Indeed, the lives of the Black residents of the East End, like those throughout North America, were shaped by race and class. Walker, Constance Backhouse, James St. G. Walker, and other scholars have documented and explained the specific ways that race was embedded in the social, economic, political, and legal systems in Canada.[4] James Walker observes, "In virtually every one of the areas of life and death, African Canadians, too, experienced exclusion and separation from mainstream institutions, amounting to a Canadian version of 'Jim Crow.'"[5] Barrington Walker further describes its broad impact, saying:

> In many parts of Canada, just as in the antebellum South, Blacks tended to live in segregated neighbourhoods that were supported by restrictive covenants, could be barred from private establishments such as pubs and theatres, or could find themselves subject to segregation in these publicly accessed private establishments. Blacks also had to contend with a gendered labour market segmented and stratified along racial lines.[6]

These racial lines and barriers were upheld by both custom and legal means, although Barrington Walker notes that in Canada the legal avenue was less entrenched than in the United States. Nevertheless, in the 1930s and 1940s, Canadian law tended to support the right of private businesses, such as hotels and restaurants, to discriminate.[7]

While the concentration of the Black population in Chatham's East End was a result of decades of racism, the neighbourhood also provided a basis for community support. Poole argues the East End was "a remarkable testament to community" providing a "fascinating entry into understanding the ways in which space becomes racialized and the manner in which the individuals who occupy those spaces respond to civic, social, and economic marginalization."[8] Poole's work explores the history of community institutions in the East End including Black churches, the J.G. Taylor Community Centre on King Street East, and the Black chapter of the Masonic Lodge. At a time when Black people faced racial discrimination in all areas of their lives, local Black institutions offered support and community connections. This included sports and recreational activities which, as sports historians Colin Howell, Rob Ruck, Ornella Nzindukiyimana, Kevin Wamsley, and others have explained, were a source of community-building, as well as relief from the daily pressures of racism.[9]

Many of the Black people from the East End came from families who had been living in what is now southwestern Ontario for several generations. The first Black people in the area would have been enslaved, arriving in the eighteenth century with white enslavers from what is now the United States or other British Atlantic colonies. As historian Natasha Henry notes, at least 500 enslaved Black people lived in Upper Canada before the British enacted the Slavery Abolition Act in 1834.[10] In the first half of the nineteenth

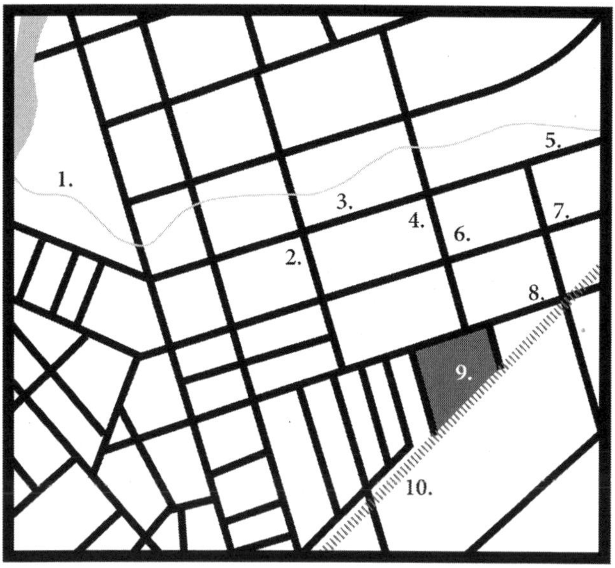

1. McGregor Creek
2. AME Church
3. First Baptist Church
4. JG Taylor Community Centre
5. King St. East
6. BME Church
7. Wellington St. East
8. Park Street
9. Stirling Park
10. Railway tracks

Fig. 2.1 ▪ Map of Chatham's "East End" neighbourhood. Photo credit: Stacie Amo, based on two maps: Government of Canada, Ministry of Natural Resources, Chatham (East), 1963, Map sheet 040J08, ed. 4; Department of Militia and Defence, Chatham, Ontario Map sheet 040J08 [ed. 3] 1934, digitized by Ontario Council of University Libraries, Historical Topographical Map Digitization Project.

century, more Black migrants came from the United States, either as self-emancipated people fleeing slavery, or as free Black people.[11] In the 1840s, two communities near Chatham were founded for American Black settlers including the Elgin Settlement at North Buxton, Raleigh Township, and Dawn, near present-day Dresden, Ontario. Other Black American migrants arrived after the US enacted the Fugitive Slave Act in 1850. This Act enabled white enslavers to travel into "free" states to capture the formerly enslaved and return them to the American South where chattel slavery was still legal. With this added threat to their security, many more Black people crossed the US border into British North America.

By the 1850s, Black people were finding their way to Chatham, a growing agricultural and transportation hub located on the Thames River in what is now southwestern Ontario. In 1861, just over 1,200 Black people lived in Chatham, comprising one-third of the community's total population.[12] As Carmen Poole observes, with Detroit just fifty miles away, Chatham became a social and intellectual centre, attracting both working-class and middle-class Black people.[13] Among the more well-known mid-nineteenth century middle-class Black residents was Mary Ann Shadd, educator, abolitionist, and the first Black female newspaper publisher in North America.[14] As a sign of the community's significance in the North American Black diaspora of the nineteenth century, when American abolitionist John Brown was organizing his 1859 raid on Harper's Ferry, Virginia, he came to Chatham to speak to people and ask for support. In the years after the American Civil War, however, Chatham's Black population began to decline. Some Black Chatham residents returned to the United States, and others left for opportunities elsewhere in Ontario.[15] By 1871, Chatham's Black population had fallen by over half.[16]

Although the end of the US Civil War had a big impact on the Black population in Chatham, the city's Black residents retained strong ties to the United States. Poole notes that despite assumptions that all American Black immigration stopped after the Civil War, Black people continued to move to Chatham from the United States, but in much smaller numbers. According to the 1921 census, 17 percent of Chatham's Black residents were American-born, with the majority arriving after the end of the Civil War. Additionally, many Black families were just one generation removed from the United States. In 1921, 52 percent of all adults (including heads of household, wives of heads of household, other adult relatives, and boarders) had at least one US-born parent. A full 44 percent reported that both their parents were born in the United States. The *Dawn of Tomorrow* newspaper, a Black-owned publication founded in London, Ontario in the 1920s, also provides clues to the continued ties to the United States.[17] A regular feature in the paper were the community "Notes," short columns with details of family news. The Chatham columns, like those from other Black communities in southwestern Ontario, contained many accounts of families receiving visitors from the United States. As well, the notes reported Chatham residents spending time in the United States either for visits or for work. Clearly, the Black people of Chatham had always been, and continued to be, deeply connected to Black people and communities on the other side of the Canada-US border.

Besides being affected by their ties and close proximity to the United States, the lives of the Black residents of Chatham were also shaped by the racialized, working-class environment where they lived. The East End was a neighbourhood where railway and industrial noises mingled with the effluent from nearby factories, hog pens, and fat-rendering operations.[18]

East End residents had complained to city council for years about the noise and smells, but as Poole remarks, classist and racist attitudes meant their concerns were largely ignored. In being marginalized, the East End resembled other Black neighbourhoods or Black-concentrated areas in Canada, such as Africville in Halifax, Nova Scotia, or the McDougall Street Corridor in nearby Windsor, Ontario.[19]

As a group, the Black people living in the East End had limited ability to earn enough money to support their families. As sociologist Tracey Adams notes, in a racist and class-based society, Black people have historically been relegated to the lowest-waged jobs available.[20] In the 1921 Canada census, just over half (51 percent) of Black adult men living in the East End were classed as "labourers."[21] In most cases, the enumerators did not give more details, but "labourers" may have included casual work, manual labour, and perhaps janitorial or factory work. Another 15 percent of Black men were identified as working in the "skilled" building trades, including carpentry and metal working. Another large occupation category for Black East End men was the service sector, at 18 percent, which included domestic work (working as drivers or cooks for wealthy families) and working in hotels. Only seven Black men declared occupations considered middle class, and five of these were clergymen, one was a book clerk and the other was a shopkeeper.

Black women worked in low-paying jobs to support their families as well. Information from the 1921 census suggests Black women in Chatham were much more likely than their non-Black counterparts to be part of the paid labour force. While nearly 25 percent of Black adult women living in the East End declared occupations, only 15.5 percent of Canadian women as a whole did.[22] As Peggy Bristow argues, historically, Black women in Chatham and nearby North Buxton were vital to the economic survival of their families.[23] She also notes that the census tended to under-count much of Black women's labour, which often included taking in washing or sewing, or serving as a midwife. Of those declaring occupations in Chatham in 1921, the majority (69 percent) worked in the service sector, which tended to be low-wage occupations.[24] Most were domestic servants, or in related areas such as laundry work and food service. A higher percentage of Black women than Black men had jobs in clerical or professional areas (21 percent), but these were largely in relatively low-paying jobs such as teaching, and office work. According to Dionne Brand, Chatham factories, with their higher-paying jobs, did not begin hiring Black women until World War II.[25] For

Black women in Chatham's East End in the interwar years, options for supporting their families remained limited.

In a 1980 oral history interview, Ken Milburn spoke about the lack of work available to young men in the 1930s. He claimed in those years all there was for "a young coloured fellow to do at that particular time was work in a hotel. There was a few other jobs... A couple of the families was working for some millionaires, but they were housemen. They were chauffeurs and such."[26] Milburn also added that those who carried luggage and shined shoes for guests did not receive wages, but were expected to work for tips only. At least three of the Chatham Coloured All-Stars, King Terrell, and Len and Boomer Harding, worked at the William Pitt Hotel, the largest hotel in the city.[27] For young Black women in that period, the options were even more limited. Wanda Milburn recalled she and her Black female friends could not get after-school jobs in dime stores the way their white classmates did.[28] Instead, she worked for a friend's mother, helping out in the kitchen on weekends.

The Black people living in Chatham's East End were also not welcome in some of the city's businesses and services well into the 1950s, an experience they shared with Black people across North America.[29] Pauline Parker Miller, daughter of former manager of the Chatham Coloured All-Stars Joseph Parker, recalled that the only hotel in Chatham that served Black people was the Merrill, located on King Street West, just outside the East End.[30] Ken Milburn confirmed that point, saying he never saw a Black customer while he worked at the William Pitt Hotel in the 1930s.[31] Beulah Cuzzens recalled, "it was unheard of to eat in a restaurant in Chatham."[32] As well, she noted, Chatham's movie theatres, the Griffin and the Princess, both had separate sections for Black ticket holders. She added that such racial segregation "was general all over Canada."[33] Parker Miller recalled that personal services like hairdressing and barbering were also divided by race.[34] Her father was also a barber who catered to the local Black population.

Racism also affected Black people's experiences at the city's schools. While Chatham public schools had been integrated since the 1890s, life could still be difficult for Black students. Cuzzens spoke about the racism at the schools in the early 1920s, and recalled one principal who would threaten to punish a whole group of Black students if he suspected just one of wrongdoing.[35] Cuzzens claimed she encountered racism from the white students as well, but added that she dealt with it by pushing back. She said, "if you could fight, you got along a little bit better. Not fighting all the time, but just fighting to make them know that you were a person."[36] Cuzzens's younger sister Wanda Milburn stated she had an easier time at school in the 1930s than her older sisters did in the 1920s. She was involved with the school track team, which she said made it easier to interact with her white peers. Still, she noted, both race and class had an impact on her experience at school. She explained, "there definitely was a lot of prejudice. We were accepted in some lights, but yet there was a class distinction, if not just in colour."[37]

The Harding family, integral to the story of the Chatham Coloured All-Stars, was in some ways typical of many of the Black families of the East End. Living on Wellington Street East, Andrew Harding Sr. and his wife Sarah (Holmes) raised a family of eight children: Florence, Georgina, Beulah, Carl, Leonard (Len), Wilfred (Boomer), Andrew (Andy), and Wanda.[38] Andrew Sr. (known in the community as Bill) was born in the late 1860s in North Buxton to Andrew J. and Frances Harding. His parents had both come to Canada from the United States, possibly Kentucky, sometime before 1865.[39] Unlike most Black men in the East End, however, Andrew Harding Sr. was married to a white woman. He and Sarah were one of just a few interracial couples in the East End during that period.[40] According to their daughter Wanda, her parents met while her mother was living with relatives at a farm where Andrew was working.[41] Both Beulah and Wanda claimed their mother's family opposed the union, but the marriage lasted; they spent the rest of their lives together.[42] Beulah, addressing what it was like for her mother marrying a Black man, indicated that her mother tried to fit into the Black community by joining the local Black Baptist church and helping out by playing the organ. Beulah claimed, however, that despite having an interracial background, the Harding children saw themselves as Black. "We became Black children, not half-white, not half-Black, we became Black. And we were raised in the community to always take pride in our Black family."[43]

Like most Black men in the East End, Andrew Harding Sr. provided for his family as a labourer.[44] For years he drove a horse and wagon daily to Erieau, eighteen miles southwest of Chatham on Lake Erie, to pick up coal from the laker boats. According to his grandson Blake Harding (son of Boomer), the family gained a work ethic from Andrew Sr., who sometimes took his sons with him on his trips to the lake. Blake recounted that "my dad recalls stories of going out there in the wintertime and how cold it was. And Erieau's not that far by car, but it's a long way by horse and wagon."[45] Blake claimed his grandmother encouraged her children to get an education. One of Andrew and Sarah's daughters, Beulah, received teacher education at the London Normal School and taught school in Essex and Kent counties for many years.[46] Her older sister Georgina worked as a stenographer and legal secretary, first for Frederick Davis,[47] a Black lawyer in Amherstburg, Ontario, and then for a Black law firm in Detroit.[48] She may have gone to Detroit because of the challenges she would have faced as a Black legal secretary looking for work in a white-owned law firm in rural southwestern Ontario in the 1920s.[49]

The way the Harding siblings spoke about their oldest brother, Carl, offers insights into the contradictory ways that unspoken racial lines worked in the community. Beulah, Wanda, and Boomer all explained that Carl had relatively light skin, which gave him access to opportunities and jobs denied his other family members.[50] They claimed that people knew he was Black—as Milburn noted, "He [Carl] would ride with my dad and there was all the difference in the world because my dad was very dark. And yet everybody still knew—we were a small town—and everybody still knew that he was a Harding."[51] The siblings suggested that simply by appearing white (or less "Black") Carl could straddle a racial line in the community. For example, Beulah said Carl could get into the "white" section of the movie theatre with his white friends, unless an usher found him and made him move.[52] She recalled her sister Georgina, whom she called a "fighter" encouraged him to defy the usher and remain in his seat. Their sister Wanda stated that Carl's lighter skin meant he could get better jobs than his father and brothers, like working in a garage.[53] Boomer spoke about Carl having sports opportunities that he himself did not, saying in a 1980 interview, "He was allowed to play with—having white skin—the Maroons" (Chatham hockey team).[54] While acknowledging that Carl had some access to the world of white privilege, the siblings spoke affectionately about him. As well, Beulah claimed that Carl's greater earning power meant he could help her financially when she attended the Normal School in London.[55]

While racism restricted the lives of Black people in Chatham in many ways, Stirling Park, a small green space located in the East End, was central for the Black community. Black people who grew up in the East End in the interwar years spoke fondly about this park where the Chatham Coloured All-Stars were formed and played. It was not initially a city-owned park, but was built on land owned and then donated for that purpose by a local white resident, Archie Stirling. Stirling had grown up in the East End, son of a Scottish immigrant father who worked as a clerk, and a mother from Kent County.[56] The 1921 census indicates that Stirling owned a grocery store (later turned into a drugstore and confectionary), a business located on Park Street in the East End.[57] The Stirling family also owned a piece of land behind Scane Street, by the Canadian National Railway tracks. Sometime before 1921, Stirling decided to use the land to make a park, and approached the Imperial Oil Company about donating some land adjacent to the property Stirling owned for the project. According to J.F. Perkins, district supervisor for Imperial Oil, Stirling financed the building of a baseball diamond and swimming pool on the land himself.[58] Originally called the "Stirling-Imperial Athletic Park" during the 1920s, it was managed by the Stirling-Imperial Association committee, comprised mainly of white, middle-class Chatham residents, including Stirling and Perkins.[59] By the early 1930s, the park had been transferred to the city of Chatham and was subsequently known as Stirling Park.

Fig. 2.2 ▪ Baseball game at Stirling Park, 1925. The team playing was likely the Stirling-Imperials or the Stirling-Imperial Juniors, who both played in the park in that period. The Junior team had a couple of Black players, but these teams were largely white. Railcars sitting on the tracks are visible at the back of the park. Photo credit: Chatham-Kent Museum 1982. 1.61C.

Stirling's lifelong attachment to baseball helps explain why he went to such lengths to create a park and baseball diamond in the East End.[60] His fascination is apparent in a short history of the game in the city he wrote which appeared in a Victoria Day baseball program in 1961.[61] A meticulous record of leagues, teams, and players dating to the 1890s, Stirling's account also recalled the city's ball parks, including those that had disappeared with housing or industrial developments in the intervening years. Stirling made use of the park he founded to organize the city's first minor baseball league for boys in the early 1920s. He also managed two teams for older youth and adults, the Stirling-Imperials and the Stirling-Imperial Juniors (under 20 years), both teams named after the park where they played. Stirling continued to be involved in community baseball throughout his life, serving as the local representative (and later, president) of the OBAA/OBA for many years. Nicknamed "Mr. Baseball," Stirling was later inducted into the Chatham Sports Hall of Fame.

While Stirling's love of baseball was critical to the creation of Stirling Park, the project, supported by Imperial Oil, was also reflective of a larger late-nineteenth, early twentieth-century North American sport and recreation movement led by the white middle class and aimed at working-class youth. Concerned about both the health and behaviour of young people, philanthropists and middle-class organizations saw sport as a way to discipline and groom working-class youth (boys and young men in particular) for life in modern industrial environments.[62] Groups such as the YMCA and amateur sport organizations sought to steer young men away from drinking, gambling, damaging property, and political radicalism, which they saw as counter-productive to civic life. Indeed, in a 1925 *Chatham Daily News* article, Imperial Oil representative J.F. Perkins praised Stirling for creating a park "where there were no facilities for keeping the children and young people off the streets."[63] Perkins's remarks about keeping youth "off the streets" suggest the concerns of the middle class in general, and perhaps East End business owners in particular, about the leisure-time activities of working-class youth. In fact, on the very same page as the *Chatham Daily News* article about Stirling Park was a piece entitled "Boys' Pranks Are Dangerous" outlining incidents reportedly involving East End boys.[64] Employing an alarmist tone, the article decried the behaviour of the young men who the author claimed were "operating slingshots and catapults with deadly aim," and loosening the nuts and bolts holding seats together at the Griffin movie theatre. Although the article did not identify the race of the boys, community knowledge of the East End's Black population would have fuelled the negative classicist and racist assumptions about the boys in that neighbourhood. Indeed, such attitudes and concerns about boys—both Black and white—in the East End may well have contributed to Imperial Oil's support of the Stirling-Imperial Park project.

An example of the Stirling-Imperial Association's outreach in the 1920s was the annual family sports day.[65] First held in 1921, the event continued through at least 1925. The day featured baseball games along with races and athletic events for all ages, with local merchants providing prizes. The *Chatham Daily News* coverage of the event suggests that Black people (mostly children) were indeed participating in the sports events. Apart from sports, generally the only times that Black people were mentioned in the community newspaper was if they had been charged with a crime. Sports day, however, presented Black people in a relatively positive way. In 1924, for example, future Chatham Coloured All-Star, 11-year-old Len Harding won races in two age categories, while Ethel Freeman, who would later marry Cliff Olbey, one of Harding's All-Star teammates, won one race and came second in another.[66] Harding collected his prizes, a baseball and a flashlight, while Freeman won two boxes of chocolates. During that same sports day, eldest Harding brother Carl, a member of the primarily white Stirling-Imperial Juniors baseball team, earned praise from a *Chatham Daily News* reporter who claimed the 13-year-old's playing was the "game's feature."[67] Harding, the reporter remarked, was "the smallest fellow on the field" who nevertheless made some "snappy catches," including one where "he backed up to the stand to catch a foul ball, and on which, no person seemed to think he had any chance of securing."[68] Although excluded in many ways, taking part in organized activities at Stirling Park provided some recognition and visibility for young Black people.

When Black people who grew up in Chatham in those interwar years shared their memories of Stirling Park, they described it as a place where people with little money and limited job prospects could find something to do. In a 1978 newspaper interview, Boomer Harding recalled, "There was no TV in those days. Few people had radios and hardly anybody who grew up in the east end around Stirling Park had a car. If a young fella didn't get himself into baseball he generally got himself into jail. The game was a kind of release from it all, for most of us."[69] Baseball, and being in the park, was a chance to forget about the daily grind of their lives for a bit. Ben Talbot, another former member of the All-Stars, while speaking to

Fig. 2.3 ▪ Carl Harding, older brother of Chatham Coloured All-Stars' players Len, Boomer, and Andy, played on the primarily white Stirling-Imperial Juniors in the mid-1920s. Carl, 13 years old when this 1924 team picture was taken at Stirling Park, is sitting in the front row (far right). Seated next to Carl is Wilf Belanger, who would later play on the 1940 Chatham Stars (as the Chatham Coloured All-Stars were known that year). Manager Archie Stirling is in the back row (centre). Photo credit: Chatham-Kent Museum 1982. 1.61B.

a newspaper reporter in 1984 claimed, "There was no place else to go but Stirling Park…During the Depression, jobs were scarce and most of [us] fellows had nothing to do. We always met at Stirling Park and played ball all day."[70] Donald Tabron, one of the All-Stars players from Detroit, also recalled long days at the park: "We either played baseball or did nothing at all. If we didn't play ball there was just the street corner."[71]

John Olbey, younger brother of All-Stars player Cliff Olbey, recalled days spent at the park. The Olbey family lived on Scane Street, which bordered the west side of Stirling Park. He remembered the swimming pool and playing pick-up games of baseball. "You'd choose up sides and play ball."[72]

Like others, he recalled that it was something they could do without any money. He remembered everyone sharing "raggedy" gloves, saying, "when you come in from the field the glove went down on the ground and the fielder from the other team picked it up and used it." Recalling the tough times growing up, he added: "It was good because there wasn't much money floating around and it got the guys together."

Others described Stirling Park as an exciting and lively place to be, a night out, and a break from everyday life. Beulah Cuzzens claimed Stirling Park was at the centre of their social life while her brothers were playing ball. She said, "every night of the week we were on Stirling Park to see a ball game. Baseball was really our breakfast, dinner, and supper at our house. We ate, drank, slept [and] played baseball."[73] Her brother Boomer recalled of those days: "We used to practice past dark. We lived at the ball park."[74] Orville Wright, who was a scorekeeper and team secretary for the Chatham Coloured All-Stars, claimed in a 1967 newspaper interview, "We had fun in those days...There was always baseball at Stirling Park...everything in town seemed to centre on Stirling Park in those days."[75]

While Black boys and men played baseball, girls and women more often played softball, which grew in popularity for both men and women in the 1920s and 1930s.[76] Black women in Chatham and North Buxton had softball teams in the 1920s. Boomer spoke about his sister, Beulah, playing softball for the "Bloomer Day Girls" (referring to the bloomer uniforms they wore) in the 1920s.[77] He said they played at Stirling Park and had exhibition games with the women's team from nearby Buxton on Labour Day holidays.[78] One such game between the Chatham and North Buxton's women's teams took place in Chatham during the Emancipation Day celebration (August 1 commemoration of the end of chattel slavery in the British Empire) in 1927.[79] Beulah remembered the other young Black women she played with on the softball team, including Hazel Shadd, Rita Lynn, and Evelyn (Williams) Wright.[80] The Buxton team included June and Alma Robbins, sisters of future Chatham Coloured All-Stars players Hyle and Stanton. June, in an oral history project directed by Dionne Brand, recalled she and her sister had to finish washing supper dishes before they were allowed to play ball with their team in the evenings.[81] Although they may have played some exhibition games, evidence does not suggest that the Black women's softball teams were members of the primarily white organized leagues in the 1920s and 1930s. Later in the 1940s and early 1950s, other Black women's softball teams played out of the J.G. Taylor Community Centre, and competed in city leagues.[82]

Life for the Black families of Chatham's East End was difficult in the 1920s and 1930s. With racism constraining employment options, Black people worked in low-paying jobs, struggling to support their families. Racism also meant that these families lived in a largely segregated world, where Black people were not welcome in some public spaces like restaurants or hotels. They were also not widely accepted on white sports teams or clubs. In that environment, places like Stirling Park were particularly important. They offered leisure and recreation, a safe space where young Black people could gather, play with friends, and toss a baseball around. With few other opportunities, a day at Stirling Park was, as Wilfred Harding noted, a "release from it all, for most of us."[83] It was in this space that a group of young Black men formed a baseball team that would remain rooted at Stirling Park and the East End, but also take them far outside it.

Fig. 2.4 ▪ Children playing in Stirling Park pool, c. 1920s. The pool was built by Archie Stirling, who also donated part of the land for the park, which was transferred to the city by the early 1930s. Photo credit: Chatham-Kent Museum 1982 1.24.7.

3

Origins

Early Black Baseball in Chatham, Buxton, and London, 1915–1927

When asked by Chatham student Dan Kelly in the late 1970s about the origins of the Chatham Coloured All-Stars, Wilfred "Boomer" Harding gave few specific details, but he claimed the team started as a group of friends playing at Stirling Park. "We was playing over in Stirling Park is where it all started...[it was] something to do mostly."[1] While Len and Boomer Harding, Kingsley Terrell, and Ross Talbot formed the Chatham Coloured All-Stars in 1933, the roots of Black baseball in Chatham can be traced to earlier Black teams in the community, as well as to Black American baseball culture. On the American side of the border, Black ball players, excluded from professional league play in the late nineteenth century, formed exhibition teams that travelled throughout the United States and the border regions of Canada. Developing a distinctive baseball style featuring speed and dynamism, these ball players marketed themselves to attract paying white audiences. Elements of that distinct baseball style carried into separate professional Black leagues (known as the "Negro Leagues") formed in the 1920s. As part of the North American Black diaspora, Black people in Chatham and southwestern Ontario had many ties, both familial and economic, across the border, and they would have been well aware of these American Black baseball traditions and teams.

While Black people had been playing baseball in Chatham since at least the late nineteenth century, the Chatham Colored Giants, formed around 1915, raised the profile of Black baseball in the community. While the team was not part of an organized league, the Colored Giants played numerous exhibition games in the community. During its most active years in the mid-1920s, the Colored Giants linked into a wider, regional baseball network, recruiting players from London, Ontario, and regularly inviting Black teams from Detroit to play. As they dazzled crowds with an array of talented players, the Colored Giants helped create a visible presence for Black baseball in Chatham. When the Chatham Coloured All-Stars formed in the early 1930s, several members of the former Colored Giants helped launch the new team. Indeed, the knowledge and experience from the Colored Giants helped propel the Chatham Coloured All-Stars into a wider spotlight.

Black Baseball on Both Sides of the Canada-US Border

Although associated with American culture, baseball, Alan Metcalfe argues, was widely embraced in late-nineteenth century Canada, and became "part of the communal celebrations and a vehicle for the demonstration of community spirit."[2] This included Canadian Black communities and areas of Black settlement which began forming teams in the last thirty years of the nineteenth century.[3] Baseball historian Bill Humber has identified one early team in London Ontario, the Goodwills, who played in 1869.[4] In Atlantic Canada, Colin Howell notes that by the 1880s, Black teams had formed in communities with larger Black populations, including Halifax, Fredericton, and Saint John.[5] In Chatham, Ontario, one of the earliest recorded reports of Black baseball happened in 1871, when a local Black team, the Royal Oaks, played the Unexpected Base Ball Club of Detroit.[6] As Metcalfe notes, cross-border challenge matches and tournaments were common between Canadian and American teams (both Black and white) in border regions during this period.[7]

By the late nineteenth and early-twentieth centuries, semi-professional American Black touring teams began travelling to Canadian communities.[8] After the major professional baseball leagues barred Black athletes in the 1870s, talented Black players instead earned some money playing for travelling "barnstorming" teams. Playing mainly white opponents in front of white audiences, some of the most well known of these teams included the Page Fence Giants from Michigan and the Cuban Giants of New York City. As Howell and others have noted, these Black touring teams marketed themselves to white audiences by highlighting their race, promising a different and exciting game. Howell argues, "In order to attract fans, they often had to cultivate an image of 'otherness' that played upon white racial theories about the different characteristics of the races."[9] While Howell claims Black players brought a "smooth and slick" style to the game, they also had to straddle the line between entertaining white audiences and falling into racial stereotypes.

By the 1890s, Black touring baseball teams were playing regularly in southwestern Ontario. Local newspapers heralded the arrival of these teams, building anticipation and encouraging people to attend. In 1895, for example, the *London Advertiser* promoted an upcoming visit by the Page Fence Giants, claiming they were "good ball players" who reportedly travelled in their own rail car.[10] Likewise, in 1905, the *Amherstburg Echo* advertised an event featuring a Black baseball team playing in Leamington, Ontario, which is less than forty miles from Chatham. The newspaper promised an exciting time, saying, "It is a fast team and a good game is assured."[11] These travelling teams would have exposed white audiences in late-nineteenth and early twentieth-century, small-town Ontario to a new style of baseball, and perhaps fostered expectations and assumptions about Black athletes.

As sports became increasingly commercialized after World War I, American Black entrepreneurs such as Andrew "Rube" Foster organized separate professional Black baseball leagues.[12] The "Great Migration," which brought tens of thousands of Black people from the American South to northern cities in the early years of the twentieth century, created a ready market for these professional Black teams.[13] During the "golden age" of the Black leagues in the 1920s and 1930s, teams such as the Kansas City Monarchs and the Detroit Stars developed large followings, helped along by star players including Leroy Robert "Satchel" Paige, Josh Gibson, and James Thomas "Cool Papa" Bell.

The teams, players, and style of play of these leagues became part of Black culture and identity in the interwar years. Scholars of Black American sport and culture, such as Gerald Early and others, argue that Black players developed a distinctive style of baseball which was more athletic and dynamic than the baseball played in the white major leagues. Early identifies "speed and aggressive base running" as one of the features of Black baseball.[14] Baseball historian Larry Lester argues that Jackie Robinson, who had spent time playing in the Black leagues before joining the Brooklyn Dodgers in 1947, helped popularize that Black style, and base stealing in particular, in Major League Baseball (MLB). Lester claims, "The Negro Leagues' more aggressive approach made baseball a better version of itself. It resonates to this day."[15] When the Detroit Stars played an exhibition game against an amateur white team in nearby Windsor, Ontario, the reporter from the

Border Cities Star was impressed with the level of play, marvelling at the team's pitcher Nelson Dean, a "dazzling speedball artist."[16] The Black team, observed the reporter, "outclassed their opponents in every department of the game."

By the early 1930s, many of the Black leagues were facing financial trouble, a result of the Great Depression, and many leagues and teams, including the Detroit Stars, folded.[17] Neil Lanctot argues that after the collapse of the Black leagues in the early 1930s, unaffiliated Black semi-professional teams emerged to fill the gap, playing exhibition games wherever they could find paying audiences.[18] During the 1930s, many of these Black touring teams, mostly from Michigan, played in Windsor each year, looking to earn a few dollars. They included the Ecorse Colored Giants, the Hamtramck Colored Stars, Quinn's Colored Stars of Detroit, and a Black team from Saginaw, Michigan, among others.[19] A few of the men on these travelling teams had previously played in the Black leagues, but most would have been local Detroit-area men. The fact that so many Black exhibition teams played in Windsor in the 1930s speaks to the popularity of Black baseball among mostly white audiences. It also reflects the scarce options in the labour market, as Black men scrambled to find work during the hard times of the Great Depression.

Early Black Teams in Chatham, North Buxton, and London

While American Black baseball teams were making an impact on both sides of the Canada-US border, Black players in southwestern Ontario were also forming baseball teams. Baseball was popular in the Black community in early twentieth-century Chatham, and was most often played as part of community or holiday events. Emancipation Day was widely celebrated in southern Ontario, and it often featured baseball games.[20] For example, Chatham's Emancipation Day festivities in 1903 included speeches, a concert band, an evening dance, and a baseball game between a Black team and a white team.[21] According to the *Chatham Daily Planet*, it was an "interesting game" with the score going back and forth in the eighth and ninth innings. When the Black team finally pulled ahead, taking the game 12–11, they claimed the prize, a box of cigars. While baseball appeared popular, it was not clear if the men were playing on organized teams, or if they came together casually for special occasions. The local newspaper rarely identified the Black teams by name—the one exception being a team which played exhibition games during the 1906 baseball season called the East End Knockers.[22] Whether they were organized teams or not, the Black players were not part of the primarily white, local organized amateur baseball teams or leagues in this period.

In 1915, a new Black team called the Chatham Colored Giants increased the profile of Black baseball in the city.[23] Although not part of the white baseball league, the Colored Giants nevertheless played exhibition games in the local area. According to the *Chatham Daily News*, the Giants had played "quite a number of games with colored and other teams in this vicinity this year and have made an excellent showing."[24] Their very name, the Chatham Colored Giants, recalling the American touring teams, suggested they wanted to make an impression in the regional baseball scene.

The men who played on the Chatham Colored Giants in 1915 came from Chatham's East End, and many were related to each other by blood or marriage. Indeed, the rosters of the Colored Giants and other Black teams from the area reveal these family and community networks that were the heart of Black baseball. Joseph Parker, a twenty-two-year-old barber who was raised in the East End by his widowed mother, was the Colored Giants' manager and first-base player.[25] Parker's brother-in-law, Duncan Williams, was also on the team. Williams was born and raised in nearby North Buxton, and played outfield with the Colored Giants. His daughter, Evelyn, would later play with the East End Black women's softball team in the 1920s.[26] Infielder Percy Parker (no relation to Joseph) was also born in North Buxton, but he grew up in the East End where his father, Alfred, worked as a teamster.[27] Other players from the East End included Charles Terrell, Herbert Crosby, and Ray Ward.

The Colored Giants were also close to another Black team in the region, the Invincibles from North Buxton.[28] North Buxton (along with South Buxton, another small community a short distance away) had once been the site of the Elgin or Buxton Settlement, founded for Black freedom seekers in 1849 by white abolitionist Reverend William King. Although the Black population in the community had declined in the intervening years, many Black families remained around North Buxton, often referred to locally as "Buxton." As A.C. (Arlie) Robbins, author of *Legacy to Buxton,* argues, the Black families of Buxton had a deep connection to baseball. She explains that, "from all accounts, it seems as if there had always been ball teams in Buxton."[29] Robbins describes the intergenerational ties, where the "teams of the 1920s were the followers of the earlier teams and the forerunners of the teams of the 1930s."[30] In researching her 1983 book, Robbins collected information on the community's baseball history from William Rhue and Stanley Prince, who named some of the standout players from the past, including six members of the North Buxton Invincibles who played the Chatham Colored Giants in 1915.[31] Baseball, and later softball, were integral to Buxton community events, such as the annual "Homecoming" celebrations held each Labour Day weekend since 1924.[32]

While baseball had deep traditions in both the East End and Buxton, when the North Buxton Invincibles and the Chatham Colored Giants played each other in 1915, the local newspaper covered the game as if it were an exotic curiosity, rather than a "normal" sports event. As Howell and others have noted, the early white press often portrayed Black ball players as clowns, or entertainers, rather than serious athletes.[33] In a notice about the upcoming game between the two Black teams, the *Chatham Daily Planet* promised the game would be a "mirth-provoking exhibition of the national pastime."[34] In covering the game itself, the reporter exclaimed it was "weird from start to finish and baseball such as was never seen in the major league nor ever dreamed of by a Cobb or a Daubert" (Ty Cobb and Jake Daubert, early twentieth-century professional baseball players).[35] In fact, the reporter used the term "weird" three times in the article, suggesting they had found the game unusual, and outside the norms of "white" baseball. The reporter also remarked on what they saw as a highly physical game, with the players from both teams hitting the ball hard. The ball, the author claimed, was "fished out of the creek at least a dozen times, slammed with great gusto against different right field trees on other occasions, fouled up against the brick wall of the armoury too often to mention, and twisted out of its ordinary shape by the agonizing deliveries of the respective pitchers."[36] The reporter concluded by remarking that the players appeared to have fun, describing the victorious North Buxton team as leaving in "high spirits" while the defeated Colored Giants were "not a bit downhearted."[37]

Possibly the game between the Colored Giants and the North Buxton Invincibles was intended to be humorous, as white teams in the city also put on "novelty" games for fundraising efforts.[38] Reporters, however, did not describe the humorous games by white players as "weird," or emphasize the physicality of the game. The game the Colored Giants and Invincibles played may very well have been faster than the baseball played by white players in the community. Some of the Black people in Chatham would have had opportunities to see American Black teams either in Detroit or elsewhere.

At the same time, however, the reporters may have been exaggerating or accentuating physical play because of their own expectations about Black athletes. As Janelle Joseph argues, prevailing images of Black athletes "typically celebrate Black physical superiority, sensuality, and greater bodily—but not mental—self control."[39] She notes, as have other scholars, that portraying them in simplified, stereotypical ways, serves to "strip Black athletes of agency, exaggerate their social differences, and reinforce the status quo."[40] While the Chatham Colored Giants and the North Buxton Invincibles may have been playing a more physical style of ball, similar to that of the American Black touring teams, the white reporter's expectations of how a "Black" team played could also have affected the reporting. Whatever the case, the reporter's take on the game between the Black teams is a reminder of the way that playing baseball brought Black athletes under the gaze of the white press and white audiences.

Besides the North Buxton Invincibles, the Colored Giants also played exhibition games with teams from local First Nations, who also faced racist and racialized press scrutiny. As Janice Forsyth argues, the history of sports and Indigenous Peoples in Canada is tied to a larger history of colonialism and residential schooling.[41] Residential and day schools run by the Canadian government and the churches since the nineteenth century used Western-style games and sport to replace Indigenous cultural and spiritual practices. They were also used to instill discipline and assimilation into the dominant white culture. Sports and games were "pivotal sites through which power was legitimated and exercised through Aboriginal bodies in the residential school system."[42] Forsyth argues that the enjoyment and relief some got from taking part in sports "can be understood as the expression of creative responses to conditions of marginalization and duress."[43] Physical practices had long been part of Indigenous culture, and as she notes in her book, *Reclaiming Tom Longboat,* they remain a key part of their [Indigenous Peoples'] identities as distinct groups and nations."[44]

Wherever or however they came to play baseball, the game was popular in First Nations communities in early twentieth-century southwestern Ontario.[45] In 1915, the Colored Giants played a team from the Delaware Nation (Eelünaapéewi Lahkéewiit) at Moraviantown.[46] The *Chatham Daily Planet*'s coverage of the game, however, displayed a typical focus on the race of the players.[47] While the reporter praised the game and the skills of the players, they rarely called them by name, instead referring to the team members as either "colored" or "Indians." According to the reporter, the game was "resplendent with snappy fielding. The Indian infielders and particularly Crosby, the colored team's short fielder [likely Herbert Crosby, who also pitched] being in the limelight." As Ornella Nzindukiyimana notes about early twentieth-century sports reporting, whiteness was the "norm" and only Black and non-white athletes were referenced by race.[48] While continually using racialized terms to describe the athletes, the *Chatham Daily Planet* reporter remarked on the strong players from both teams including "Chesley," the pitcher from Moraviantown, who began the game "like a house on fire." As well, Percy Parker of the Giants impressed the reporter with his ninth inning "ringing two ply clout to left centre" which led to the game-winning runs. According to the article, a large and enthusiastic crowd had come to see the game.

Although the Chatham Colored Giants were not members of Chatham's city baseball league, a notice that Joseph Parker sent to the *Chatham Daily News* at the end of the 1915 baseball season suggests they wanted to engage more directly with teams within the league. The *Chatham Daily News* reported that the Colored Giants, "representing the colored population of the city is anxious to prove their worth on the baseball diamond and have challenged the Regiment team to a game."[49] The Regiment team was a finalist in the city's baseball championship, playing for the Wanless Trophy. The article noted, "Should the soldiers refuse to play it is hinted in some quarters that the colored team will claim the city championship." Through that challenge, the Black team was signalling that trophy or not, no one could call themselves the best without playing the Colored Giants. Whether or not the Colored Giants wanted to be part of Chatham's city baseball league, the incident suggests they wanted to connect and interact with the city's white teams. While it is not known if the game ever took place, the Colored Giants had sent a message, insisting that they be noticed.

Although the Colored Giants made an impact in the 1915 baseball season, the team played infrequently (or at least, their games were not covered by the newspapers) over the next several years. World War I may have led to this hiatus, as at least two of the Colored Giants' players, Ray Ward and Herbert Crosby, enlisted with the Canadian Expeditionary Force, No. 2 Construction Battalion.[50] The No. 2 Construction Battalion was an all-Black unit the Canadian government created in response to complaints that local regiments were turning away Black men who tried to enlist. Many young Black men from the Chatham area, including Ward and Crosby, joined the

No. 2. Construction Batalion, which actively recruited in Chatham and Windsor. After the war was over, the Colored Giants got back together, playing exhibition games with local white, Indigenous, and Black teams.

When the Colored Giants regrouped in the 1920s, they retained some players from the 1915 season, while recruiting new members.[51] Leading the team was Duncan Williams, who took over managing duties from Joseph Parker.[52] First World War veterans Ray Ward and Herbert Crosby returned to the team, with pitcher Crosby bringing his younger brother, Clarence, who was also a pitcher. After one game in 1925 in which they both played, the *Chatham Daily News* claimed, "the Crosby brothers staged a very fine battle in the box."[53] Herbert Crosby's brother-in-law, John Lewis, an infielder (shortstop and first and second base) also joined the team, playing for the Colored Giants in 1925 and 1926.[54] Second baseman, Percy Parker, another returning player from the 1915 team, recruited his younger brother, Caspar.[55] Charles Terrell, who had played in 1915, was occasionally joined on the field by his nephew (and future member of the Chatham Coloured All-Stars) King Terrell in the 1926 season.[56] According to a 1967 newspaper article, the Terrells were a "family of baseball background," suggesting that perhaps other family members had also played the game.[57]

The Colored Giants also reached out to players in other communities, inviting members of a Black team in London, Ontario, the London Colored Stars, to join them. The London Colored Stars were active at about the same time as the Colored Giants. According to the *London Free Press*, the Colored Stars had won fifteen of nineteen games during the 1923 baseball season, and they were "looking for more engagements."[58] Several members of the London Colored Stars joined the Colored Giants for games, particularly when the Chatham team was playing teams from Detroit.[59] As well, it seems members of the Colored Giants occasionally went to London to play for the London Colored Stars. In July 1923, the *Dawn of Tomorrow* reported that Ray Ward, Percy Parker, and John Lewis, all of the Colored Giants, had come to London for a few days to join the London Colored Stars for a game in Goderich, Ontario.[60] It is not clear how the London and Chatham players knew each other, but a couple of the London players were born in Chatham, suggesting community connections and networks of friends fostered the relationship between the teams.

Harry Coursey, who played for both the Colored Giants and the Colored Stars, was also one of the very few Black ball players who also played on white teams in the 1920s. Born in Chatham but raised in London, Coursey attracted press attention while still in his teens for his performances at track and field meets.[61] Specializing in sprinting, Coursey was invited to try out for the 1924 Olympic Games. That same year, he also pitched for a white, OBAA-affiliated Junior team in London.[62] In 1925, Coursey managed and played for the McCormick's, another white team in the Middlesex-Oxford League.[63] The *Dawn of Tomorrow* ran several stories about his achievements, proudly noting that Coursey was the first Black man to manage a white baseball team in the city.[64] By 1926, Coursey was pitching for the London Braves of the Intercounty Baseball League.[65] The Braves were the city's premier baseball team, and pitching for them would have increased his visibility within the white baseball community.

One of Coursey's teammates was Herbert Wilson who, like Coursey, was born in Chatham but had since moved to London.[66] Years later, Boomer Harding recalled Wilson coming to watch him play while Harding was a member of a London-based Canadian Armed Forces hockey team during World War II. Harding, noting that Wilson was hearing impaired and could not speak, remembered the older man communicating with him by using gestures. Harding recalled Wilson supported him at the hockey games, and claimed he "gave me the sign to 'go get them' every time when I'd be sitting in the penalty box or in the players' box. He'd come down and make conversation with me in his own way."[67] Harding's brief anecdote about Wilson offers a glimpse into the role of sport in developing social ties and support among Black communities in the region.[68]

The Colored Giants were particularly active in 1925 and 1926, increasing their visibility in the city. Although still not members of Chatham's city baseball league, they frequently played exhibition games against white city and Kent County teams.[69] The press coverage of the Colored Giants in this period was largely flattering, particularly with standout players like Coursey.[70] A *Chatham Daily News* reporter described a game between the Chatham Colored Giants and a Black team from Detroit at Buxton's Homecoming in 1925 as "the best exhibition of amateur ball seen in this vicinity for years."[71] The reporter noted that Coursey struck out twenty-one batters, and that Duncan Williams thrilled the crowd when he caught the ball "after he had fallen on his back." Coursey received a lot of attention, and one reporter called him "one of the best amateur hurlers in the province."[72] The following year, reporters remarked on his playing with the London Intercounty League team, saying he "showed some mighty fine stuff with the London Braves this season."[73]

LONDON, CANADA, AUGUST 2ND, 1924.

HARRY COURSEY, who finished a close second to A. Vance, Canadian Champion sprinter in the 100 metre dash. Coursey qualified for the Olympic, recently held in Paris, but since this is his first year in training, he was advised by trainers Lightfoot and Cornellius to forego the Olympic in order to improve his style. Coursey's time was eleven and two fifth seconds.

Fig. 3.1 ▪ Harry Coursey, member of the Chatham Colored Giants and the London Colored Stars baseball teams, may have been the first Black man on the London Braves (later renamed the London Majors) of the Intercounty Baseball League when he pitched for them in 1926. He was also a track and field athlete. Photo credit: *Dawn of Tomorrow*, August 2, 1924, 1. London, Ontario. Canadiana https://www.canadiana.ca/view/oocihm.N_00229_192307.

The Colored Giants also helped showcase Black baseball, frequently inviting Black exhibition teams from Detroit to play at Athletic Park (now Fergie Jenkins Field, named after former MLB player Ferguson Jenkins Jr.) the largest baseball park in Chatham. The Matthewson's All-Stars and the Taylor's Stars of Detroit, along with a team from Detroit's Second Baptist Church, were among the teams playing in Chatham in these years.[74] In both 1925 and 1926, the Colored Giants hosted an event billed as the "Colored Amateur Championship" of Michigan and Ontario.[75] The local white press actively promoted these games and tournaments. One reporter assured readers that an upcoming game between the Matthewson's All-Stars of Detroit and the Colored Giants would be "hotly contested," while another claimed a scheduled meet between Black teams was generating interest in "baseball circles."[76] Reporters from the *Chatham Daily News* even contacted the managers of the Black teams in advance to ask them about their lineups.[77]

Clearly, Black baseball was no longer "weird," at least in the eyes of the local press, as it had been when the Colored Giants played North Buxton in 1915. At a game between the Colored Giants and the Taylor's Stars of Detroit, a *Chatham Daily News* reporter claimed, "The attendance was large and the game was fast while players on both teams kept up a running barrage of humor which added much to the interest displayed in the contest."[78] Although the reference to the fast game and the humour reinforces white expectations for "entertainment" at Black baseball games, it also suggests the reporter was recognizing a different baseball culture. Indeed, by the mid-1920s, the Colored Giants had carved out a space for Black baseball in Chatham, making it more familiar to white audiences.

While the Chatham Colored Giants were making a mark in Chatham baseball, the London Colored Stars were also increasing their visibility in London and the surrounding region, not just through baseball, but through music. As scholar Cheryl Thompson argues, music with its strong association with the church was central to the Black community.[79] She notes that in the 1920s and 1930s, the *Dawn of Tomorrow* newspaper featured many notices about musical performances. The newspaper also reported on the musical efforts of the Colored Stars baseball team, who used their proceeds to help fund the club or raise money for various causes.[80] In 1923, the Colored Stars held at least two concerts after baseball games in West Lorne and Arkona, two small towns near London.[81] Their concert in Arkona in August 1923, was a joint program with the Elites, a Black women's ball team which also gave concerts in the London area.[82] An advertisement for the event in the *Watford Guide-Advocate* provides some insights into the group's musical performances.[83] For thirty-five cents admission, audiences could expect "vaudeville" acts in the first half, and vocal numbers including solos, duets, and a full chorus in the second. The advertisement also proclaimed that a "First-Class Orchestra" would be accompanying them. According to the *Dawn of Tomorrow,* the Arkona concert attracted 500 people.[84] Although there is no record of the musical programs, other concerts by Black performers of that era featured spirituals and popular songs.[85] The notice billed the performers as the "Elite Colored Minstrels," but it is not clear if this was a name the group itself used, or if it was used in the advertisement to generate interest. The *Dawn of Tomorrow* never used the term "minstrels" when describing the group, rather calling them a ball team that gave concerts. "Minstrel shows," commonly performed by white singers in blackface, were popular among white audiences in the 1920s.[86]

Playing baseball, and performing musical numbers, were perceived as non-threatening ways of presenting themselves to the white community, as sports and entertainment were considered acceptable venues for Black people in that period. At the same time, music gave the players and performers opportunities to earn some money and display hard-earned talents.

By the mid-1920s, Black baseball had become firmly established in Chatham, aided by the Chatham Colored Giants who brought interest and a distinctive culture and style to the game. Through this larger network of players and teams from North Buxton, Detroit, and London, Black baseball developed a higher profile in Chatham, attracting the attention of white audiences and the local white press. Despite this attention, however, the Chatham Colored Giants were still on the outside of organized amateur baseball in the community. Whether or not the Colored Giants or any of the other regional Black teams like the London Colored Stars wanted to play in a league is unknown. After all, playing in a league meant having to follow the league's schedule, which took away some independence. Making time for games was always challenging for precariously employed Black men. In any case, by the late 1920s the team was no longer playing for reasons that are not clear. Nevertheless, the Colored Giants, through their strong presence in the city for some years, had helped create an interest in Black baseball, which would revive some years later when the Chatham Coloured All-Stars took to the field in Stirling Park.

4

A New Black Baseball Team in Chatham, 1933

In 1933, several years after the Chatham Colored Giants disbanded, a new Black team known as the Chatham Stars (as the Chatham Coloured All-Stars were known then) emerged in Stirling Park. Comprised of a group of young men who had grown up in the East End playing and watching baseball, the young team would also rely on help from older, more experienced ball players in the neighbourhood. Some of these included former members of the Colored Giants, who provided management and coaching in their first year. Unlike the older team, in 1933 the Chatham Stars joined the primarily white, OBAA-affiliated Chatham City Baseball League. What had changed by 1933 that brought a Black team into the Chatham City Baseball League for the first time? While not all the reasons are known, in the early years of the Great Depression, baseball in the city had fallen on hard times, and organizers' desperation to rebuild the sport explains much about why the Stars were welcomed. The new Black team also had the support of Archie Stirling, an influential figure in Chatham baseball.

Although they were accepted into the OBAA-affiliated Chatham City Baseball League, the Stars faced challenges that the white teams did not. First, they had no experience with OBAA regulations and protocols. While the former members of the Colored Giants who helped the Chatham Stars had baseball experience, they had never played in the OBAA. As well, the new Stars faced financial difficulties; unlike some of the other teams, they had no dedicated sponsor to pay for uniforms and equipment. To help fill the club coffers, the Stars turned to exhibition play. Drawing on the same traditions of Black baseball culture as their predecessors, the Chatham Colored Giants, the Chatham Stars learned first-hand of the ambiguities and contradictions of marketing themselves to white audiences.

Finally, the Chatham Stars had to prove themselves as a legitimate team. As a Black team, the Stars still had to justify themselves in the new league, to the press (who reported on the league closely), and to community fans. Their first year in the league was difficult and they lost more games than they won. Despite their record, the Stars gained a reputation as a hard-working team, and they received support from the local press who portrayed them sympathetically. In the 1930s, sportswriters looked for ways to engage audiences and sell newspapers, and the Stars fit the "worthy underdog" narrative. By the end of their first season, the Stars started winning more games, in part with the help of a new recruit, Earl "Flat" Chase from Windsor. His pitching and batting prowess would not only make the team stronger, but his play would also become part of "the Flat Chase legend" developed years later in the local press, and in the collective memory of the former players.

Chatham Stars Join the Chatham City League

Why a Black team was invited into the Chatham City Baseball League in 1933 can be explained, at least in part because organized baseball in the city was on the verge of collapse. Although Chatham had a city league and teams playing in OBAA-affiliated leagues in the county in the 1920s, most of that had been lost by the early 1930s. According to Stirling, the city league disbanded after the 1929 season when the OBAA suspended one of their four teams for a rule infraction.[1] As the city league was small, losing a team made it hard to continue. In the early 1930s, Chatham no longer had an Intermediate-level team playing in the OBAA-affiliated county league. In fact, strong baseball players of Intermediate age joined teams in other Kent County towns.[2] Carl Harding, for example, who had played on Stirling's Stirling-Imperials Junior team in the 1920s, played for a team in nearby Blenheim in 1932.[3] By 1932, the only baseball team in the city was a Junior (under 20 twenty years) team, which played in an OBAA-affiliated Junior league in the region.

Chatham's difficulties in maintaining a city league, however, were common in organized baseball in that period. As Alan Metcalfe notes, baseball leagues were precarious in late nineteenth- and early twentieth-century Ontario.[4] Metcalfe explains that even after the OBAA was founded in 1918, baseball in interwar, rural Ontario was characterized by "a proliferation of short-lived leagues, independent leagues, and a lack of organizational stability."[5] This was partly due to baseball being a summer sport which coincides with the busiest time of year in agricultural regions such as southern Ontario. The demands of work in agriculture and agricultural-based economies simply made it hard for players and teams to commit to a set schedule. Although baseball players living in Chatham were not farmers, much of the city's economy was tied to agriculture, and much of this work was either seasonal, or its pace intensified during the summer.

Another reason that organized baseball was declining in Chatham was the rising popularity of softball.[6] A relatively new sport, by the mid-1920s softball had overtaken baseball in numbers of teams and players in Chatham.[7] Softball's popularity continued in the 1930s, when the city featured a six-team men's league, a church league, and a women's league.[8] As well, the city's main softball venue, Tecumseh Park (formerly a baseball diamond), had been outfitted with floodlights, allowing teams to play at night. Night games, held when people were off work, were an advantage when looking to attract paying spectators. Chatham's baseball parks, however, never had lights in the 1930s, and most games were played in the daytime. Whatever the cause, softball games in Chatham in this period regularly attracted between 4,000 and 6,000 spectators, while baseball games normally drew a few hundred. While admission fees for baseball games were just ten cents for most games, even those fees could make a difference.[9]

Despite these challenges, local baseball organizers decided to revive the city league in the spring of 1933.[10] A reporter with the *Chatham Daily News* covering the inaugural meeting of the new league noted the optimism, remarking that "baseball will within the next year or two again occupy its former place on the sports map of the Maple City."[11] Signalling they wanted to bring back competitive play to Chatham, the league organizers also planned to apply to join the OBAA. Despite their ambitions, the new league was still relatively small, with just four teams, including the Stars. Of the three white teams, one was a Junior-level outfit that also played in the county Junior League. After failing to operate for several years and seeing some of their strongest baseball players join teams in other communities, the Chatham City Baseball League was clearly prepared to accept a Black team to bring the sport back to the city.

While it is not known who approached whom when proposing to bring the Chatham Stars into the new city league, Archie Stirling was most likely involved. Stirling was not on the executive of the Chatham City Baseball League, but he had become a local representative of the OBAA (a position he would hold for many years). He was also at the inaugural meeting of the relaunched city league, and it is hard to imagine that a Black team would have been accepted if he had been against it. Stirling's role and relationship with both Black ball players and the Chatham Stars/Coloured All-Stars is important and complex. In the 1920s, he recruited several Black players (including Carl Harding and future Chatham Coloured All-Star player King Terrell) to join the Stirling-Imperial Juniors.[12] As organized baseball was otherwise all white, Stirling brought some (but not many) Black players into a white environment. As will be discussed later, Stirling would also play a behind-the-scenes supportive role for the Chatham Coloured All-Stars. In his oral history interview in 1980, Terrell claimed that Stirling was "one of the nicest men that you'd ever want to be around or meet."[13] Indeed, he was highly regarded within the community as well—people who grew up in the East End recalled he would give free bricks of ice cream from his store to anyone who hit a home run in Stirling Park.[14]

At the same time, it is important to place Stirling's support for a few Black players in the 1920s, and the Chatham Coloured All-Stars in the 1930s, in the context of his efforts to build and rebuild baseball in the community. The previous chapter outlined that Stirling devoted much time, money, and energy to developing baseball programs, creating Stirling Park and managing the Stirling-Imperials, and the Stirling-Imperials Juniors. Then as baseball declined and the league collapsed, he worked to bring it back. He wanted baseball to survive, and encouraging talented Black players and a Black ball team was one way to do that. Recalling his encounters with Stirling, Terrell explained, "That's one thing about him. He wanted a ball club. And he didn't care who you were, or what you was, or where you came from, or anything else as long as you could play ball and you was decent and respectable, and you didn't put yourself above anybody else."[15] While oral history accounts of Stirling confirm community regard for him, it is also important to be aware that he also needed those Black players and the Black team, or felt he needed them, to keep baseball viable. He was getting something out of his relationship with the Black players—a more robust baseball program in the city. It was a supportive relationship, but also transactional, as the relationships between many white allies and Black athletes were.[16]

King Terrell's memories about how Stirling got him to join the Stirling-Imperials in the mid-1920s offer some insights into the care he took to recruit the young player. It is not clear how Stirling first took notice of Terrell, but he was the young nephew of well-known Chatham Colored Giants player Charles Terrell (and King himself had played some games with that team). As well, King Terrell had been a high school track and field star, a sprinter, which is helpful in a baseball player.[17] Whatever led him to approach the young man about playing baseball, Stirling took care to first secure Terrell's grandmother's approval before even approaching him. Terrell recalled that when Stirling arrived at their house that day, he came with a well-known Black East End resident, Charles Lynn, a mail carrier.[18] Terrell claimed his grandmother knew both men well, which suggests that Stirling had enlisted Lynn's help to gain her trust. Terrell recalled, "They talked to my grandmother and they said, 'Mrs. Terrell, can King play baseball for the Stirling-Imperials?' And that was the beginning of me knowing Mr. Stirling."[19] Terrell also remembered that Stirling gave the players rides to the games and bought them sandwiches and drinks. While giving Terrell and others rides and refreshments was generous, the gesture also helped ensure that the young men could play. The Stirling-Imperials played in a county league where travel was necessary, and few in the East End had cars or extra money for snacks.

The Chatham Stars Players

Aside from Stirling's support, the involvement of several former members of the Chatham Colored Giants with the Chatham Stars may have helped ease the new team's way into the Chatham City Baseball League. The Colored Giants had been popular, even if they had not been part of the city league. Local white baseball organizers would have known them or been aware of the skills they brought to the game. Duncan Williams, who played with the Colored Giants in 1915 and managed them in the 1920s, became the Stars' first manager in 1933. Williams's former Colored Giants teammate, infielder Percy Parker, joined the Stars as a third-base coach. In an oral history interview, Boomer Harding indicated he was aware of Parker's longer baseball history, saying Parker "knew all about baseball being a former great player in that old league."[20] Another former Colored Giants player, Clarence Crosby pitched for the Chatham Stars for the first half of their inaugural season.[21] Harding recalled that Crosby had played with the Colored Giants, saying "Clarence was the pitcher. Southpaw pitcher, was very good. Had former experience with the older fellows and was trying out with us."[22] And finally, King Terrell, who had followed his uncle Charles onto the Colored Giants in 1926, was one of the founding members of the Chatham Stars in 1933.

Besides the former Colored Giants, other young Black men from the East End joined the new Chatham Stars. Harding brothers Len and Boomer would have a profound impact on the Stars/All-Stars over the eight-year history of the team. Len, a high school track and field champion, was known for his speed.[23] "He was as fast as lightening [*sic*]," confirmed Orville Wright in a 1967 newspaper interview.[24] A versatile player, Harding played almost every position except pitcher. He was the team's catcher for the most part, and in the 1933 season he quickly settled into that role. While he was an all-around player, he was also known as one of the leaders of the team. By the late 1930s, Len had become the team's official manager.[25]

Like his older brother, Boomer was also a high school track and field champion, winning the city-wide Senior Boys' title in 1933.[26] He was also a hockey player, one of the very few Black people involved in the sport in Chatham during that period (his older brother Carl was another). His hockey playing was considered so exceptional that when he broke his collarbone, taking him out of the lineup of the Chatham Vocational School team, it made the *Chatham Daily News*.[27] Like many of the Stars in 1933, Harding played a variety of positions, but he played mostly outfield. He explained years later that he wanted to play first base, but his brother Len told him, "You'd have to earn the position."[28] Harding continued to play outfield in the 1933 season, and moved to first base the following year.

The oldest Harding brother, Carl, had been among the first Black players to play in white organized baseball in Chatham, but he had already left the city when the Chatham Stars formed. When he became too old to play for the Stirling-Imperial Juniors, Harding began playing for OBAA-affiliated teams outside Chatham (as Chatham did not have any intermediate-level, OBAA-affiliates in that period). By 1933, he was playing baseball in Rodney, in nearby Elgin County.[29] He then moved to St. Thomas, Ontario, where he worked for a garage, and played both baseball and hockey. He also spent some time working (and playing sports) in Kirkland Lake before returning to St. Thomas. Harding's daughter, Jennifer Miss, suggested that despite being light-skinned, racial prejudice had limited his opportunities in Chatham, which contributed to his decision to leave.[30]

Another pair of brothers, Ross and Benjamin (Ben) Talbot, also played with the Chatham Stars. Although their father was from nearby Dresden, the Talbot brothers, who both worked as chauffeurs in the 1930s, grew up in the East End.[31] They were also first cousins of fellow teammate King Terrell.[32] Ross played first base that season, while Ben played a variety of positions. Both Ross and Ben would remain with the Chatham Coloured All-Stars throughout the 1930s. Two other East End men, Clifford (Cliff) Olbey and Gouy Ladd, joined the Chatham Stars a few weeks after the start of the season. Olbey was one of seven children raised in the family home on Scane Street, close to Stirling Park.[33] Like several of his fellow players, Olbey worked at the William Pitt Hotel. He played right field, a fact his younger brother John recalled in an interview over eighty years later.[34] He also remembered his brother was a fast runner, as did King Terrell.[35] Boomer Harding laughingly described Olbey sliding headfirst into first base, saying, "he never learned to slide. He went only head first [laughing]. It was—he usually got to the bag."[36] Gouy Ladd, who was born in Chatham and raised in the East End,[37] played several infield positions in that first year, but later was known for his work in outfield. Both Boomer Harding and King Terrell remembered him as a solid player.[38] Terrell recalled he "couldn't run very fast but he was a pretty good ball player and he was a pretty good batter."[39] He also recalled that Ladd was a reliable member of the team, showing up for most games. Indeed, Ladd continued to play for the All-Stars as long as they were together.

Coming from Buxton, Sagasta Harding joined the Stars in mid-July, 1933. Harding, no relation to Len and Boomer, came from a strong baseball family. His older brother Robert (Bob) had been a member of the North Buxton Invincibles, who played the Chatham Colored Giants in 1915.[40] Their first cousin, George Harding, was a well-known pitcher in the region. He lived in Windsor, but according to Ferguson Jenkins Sr., Harding always came back to Buxton for the Labour Day Homecoming baseball games.[41] Jenkins described George as "a major league baller…he was the same type of pitcher as Flat [referring to Chatham Coloured All-Stars pitcher, Earl "Flat" Chase]. And I used to catch him, and that was when I was going to school."[42] Baseball clearly ran in the family. Sagasta's fellow players, however, remembered him as much for his piano playing as for his baseball skills (although Terrell did recall Sagasta had an unusual way of gripping the bat).[43] Terrell, a piano player himself, said he used to play piano with him, adding "I used to love his playing."[44]

Playing in the Chatham City League

Although the Chatham Stars had experience and youth represented in their roster, as a Black team they faced several challenges moving into organized amateur baseball. Besides dealing with more overt forms of racism (which will be discussed in the next chapter), the Stars had no experience with protocols and league officials. In meeting these challenges, the Chatham Stars sought help both from within the Black community of the East End, and from Archie Stirling. In an oral history interview, Boomer Harding recalled that Stirling avoided publicly cheering for one team or another, as his sons played on different teams in the city.[45] Nevertheless, Harding claimed that Stirling supported the All-Stars behind the scenes, freely providing advice as they navigated the politics of amateur baseball. Harding remarked, "Any little advice we wanted, the boys would slip around the store and Archie'd keep us on the inside track. Which we needed because baseball played off the field is a very different game than the one played on the field and you had to know what was going on. Archie had all that information and he passed his knowledge on to us willingly."[46] Knowledge was indeed important for a Black team on the outside of organized amateur baseball. Stirling, who clearly wanted to see the team succeed (as their success also bolstered Chatham baseball), shared his inside knowledge with the new team. As well, as Harding laughingly claimed, Stirling helped them out of tough situations "a few dozen times."[47]

On joining the city league, the Chatham Stars also came under the regular scrutiny of the local press, particularly the sports department of the *Chatham Daily News*. In the 1930s, the paper had a dedicated sports section with two to three pages featuring local and professional sports in equal measure. The pages, clearly aimed at men, also included with advertisements for automotive-related products and services, men's clothing, and sports equipment. As sports historians Don Morrow and Kevin Wamsley, Colin Howell, and others have noted, sports reporting expanded in the interwar years, coinciding with the increased commercialization of sport. Morrow and Wamsley argue that the relationship between sport and newspapers was "symbiotic," as promoting sport, and getting readers engaged with sports, helped sell newspapers.[48] Sports historians Stacy L. Lorenz and Jay Scherer also observe that community newspapers used sports pages to sell advertising.[49] Making the print stories about sports interesting to readers was critical, and competent sportswriters used various strategies. One approach was focusing on individuals, the "sports hero," as seen in the way American journalists wrote about George Herman "Babe" Ruth. As Howell notes, "Sports heroes were the idols of a consuming society and were themselves to be consumed and emulated."[50] Lorenz and Scherer also explain that both style of play and personality were part of the sports hero narratives developed in the earlier twentieth-century press that have continued into the present.[51] Nzindukiyimana also reminds us that models of masculinity and femininity, intersecting with race and class, also shaped sports coverage.[52]

In covering the Chatham Stars in their first season, the *Chatham Daily News* reporters generally portrayed the new team favourably. The Chatham Stars' record was uneven, as they lost more games than they won.[53] Perhaps trying to support the newly-revived Chatham City Baseball League, the sportswriters avoided referring directly to race in that first year. Considering the racist environment of 1930s Chatham, drawing attention to one of the four baseball teams in the city league being Black may have alienated potential white baseball audiences. Instead, the paper presented them as "worthy underdogs," players who worked hard and never gave up. Using language that may have appealed to a white readership, they emphasized traits such as persistence that were widely valued in white, middle-class society. For example, in one early season game, the writer asserted, "Dunc Williams [*sic*] team went down fighting. They never gave up…"[54] In another game the Stars lost 9–4, the reporter noted that although the Stars trailed, they tied the game three times. According to the *Chatham Daily News* reporter, "The Stars put up a hard battle for six frames during which time they knotted the score on two occasions."[55]A report on another game, which the Stars lost by one run, claimed they "whittled" away the Merchants' early lead, nearly reaching a tie.[56] They were, as portrayed in the press, worthy opponents, embodying characteristics of mainstream white culture. That language suggests what Patrick Miller has described as "muscular assimilationism," employed by Black American activists in the early twentieth century.[57] Faced with renewed racism and terror directed against Black Americans in that period, Black leaders pointed to the promise of sport as a proving ground for Black men. Tying Black masculinity and sport with respectability and excellence, "muscular assimilationism" was a way to prove they deserved to be accepted into the wider society. Although that language is associated with the early twentieth-century Black press, who championed the achievements of Black athletes, the white sports reporters also reflected these ideas in their coverage of the Stars. As will be discussed in the next chapter, sports reporters and columnists still used racialized language to describe the Black players, but direct references to race in 1933 were rare.[58]

When Boomer Harding described his team's appeal to fans, he, like the *Chatham Daily News* reporters, remarked on their willingness to work hard. He also claimed that they offered fans unexpected excitement. In a 1980 interview, he explained: "They [the spectators] didn't know what was going to happen. In a ball game, nothing was taken for granted. When we were playing, we could be five or eight runs behind and nobody give up and at any time we could explode."[59] Harding argued that the element of surprise was also what attracted fans to their games. He explained, "Well you didn't know how it was going to happen in a game. Something was going to break loose before somebody could hold us for a little while. Then the bats would break loose and we'd make some little excitement some way. Run the bases or something else."[60] Indeed, a number of the games in that first season were similar to what Harding described, with close scores and come-from-behind wins. For example, in a regular season game against the Duns, the Stars were behind 5–0 in the fifth inning, but rallied in the latter half of the game with "King Turrell's [*sic*] home run drive over the right field fence in the last of the seventh, with two men aboard and two men out, knotted the count at 5–5."[61] Several times, the Stars scored multiple runs in a single inning, such as when they scored six runs in one inning in a game against the Juniors.[62] Clearly, Harding's memory of how his team played matched, at least in part, some of these games in their first season. As well, Harding's comments about the team working hard and not giving up suggests the burden of a Black team having to prove themselves in white spaces. In a racist and racialized environment, a Black team would need to prove they were legitimate, that they had a right to be there. A Black team that did not appear to "fight" or work hard may have been stereotyped as "lazy," and risked losing support from key figures or sponsors (as well as fans). Whatever the motivation, the Chatham Stars were able to use their enthusiasm for the game to develop an identity and attract fans.

Exhibition Games and Playing in a White Marketplace

While the Chatham Stars were adjusting to playing in the Chatham City Baseball League, they also occasionally took to the road as an exhibition team. As Harding explained, they played exhibition games to earn cash to support the club: "We had to go on the road and sort of barnstorm across the province to pick up enough money to buy our bats."[63] These were games organized in other communities, small towns for the most part, where people paid 50 cents admission to see the Black team play against a local outfit. For their efforts, both teams took home a share of the gate. Although known as the Chatham Stars in the Chatham City Baseball League in 1933, when the team played exhibition games that year they adopted names that reflected Black American touring team culture. When they played against a Black team in London in July, 1933, for example, they called themselves the "Canadian Colored Champions of Chatham."[64] Later in the summer, when they played against a team of London postal workers, they settled on the "Chatham Colored Stars."[65] With those names, the team was signalling their difference, entering a marketplace where race carried some value.

Harding acknowledged that white audiences came to see them because they were Black, saying, "We were an attraction because we were colored but teams figured if they could make some money on us to play against them, they would pay us to get down to their parks."[66] Colin Howell, in *Northern Sandlots*, notes that "barnstorming black teams found themselves caught in the contradictions of a predominantly white market-place," having to attract an audience by cultivating an exoticism, while also showing off baseball skills.[67] Harding claimed the audiences were "coming to see us get beat and they also wanted a clown about it."[68] In a 1984 newspaper interview, Ben Talbot admitted people saw their Black team as a "novelty," but it helped to attract crowds.[69] King Terrell, however, asserted that while people may have come out partly because of their race, the team showed the crowd quality baseball: "Yeah, we had a good ball club and sure people acted funny when you went there, look at you as though they were looking at a bunch of clowns...But when you got out on the baseball field to play baseball, those guys played baseball. They knew how to play baseball and they played baseball."[70] Terrell suggested that while white audiences may have come with preconceived notions of what a "Black" team was like, he thought it was important that through their playing they upended those expectations.

Although the Chatham Stars played exhibition games to earn money for the club, sometimes the games were also social times for the players. Several times during the 1933 season, the Chatham Stars caught up with old friends from London who were playing on the Hotel London team.[71] Comprising employees of the hotel and their friends, the Hotel London team also featured several former players from the Chatham Colored Giants, including Harry Coursey (who was also the team manager), Herbert Wilson, and Harry (Hank) Anderson.[72] As well, the Hotel London team included two sets of brothers from longstanding London baseball families: the Moxleys (Melvin, Ken, and Jim), and the Andersons (Harry, Roy, and Allen).[73] Like the Chatham Stars, the Hotel London team was playing in an organized amateur baseball league in the city, although it was not affiliated with the OBAA. Many of the players lived in a working-class neighbourhood in London's east side, and they played in a park off Trafalgar Street. Lloyd Campbell, a white man who grew up in the same neighbourhood as the Black ball players, remembered watching them play. "They were such a good team," he recalled.[74]

The Chatham Stars and the Hotel London team got together at least twice during the 1933 season. According to the *Dawn of Tomorrow*, the Stars hosted the London team in Chatham in the spring, holding a social evening and dance for their guests.[75] Then in July, the Stars came to London for an exhibition game that reportedly attracted 5,000 spectators.[76] That time, the Chatham Stars held a picnic at London's Springbank Park before heading over to the Trafalgar baseball diamond.[77] The game was a Colored Giants reunion of sorts, as former members of that team were playing on both the London and Chatham teams. Besides Coursey and Anderson playing for Hotel London (Wilson was unable to play because of a broken foot[78]) the Chatham Stars' lineup included former Colored Giants Herbert and Clarence Crosby. Herbert Crosby, who was in his late thirties, pitched for just a couple of innings before handing off to his younger brother, Clarence. As Herbert Crosby was not a regular member of the Stars, he likely came just to play against Hotel London. Terrell, who played for the Colored Giants in 1926, was there in London that day, playing third base. The Stars were also accompanied by their manager, former Colored Giants manager Duncan Williams, and either he or his son, Duncan Williams Jr., played as well.[79] The Chatham Stars won 7–5 in a six-inning game.

Although they lost their game against Chatham, Hotel London won their city league championship that year.[80] It was also their last season together, as the following spring the Hotel London fired the Black men who were working as luggage porters and the Black women who worked as elevator attendants.[81] The *Dawn of Tomorrow* claimed that the hotel, which had just changed management, replaced their Black employees with white World War I veterans and other white people. The men who worked for Hotel London lost both their jobs and their team, a reminder of the precariousness of Black employment in that period, and the challenges Black teams faced finding financing. Reports in the *Dawn of Tomorrow* suggest that at least some of the members of the former Hotel London team founded a new team, the Harlem Aces, and that they played in the 1934 season.[82] They had, however, lost their main financial sponsor.

Flat Chase, and Memories of Baseball Skills

Late in the Stars' first season, they recruited a new player from Windsor: Earl "Flat" Chase. Born in North Buxton, Chase was raised in a downtown Windsor neighbourhood where Black people had settled since the nineteenth century.[83] The Chase family lived across the street from Wigle Park, with its baseball diamond, where young Chase learned to play.[84] Besides playing in Windsor, Chase also played in church baseball leagues in Detroit. After the Detroit-Windsor tunnel opened in 1930, getting from Detroit's historic Black neighbourhood in the city's east side to Chase's home in downtown Windsor would have taken less than half an hour by car. According to his son, Earl Chase Jr., "He was picked up, you know, a team from Detroit just come over, and they would get him to come play with certain teams on weekends."[85] Ferguson Jenkins Sr. also remembered going across the border with Chase to play in Detroit church league games.[86]

Earlier in the summer of 1933, Chase played for the Windsor Colored Stars, a team based at Wigle Park and managed by William Bush. That summer, the Colored Stars were playing in the Blue Water League, a non-OBAA league comprised of white teams from rural communities in northern Essex County.[87] In the 1930s, organized baseball in Windsor, much like its counterpart in Chatham, was unstable, with city leagues operating some years and not the next. As in Chatham, Windsor had more softball teams (including a Black team, the BME Rangers) than baseball teams.[88] While playing in the Blue Water League in 1933 and 1934, the Colored Stars were often at or near the top of the standings. Their pitcher, James (Jim) Pettiford, of Sandwich, was described in the press as "one of the best pitchers in the league."[89] When a new Windsor city league (unaffiliated with the OBAA) emerged in 1935, the organizers admitted the Colored Stars. A *Border Cities Star* reporter suggested they were a promising addition to the new league, calling them "one of the busiest and most capable aggregations in the district."[90] As strong as the team was, however, it never played in OBAA-affiliated leagues, such as the Essex County Baseball League, and never competed for a provincial championship like the Chatham Coloured All-Stars.[91]

When Chase played for the Windsor Colored Stars, he began to attract press attention, mostly for his batting and infield play.[92] That press attention continued when he moved to Chatham, where he was often among the top batting leaders,[93] and made his mark as a fastball pitcher. While Chase would be covered extensively in the local newspaper for his baseball skills over the

Fig 4.1 ▪ Earl "Flat" Chase, born in Buxton, and raised in Windsor, Ontario. Chase moved to Chatham late in the 1933 season and joined the Chatham Stars (as the Chatham Coloured All-Stars were known that year). This picture was taken in the 1940s, as he is wearing a Shermans uniform, a team he played for from 1942–44, and again in the later 1940s. Photo credit: Leddy Library Archives and Special Collections, F1033 (Wilfred "Boomer" Harding Collection), Scrapbook 1.

next fifteen years, he was also a big part of the oral history of the team. His former teammates, interviewed at various times from the late 1960s through the early 1980s, spoke at length, and in great detail, about Chase. In fact, one of the striking features of those oral history and newspaper interviews is how much the players could speak about distinctive features of each other's playing, many decades after they had last played together. As Bruce Kidd has suggested, to perform a sports skill is to "embody, express, and elaborate a complex code about self and culture—in short, to acquire an identity."[94] It was part of who they were, and how they were remembered by their teammates. Within a racialized community these styles or skills also took on another meaning. As Janelle Joseph has explained, Black athletes sometimes cultivated distinctive moves or stances to express individuality and defiance, arguing "when athletes embrace an ability to move their hips sensually or shout out to their peers and see these acts as resistant to dominant—that is, white Canadian—ways of being masculine, they use their agency to generate space to challenge dominant gender scripts."[95] In a white-dominated society, making an impression, a mark, even through baseball, was important and helps explain why the former players focused on their memories of their teammates' skills.

Although Chase came to the Stars as a pitcher, his fellow players most often spoke about his batting and ability to hit home runs. Although he pitched right-handed, he batted left (which is not unusual, but still relatively rare in baseball), giving him an advantage when facing right-handed pitchers.[96] Chase's batting was also a challenge to the opposing team players, as, according to King Terrell, Chase was a "spray hitter," meaning that "you can hit a ball in any part of the field."[97] While most left-handed batters will generally drive the ball into right field, with Chase, according to Terrell, "you didn't know where the ball was going to go."[98] Boomer Harding also noted that he could hit the ball anywhere, even far into left field. He explained:

> He could hit a ball low and he could hit it high or he could—there's no weak spot. He could—he'd hit the ball where it was pitched. If they thought, well, we'll pitch him outside—he'd hit it hard, he'd hit it out of the park, in left field just as easy as in Stirling which was small. But he'd still hit it further out of the park than a right-hand batter would hit it out.[99]

Observing a home run Chase hit over the left-field fence in a game in 1939, *Chatham Daily News* sports reporter and columnist Art Cartier declared it was something "you see no more than once or twice in a lifetime."[100] Noting the game took place at the larger Athletic Park, Cartier declared "It's hard enough for a right-hander to pull one that distance."[101] Orville Wright recalled years later that he had "never seen a man hit' em as far as Flat did."[102] That these men could speak in such detail about Chase's batting—the nuances of where and how he hit the ball—suggests how much those memories were tied to the man himself.

Another Chatham Coloured All-Stars player whose unique skills were part of the oral history of the team was King Terrell. Terrell was a left-handed third-base player, a rarity in baseball.[103] Right-handed batters tend to hit the ball toward third base, and it is generally easier for a right-handed third-base player to retrieve and then throw the ball back to the left (throwing either to the catcher or to the first base player) than it is for a left-handed player. Terrell, however, regularly played third base, and did so throughout his team's eight-year existence. In fact, his unusual skills at third base became part of the oral history of the team, and his fellow players and others often spoke proudly about it. When she was interviewing Terrell, Wanda Milburn mentioned his third-base playing several times.[104] Milburn, who had grown up watching Terrell play, said, "And we know that you were the left-handed third baser who was really quite unique." Boomer also recalled Terrell's skills, explaining, "I caught a lot of his pitches standing on first base. He could throw them around, curve ball around the pitcher usually."[105]

Although many years had passed since he last played baseball, Terrell clearly valued that part of his life. In his oral history interview, he recalled receiving special attention for his playing, including getting his picture taken for a newspaper.[106] He also spoke about a time when he was playing out of town, when a game announcer told the crowd how rare it was to see a left-handed third baseman. Terrell recalled, "he announced my name, and everybody got up and gave me a big hand." He clearly relished that moment, as he said he remembered it, "just as well as if it was yesterday." At a time when opportunities for monetary or other markers of "success" were limited for young Black men, expressing yourself through sport, making an impression, mattered.

The Stars' third-base coach Percy Parker's humour and cheering from the sidelines also left strong memories among his fellow players and others. Boomer revealed that Parker had several catch-phrases he would use throughout a game, like "ain't that beautiful" when someone made a good play.[107] He recalled, "all during the game he'd crack you up." Boomer's sister Wanda remembered how loud Parker's voice was: "you could hear it all over the East End," she said.[108] The former Chatham Coloured All-Stars players and others remembering him as much for his cheering as his coaching suggests how important Parker's support meant to them. In the next chapter, the Black team's frequent encounters with racism at games, including spectators yelling racial slurs, will be discussed. A friendly, and very loud, voice on the sidelines to help counter that hostility, to resist it, meant a lot to the players.

Concluding the First Season: The Wanless Trophy

Although the Chatham Stars struggled in their first season in the Chatham City Baseball League and finished in last place, Chase's arrival helped the team win the Wanless Trophy.[109] Named after the Chatham City Baseball League president, Ed Wanless, the cup was awarded to the winner of a post-season tournament involving all four city league teams. With Flat Chase pitching, the Stars won the Wanless Trophy in five straight games. In the four games where he pitched, Chase far outperformed the opposition pitchers. In the first game of the series, Chase had twelve strikeouts, while the other team's two pitchers struck out twelve between them.[110] In their second game, he struck out eight, but the other team got only eight hits from him.[111] In the last two games against the Juniors he doubled the number of strikeouts of the opposing pitchers—11 vs 6 in one game, and 15 vs 7 in the other.[112] The newspaper reports suggested Chase was a controlling presence in the games. A reporter covering one game claimed the opposing team members "were unable to do much with the offerings of the Buxton boy."[113] In the final games against the Juniors, the paper observed, "It was simply a case of too much Chase, who worked on the mound in both games."[114]

In some ways, the Wanless Trophy victory provided some vindication for the Chatham Stars after a difficult first season in the Chatham City Baseball League. That they had even been part of that competition, playing in what had been an all-white league, is due in part to the declining fortunes of baseball in the region. While the Chatham Stars were able to find a place in an OBAA-affiliated league, the experiences of the Windsor and London Black teams highlight the larger challenges they faced in this period. All three teams had grown out of the strong traditions of Black baseball in the region, connected through tight networks of family, place, and community. They were created and nurtured in those environments, and all three showed signs of strong baseball talent. Only the Chatham team, however, moved into the spotlight through OBAA-affiliated leagues, enabling them to seek championships and develop a larger profile. Whether or not the Windsor and London teams would have wanted that path is unknown. Local baseball organizers had control over who had access to OBAA competition, and it is possible that the Windsor and London teams, through racism or other reasons, did not have the influence or support to move into advanced play. Certainly, the Hotel London team never had a chance to continue in

Fig. 4.2 ▪ Advertisement for the 1933 Wanless Trophy, an end-of-season baseball tournament in Chatham. Although they had a rough first season, the Chatham Stars won the Wanless Trophy that year. Photo credit: *Chatham Daily News*, September 20, 1933, 11.

the London city league after their employers fired them and stopped their sponsorship. In Chatham, however, where local organizers were anxious to rebuild the city's baseball legacy, a space opened for a Black team to compete for a provincial championship.

5

Playing in Racialized Spaces

The 1934 City League Season

From the first few games of the Chatham Coloured All-Stars' second season in the Chatham City Baseball League, it was clear the team had developed a new confidence and energy. With some experience, as well as new players they had recruited from Buxton and Detroit, the team began winning games. In fact, they won all but one of their regular season games in the Chatham City Baseball League in 1934. Flat Chase's fastball pitches and a strong batting lineup began bringing crowds, and some excitement, to local baseball. They had also developed an identity as an exhibition team, playing across southwestern Ontario to support the club. As noted in the *Chatham Daily News* sports pages late in the 1934 season, "The Stars are in constant demand in all parts of the district because they're so good a drawing card."[1] For those who hoped to see baseball flourish in Chatham once again, a team such as the All-Stars who could attract crowds was a valuable commodity. Indeed, *Chatham Daily News* sports reporters celebrated the team, believing it could turn around the declining fortunes of baseball in the community. Despite the accolades, the Chatham Coloured All-Stars continued to face the challenges of being a Black team in a predominantly white sporting space. While the local newspaper columnists praised their playing, they also sometimes portrayed the Black team in racist and racialized ways. The All-Stars also encountered conflict, racism, and occasionally physical violence on and off the field. Winning baseball games was no immunity from racism.

Second Year in the Chatham City League, 1934

As the team began their second season in the Chatham City Baseball League, they went through a few changes, one of which was their name. Throughout 1933, they had been known as the "Chatham Stars" (except when they were playing exhibition games, when they were known as the Chatham Colored Stars and the Canadian Colored Champions). Although the *Chatham Daily News* continued to call them the "Chatham Stars" in 1934, write-ups on the team from wire services or outside bureaus more often referred to them as the "Chatham Colored All-Stars" particularly when they played exhibition games. By the end of the season, they were referred to as the "Chatham Colored All-Stars" more often.[2] Only in 1935 did the *Chatham Daily News* regularly call them the "Chatham Colored All-Stars." When they registered with the OBAA, however, they were simply the "Chatham All-Stars."[3] According to Archie Stirling, the team dropped "Colored" for fear they would be rejected because of their race.[4] While highlighting their race was an advantage when promoting themselves as an exhibition team, it could be a liability when dealing with the all-white OBAA executive.

Besides changing their name in the 1934 season, the All-Stars also gained a new manager, Joseph Parker, who replaced his brother-in-law, Duncan Williams, in the role. In the years since he managed the Chatham Colored Giants, Parker and his wife, May, had adopted two daughters, Hilda and Pauline. They lived in the second-floor apartment above Parker's barber shop, on King Street West, just outside the East End neighbourhood.[5] By the 1930s, Parker was widely known in the community by the nickname, "Happy" or "Hap" Parker.[6] Joining Parker on the support team was a third-base coach, Louis Pryor. Born in Michigan but raised in Chatham's East End, Pryor had spent much of the 1920s living and working in Detroit (which also explains why he was not involved with the Chatham Colored Giants).[7] His family—wife Blanche and children—remained in Chatham while he made visits back and forth. By the early 1930s, perhaps because of declining job opportunities in Detroit during the Great Depression, Pryor returned to Chatham permanently. Percy Parker, as well, returned to the team as a third-base coach for the 1934 season.

Many of the players from the previous year returned for the 1934 season, including the Harding brothers, the Talbot brothers (although Ben missed the later season and playoffs due to work), as well as Gouy Ladd, Sagasta Harding, Cliff Olbey, Flat Chase, and King Terrell. Aside from the returning players, the All-Stars recruited several new team members for the season. Among them were another pair of brothers, Hyle and Stanton Robbins, from Buxton. According to the Robbins brothers' niece, Pauline Williams (her mother Alma was their sister), the whole family, girls and boys, grew up playing baseball (and two Robbins sisters, Alma and June,

played softball).[8] Williams recalled, "our school is right up the street from us. You know, the SS #13 Raleigh, and we had a big yard, they had a big yard, and they all of them played up there." In the 1934 season both Hyle and Stanton played outfield, but Stanton also pitched in later years. Boomer Harding recalled that Hyle was a fast runner and Stanton had a good arm.[9] Pauline Williams recalled someone she knew who used to play ball with her uncle would add padding to his glove to cushion Stanton's pitches. She also said her mother "liked to play ball with them, but she said he could get that ball and he would land it on anybody that got near him. So, he was good with the ball."[10]

Using their cross-border baseball connections, the Chatham Coloured All-Stars also recruited two players, Donald Tabron and Donise Washington, from Detroit.[11] Ben Talbot, speaking to a newspaper reporter in 1984, claimed that Tabron and Washington came to Chatham through Flat Chase.[12] The All-Stars were initially looking to fill a couple of spots on the roster for a Victoria Day game in Chatham. Talbot claimed "Flat said he knew a guy in Detroit that he played with in the Church League." The person Chase knew was Donald Tabron, who was living in the historic Black neighbourhood on the east side of Detroit known as "Black Bottom." Talbot recounted that he and Len Harding went over to Detroit to speak to Tabron, saying "we looked in every pool hall on the east side," before finding him at two in the morning.[13] In a 2019 interview, Tabron's son, Donald Jr., shared a similar story his father told him, saying Tabron had been running the card tables at his older sister's "rent party" that night when the Chatham ball players finally found him.[14] Tabron agreed to come and brought along his friend, Donise Washington, as catcher.

Although both Tabron and Washington were living on Detroit's east side in the early 1930s, like many Black Detroiters of that era they were not native to the city. Tabron was born in Princeton, Indiana, but moved to Detroit to live with an older sister when he was a child.[15] According to Tabron's son, Donald Jr., the move happened after the 1925 Tri-State Tornado which tore through their hometown. One of the buildings destroyed was a factory where Donald Sr.'s father, Henry, worked.[16] Although he was not killed, he may have lost his job. As Tabron's mother had died when he was an

Fig. 5.1 (facing) ▪ Wilfred "Boomer" Harding, taken c. 1934 or 1935. Photo credit: Leddy Library Archives and Special Collections, F1033 (Wilfred "Boomer" Harding Collection), Scrapbook 1.

infant, it was decided that he should go to Detroit. He finished his schooling there, but after graduating from high school, like many other young Black people of his generation, he struggled to find work. Donise Washington was also living in Detroit in the early 1930s, but had been born in Memphis, Tennessee.[17] Whether he moved north as a child with his parents or arrived as a young man searching for work is unknown. He was, however, one of tens of thousands who were part of the Great Migration, the movement of southern Black people into northern industrial regions. In 1930, Washington was living with his then-wife's family and working in a factory.[18]

As Tabron himself recalled, he and Washington went to Chatham "to play one game on Queen Victoria's birthday."[19] Instead, of just one game, Tabron said with a laugh, "I wound up staying two years and Don stayed for five." That Victoria Day game went well, with the All-Stars winning against the Duns. Washington's late-game hit enabled Ross Talbot, who was on first base, to score the winning run: "Washington then came to the rescue of his mates with a two-bagger scoring Ross and the game was over."[20] At some point either before or after that game, the All-Stars invited the two Detroit men to join the team, offering them room and board if they stayed. With few prospects in Detroit, both men accepted. Explained Tabron, "That was the middle of the big Depression and baseball was something to do, the only thing to do. There was no such thing as really finding a job."[21] Certainly, jobs were hard to get for young Black men in Detroit at the height of the Great Depression.

Both men from Detroit moved in with local Chatham families. Tabron spent his first year living with Len and Boomer Harding's family. While interviewing Beulah Cuzzens for the MHSO oral history project, Vivian Chavis reminded her that players from out-of-town often stayed at the Hardings' house. "Your brothers and family were sort of another home for those boys in Chatham," Chavis noted.[22] Boomer also spoke about their ball player guests: "We all lived in a big house in the East End. When the boys come into town there was no accommodations, so we always had room for them in the house."[23] Wanda Milburn claimed, "At our house the side door was always open for anybody that Len or Boomer brought home. Sometimes maybe five or six of them would stay."[24] She said her brother used to give her a nickel to clean the bathroom after the ball players came home and washed up after a game. "It was so dirty," she recalled.[25] Pauline Parker Miller remembered both Washington and Tabron staying with them for a time. She recalled they put some beds on the third floor of the building where her father had his barber shop.[26] Harding claimed that lack of work during the Depression enabled them to recruit players. He explained, "Work was kind of scarce in the Windsor district so this was how we got most of our players. Times were tough and they'd play just for a house and some place to stay."[27]

The 1934 Season in the Chatham City League

The new players—Chase, and the two men from Detroit—brought some experience to the Chatham Coloured All-Stars which contributed to a strong second season. Terrell described Tabron's playing, saying he "was smooth and he was fast for a short stop, and he had an arm like a whip. He could throw a ball from any position."[28] Over the course of the 1934 season he also began pitching, and was known for his curve balls..Tabron's son, Donald Jr. explained, "He was a junk ball pitcher. What I mean by that is curve balls, sliders, knuckle balls. He wasn't a flame thrower or a fast pitch type of guy, he was going to throw junk at you…he was going to try to fool you with a lot of movement or off-speed."[29] Over the course of the season, Tabron worked on his pitching and ended up on the mound for many of the team's OBAA playoff games.[30] Indeed, pitching was one of the All-Stars' strengths in the 1934 season. King Terrell proclaimed that their team had a whole "infield of pitchers."[31] Aside from Chase and Tabron, Terrell, Ross Talbot, and occasionally, their catcher Donise Washington, all took turns pitching. That season, Chatham Coloured All-Stars pitchers also held the top three records in the league in late July, with Chase at 7-0, Terrell at 4-0, and Talbot at 3-1.[32]

Besides a strong pitching staff, the All-Stars gained a talented catcher in Donise Washington. Although Len Harding had been the team's primary catcher in 1933, he shifted into other positions, mainly the outfield, when Washington joined the team. His fellow players praised Washington for his leadership and his skills as a catcher. Terrell claimed Washington could catch as well as any player he had seen in the major leagues, remarking, "I've seen Donise Washington cut guys down on second base when he was on his haunches; he wasn't even standing up straight."[33] Terrell also spoke about Washington's leadership role on the team, saying he "practically kept the team together and made all the arrangements to travel, and everything like that."[34] John Olbey, who watched the team play when he was a boy, claimed Washington was like a field manager, making decisions about strategies and game play. Added Olbey, "He was the solid heart of the team."[35]

Along with strong infield players such as Tabron and Washington, the Chatham Coloured All-Stars had some effective batters. City League baseball statistics compiled and published in the *Chatham Daily News* suggest that the All-Stars players were among the league's top batters. In late June, five of the top six batters were members of the Chatham Coloured All-Stars, including Len Harding, Donise Washington, Stanton Robbins, Cliff Olbey, and Flat Chase.[36] By late July, the team was still leading in batting, with five batters in the top ten.[37] Granted, it is hard to say how strong the All-Stars' competition in the city league was that year. The Merchants, the city league's top team in 1933, joined the OBAA-affiliated Essex County Baseball League in 1934, taking some of the city's more experienced players with them. Nevertheless, the All-Stars clearly had some talented players.

In the 1934 season, the All-Stars also led the league in base stealing, a tactic popularized through the American Black baseball leagues.[38] Stealing bases added some excitement to the game, as it shifted attention from the pitcher and batter to other places on the diamond. That kind of dynamism also helped attract audiences, which was so important for the touring Black teams trying to make a living in the Great Depression. In the 1933 season, the All-Stars were not known for base stealing, but in 1934 it became a much bigger part of their game. By July 23, Donise Washington was at the top of the standings with twelve stolen bases, followed by a white player, Alvin "Dutch" Scott, who played with the Braggs, with ten, then Cliff Olbey with nine, and Ross Talbot with seven.[39] Given that Washington was the league's top base stealer, it is possible that the other players on the team followed his lead. Washington had a lot of influence on the team, as the former players acknowledged years later.[40] For whatever reason, stealing bases became a feature of the All-Stars' game in 1934.

The All-Stars maintained their ties to Black baseball culture in the 1934 season, and invited a Black team from Detroit, Taylor's Stars, to play on Emancipation Day and again on the Labour Day weekend.[41] Although the team members had changed, it is possible that this was the same Taylor's Stars team that used to play the Chatham Colored Giants in the 1920s. A few of the Taylor's players who came to Chatham in the 1930s previously played in the Negro National League, including former Detroit Stars pitcher Lawrence "Lefty" Terrell.[42] At a Labour Day game in Chatham in 1934, Lawrence Terrell coincidentally faced off against another left-handed pitcher named Terrell—King Terrell.[43] For the most part, however, the Taylor's Stars were representative of the many touring teams from Detroit that were looking to make some extra cash during the precarious years of the Great Depression.[44]

Boomer Harding recalled the excitement in the Chatham Black community when a Detroit team came to play. He said, "We'd bring up some teams from Detroit and pack the park. It was entertainment for the day, we didn't have any television then."[45] If the crowds were large, both the All-Stars and the team from Detroit would benefit. In a late 1970s interview, Harding explained they normally played for a share of the gate: "It was usually 60/40 or they'd play you 60/40, winner takes the 60, loser 40. Or else they'd want a fifty dollar guarantee or something, which was a lot of money. It would pay their way across the border, you know. Three or four cars. And we put on some good exhibition."[46] The All-Stars would charge admission, about fifty cents recalled Harding, and use that money to buy equipment or cover expenses for the club.

According to the *Chatham Daily News*, the crowd of 1,400 at the Emancipation Day game in 1934 was "treated to an all round entertaining spectacle."[47] Detroit won the first game 9–6, and Chatham took the second by a score of 7–6. As Boomer Harding later recalled, the Taylor's Stars of Detroit were a strong team. He said, "They had a lot of good talent. Of course, they had a lot more to draw from than we did in our little town but we always had the pitching to hold them."[48] He added that they sometimes recruited some white players from the city league to help when they played the Detroit team. "They were a powerful team and they played ball for keeps," he recalled.[49]

Although the Chatham Coloured All-Stars were having a successful year, two incidents in early June 1934 are examples of the conflict they sometimes experienced with the white teams in the Chatham City Baseball League. The first incident involved a complaint the Kent Bridge team (Kent Bridge is a small community a few miles from Chatham) lodged against the All-Stars during a city league game.[50] The Kent Bridge managers claimed that Cliff Olbey had shoved their third-base player as the All-Star ran from second base and headed toward home plate. After the game, Kent Bridge representatives took their case to a Chatham City Baseball League executive meeting. When asked about that specific incident in a late 1970s interview, Harding acknowledged, "Well this is what we had to do a lot was fight. There's no easy game."[51] Rob Ruck and others have argued race and racial conflict could rarely be separated from sports.[52] Harding elaborated on the sometimes rough, physical nature of their games. He said, "Oh yeah and there was spikes and everything else. You—it was played pretty rough [laughs]. We just had to play it rough, we did. You get recognition there."[53]

As Black men on a baseball field with white opponents, white officials, and mostly white spectators, the unequal power dynamic of Black against white was always there, whether actions or conflicts directly referenced race or not. Fellow player Ferguson Jenkins Sr. did not recall the physical fighting Harding described, but he did remember people arguing at games. He said in a 1980 interview, "There was arguments in baseball years ago, just like there's…it didn't come to blows but there was always a lot of discussion and cussing."[54] He then clarified, "We were talking to people what the right thing was. And being coloured, it was that you had to beat any team by ten runs pretty near."

Black teams also faced challenges when trying to defend themselves from complaints brought to league officials. While the *Chatham Daily News* article about the incident suggested that Olbey deliberately shoved the Kent Bridge player, the report did not give the All-Stars' views on what had happened.[55] As well, the article did not say if the All-Stars had a representative at that executive meeting where the Kent Bridge team made the complaint. Neither is it clear if the All-Stars disputed the charge, or if they had any other comments about other conflict or incidents at that game. Having to interact with an all-white group of league officials would not have been easy for a Black team disadvantaged by class and race. As well, assumptions and stereotypes about Black men being inherently violent would be an unspoken factor in any charges of violence the All-Stars would have faced. Even the language the *Chatham Daily News* reporter used to describe the incident emphasized Olbey's physicality: "Olbey pounded the keystone sack [second base] and headed for third. Stevens threw to third to flag the runner but the ball went between Millen's [Kent Bridge third-base player] legs…Olbey shoved Millen, toppling him over and scored."[56] Whatever happened at that executive meeting, the city baseball officials ordered the game replayed.[57] While it is not known how the All-Stars reacted to this ruling, in the later years of the team they defended themselves more openly in their interactions with league officials when they felt they had received unfair or unequal treatment.

Just a few days after the incident with Kent Bridge, another conflict arose at a city league game between the All-Stars and the Duns when two spectators got into a fight. The *Chatham Daily News* reporter was somewhat bemused by it, remarking that the two "got into an altercation which resulted in one of them being shoved off the stand. Several of the other fans showed a willingness to 'mix' but there was no damage."[58] While this incident did not appear particularly violent (apart from the shove off the bleachers) it is a reminder of the conflict, often racialized, that was part of the experience of Black fans. Although the newspaper report did not mention it, one of the spectators who got into the fight was Black.[59] In their article on Black women and sports in early twentieth-century southern Ontario, Nzindukiyimana and Wamsley explain that being a Black spectator meant having to deal with racial slurs, insults, and provocations. They note the way that Beulah Cuzzens described the verbal assaults she regularly encountered at sports events. They argue her experience "further underscores how much racial tensions dictated Black people's combative outlook and behaviour. The ballpark was often a 'fighting' arena."[60] Cuzzens's younger sister, Wanda Milburn, recalled hostility from white spectators while watching her brothers play in Bothwell (Kent County) when she was in her teens. She said, "And some kids were calling us names and throwing apple cores and stones at us. I finally got tired for one and got up and chased the little boy and when I caught him, I beat him. And I beat him so hard that they had to stop me. They stopped the ball game and sat me on the bench with the ball players."[61] Physical violence was sometimes part of the game, on the diamond and in the stands. The fight among the spectators on that June day in 1934 is a reminder of the extra burdens of playing or watching baseball for Black and racialized people.

Indeed, a factor in both the physical conflict on the ball diamond and fighting in the stands was "whiteness," an identity that was historical and varied over time, but nevertheless was part of the larger context of a racialized society. Nell Irvin Painter and others have explored the ways that ideas of whiteness and racial superiority have shaped interactions between people of European and non-European descent.[62] Historian Craig Heron, in his study of working-class boys and masculinity in early twentieth-century Hamilton, Ontario, has reflected on the more specific ways that whiteness affected working-class life. Public education that glorified the British Empire and its white, male "heroes," he argues, "helped shape their [white, working class boys'] identity as white males."[63] Moreover, he claims, this identity helped develop "a sharper sense of gendered and racial superiority that could seep into their after-school play and began to frame not only their consciousness of Empire, but also their attitudes to small African-Canadian and Chinese populations." Although conflicts on the ball diamond and in the stands were instigated by many factors, race was always part of the power dynamics embedded in the conflicts.

Through the Lens of the *Chatham Daily News*

As discussed in earlier chapters, ideas about race also affected the way newspapers covered the Black baseball teams. In 1934, the sports pages of the *Chatham Daily News* introduced a new feature, a regular sports opinion column that brought more direct attention to the Chatham Coloured All-Stars. "Analyzing Sport," written by 19-year-old John (Jack) Calder, was one of many opinion columns appearing in Canadians' sports pages to engage readers and sell newspapers. These columns featured lively writing and strong opinions from personalities such as the *Toronto Star*'s Lou Marsh and the *Globe and Mail*'s Fanny "Bobbie" Rosenfeld.[64] These columns were tied to the growing commercialization of sport and the rise of the sports journalist as celebrity. As Morrow and Wamsley note, Marsh, one of Canada's pre-eminent sports columnists, attracted readers with his punchy, catch-phrase-laden prose and his humorous asides. His writing was also peppered with ethnic stereotypes and racist slurs.[65]

Calder would undoubtedly have been aware of Marsh and other columnists making their names in 1930s sports journalism.[66] Although his writing style differed from Marsh's, Calder's evocative prose and wry humour suggested he, like Marsh, used his columns to speak directly to the public, and tried to engage them in sports stories both amateur and professional. A public invested in these stories were more likely to attend local sports events and buy newspapers. Calder wanted to see the declining status of Chatham baseball reversed, and he used his columns to promote the sport and get spectators to attend games.[67] He spoke glowingly of white baseball traditions in Chatham (he never mentioned the Chatham Colored Giants) while decrying the loss of fans and revenues. In one column, for example, he encouraged readers to attend a game to "help baseball regain its feet financially."[68] In another, he called on readers to "help baseball a little to return to its lost prestige here."[69] This overriding concern about the relative weakness of baseball shaped the way he covered the sport, and how he came to see the Chatham Coloured All-Stars.

During the 1934 baseball season, his first covering local baseball, Calder's initial focus in his columns was not the All-Stars, but a white team, the Merchants, playing in an OBAA-affiliated league in nearby Essex County.[70] Initially, he saw the Merchants as the team that would help Chatham regain its stature as a strong baseball town. Only after the Merchants failed to make the league playoffs did Calder turn his attention to the Chatham

Coloured All-Stars, who were the season's runaway frontrunner in the Chatham City Baseball League. As Calder began promoting the All-Stars, his columns suggest that he greatly admired their ability to attract fans to baseball games. Paying customers also gave the teams and the league some financial stability. In one column, for example, Calder praised the All-Stars for working hard to make their games interesting and exciting, adding that, "Those qualities are necessary to an outfit that's going to break even in these days of strain and stress."[71] In a column later in August, Calder remarked that the All-Stars, by attracting crowds, were also helping the finances of the other teams they played, saying: "Wherever they go the Stars bring out a big crowd and many teams which have been just managing to get along financially this year will go over the top when the Stars play them. Chatham too will see bigger crowds than in several years when the colored team begins its O.B.A.A. campaigning on September 6."[72] As the All-Stars began their first series in the OBAA playoffs in early September, Calder proclaimed that the All-Stars had been "largely responsible for a revival of baseball interest in the city."[73] Later, as the All-Stars were moving through the OBAA playoff rounds, Calder remarked "There'll be a lot of ball around here next year if the Stars win the provincial title."[74] While he openly admired the team's skills, Calder clearly saw them for what they could do to revive local baseball.

In promoting a Black team to a largely white readership, Calder's narratives about the Chatham Coloured All-Stars often featured white, middle-class values. A member of the middle class himself (his father was an Anglican minister),[75] Calder praised the All-Stars for their ambition and hard work. Reminiscent of the "muscular assimilationism" described by Patrick Miller, Calder's promotion of the team emphasized traits seen as a path to respectability and acceptance in mainstream white culture. For example, in a late July 1934 column (his first column devoted specifically to the All-Stars), Calder proclaimed them "Chatham's Most Ambitious Team."[76] He spoke approvingly of the team's busy exhibition schedule, noting their coach, Joseph Parker, had to convince the All-Stars to limit themselves to two games a week. Using a cultivated folksy tone, Calder remarked on how hard the All-Stars played, wondering how they were not "hobbling on crutches with charley horses that whinny plenty loudly."[77] In another column, published shortly before the All-Stars began their OBAA playoff rounds, Calder again emphasized the work ethic of the team, arguing they could "instill in the minds of some of our delinquents the idea that baseball can be made most attractive when energy and drive are injected into the playing of the game."[78] As a white columnist trying to promote a Black team to a largely white readership, Calder may have featured the team's work ethic to counter prevailing racial stereotypes about the work habits of Black people.

Calder also emphasized white middle-class values including ambition, reliability, and a strong work ethic in player profiles in his columns. For example, Calder identified Donald Tabron as ambitious, and called him one of the "Most Improved" players of the Chatham City League.[79] Hard work, he noted, transformed Tabron from a fair, to a more focused athlete whose "arm is more deadly and he's a surer man on ground-hit balls." He again praised Tabron, and a white player on another team, as "willing workers, as ambitious as they come." Later that same month, Calder featured King Terrell in a column, calling him one of the most "reliable" on the team.[80] He claimed Terrell's "left-handed shoots and curves are as baffling as any deliveries offered up by any pitcher in the circuit." Calder also frequently praised Donise Washington for his leadership, his work ethic, and his judgment. For example, in a write-up of a game (likely written by Calder), the author called Washington the "brains of the team."[81] In an "Analyzing Sport" column, Calder again called Washington a "clever catcher," and noted that he and Tabron "have toiled for hours together in the mornings whipping themselves into shape for the O.B.A.A. campaign."[82] Hard work, practice, and leadership were all qualities Calder wanted to convey to his readers.[83]

While Calder often praised members of the Chatham Coloured All-Stars, his coverage of the Black team was nevertheless racialized and racist. Although Calder rarely mentioned race directly, he sometimes described and wrote about the Black players differently from the white players. Janelle Joseph and others have noted the way mainstream white press and culture emphasize the physicality of Black athletes, and Calder followed that pattern.[84] While evidence suggests that the All-Stars were an athletic team with fast runners and strong hitters, Calder accentuated those traits when describing them. For example, in one column, Calder asserted that the All-Stars had "a steam-roller attack, a penchant for grabbing the breaks," suggesting an overpowering physical force.[85] Calder also used machine metaphors, at one point calling them a "well-knit machine," suggesting a physical, but unthinking athletic drive.[86] While he occasionally described the white Merchants as "fighting," while they were aiming for the league playoffs, he did not use the same physical language with the white team as he did with the All-Stars.

Calder's emphasis on the physical was most noticeable when he wrote about Flat Chase, often commenting on his size. In one column, for example, he referred to him as a "strapping right-hander."[87] Later in the same piece, Calder called him a "speed-ball demon," suggesting a physical power over which the Black player had little control. In another column, Calder described Chase as an aggressive, physical force, saying: "it was big Flat Chase, who played at shortstop for the Stars yesterday, who predominated on the attack." [88] To accentuate the point, Calder also invoked racist imagery (and a possible reference to the Ku Klux Klan) when he asserted that "The Kolored King of Klout rapped a triple, a double, and a single in five attempts." While admiring Chase's skills, Calder also reduced him to a racist stereotype. When covering white players, by contrast, he sometimes referred to their height, but otherwise did not talk about their bodies in the same way.[89] In nearby Windsor, Ontario, the *Border Cities Star/Windsor Daily Star* also described Black ball players in similar ways, avoiding overt references to race, but remarking on the physicality of the athletes.[90]

Calder used entertaining stories to connect with readers, but his anecdotes about the Black ball players sometimes veered into stereotypes and mockery. In one column, Calder commented on Flat Chase's batting stance, describing him as doing a "rumba" when he got up to the plate. Calder then joked Chase's movement should be set to orchestral music.[91] Boomer Harding, in a late 1970s oral history interview, recalled that Chase did have a distinctive way of getting ready to hit a ball, saying, "he get set there and the rump would go like this and when that guy threw the ball he was set. And he got the prettiest follow through and everything."[92] While Harding admired Chase's signature move, Calder exaggerated it for comic effect and played into the stereotypes of Black people as entertainers. Calder also commented on Percy Parker's humorous remarks during games. As mentioned earlier, the former members of the Chatham Coloured All-Stars and others recalled Parker's sense of humour and loud support for the team. In Calder's column, however, Parker appeared clownish, described as a "box vaudevillian," who put on "a little floor show by himself during the game on Saturday."[93] The former members of the Chatham Coloured All-Stars who spoke about Parker had a lot of respect for his baseball knowledge and experience, and they appreciated his sense of humour. While Calder was trying to amuse his readers, he never made similar personal remarks about the white ball players he covered.

How much members of the Chatham Coloured All-Stars paid attention to Calder's columns and commentaries is unknown. Moving into public spaces such as organized baseball, however, meant the players faced increased scrutiny from the press. According to Harding, the All-Stars team members enjoyed seeing the newspaper articles summarizing the games. In a 1984 newspaper interview, Harding noted "the players appreciated picking up the paper the next day seeing the report on our games right up there with the Tigers who were hot that season too."[94] Seeing their names and the record of their games was a validation, a legitimacy in a world that excluded them in many ways. Whether or not they paid attention to the more focused commentary and judgment from newspaper columnists, however, is unclear. The scrapbooks compiled from newspaper articles by family members of the Chatham Coloured All-Stars, however, may offer some clues. What people do not save can be as revealing as what they do. While the scrapbooks belonging to the Harding and Chase families featured dozens of articles summarizing the games, they included very few of the "opinion" columns by Calder or others, at least during the 1934 season.[95]

As the Chatham Coloured All-Stars finished their second season in the Chatham City League, they were in a more secure position than they had been a year earlier. With their strong season record, and crowds coming to see Flat Chase, Donise Washington, and others, the All-Stars were carving a space for themselves in the predominantly white environment of Chatham amateur baseball. At the same time, this higher profile meant increasing expectations and demands from white audiences, whether it was game spectators, league officials, or columnists with the *Chatham Daily News*. These demands would intensify in the weeks that followed, as the Chatham Coloured All-Stars moved into OBAA playoff contention.

6

Becoming the All-Stars

The 1934 OBAA Championship

By the end of their second season playing in the Chatham City Baseball League, the Chatham Coloured All-Stars had won the right to represent the Chatham City Baseball League in the OBAA playoffs. Although they had gained experience in white amateur baseball over two seasons, moving into OBAA playoff contention meant having to deal with a range of new problems and challenges. First, they had to travel outside Kent County to play the various regional winners. Extra travel meant having to find more money, which was always a problem for a Black team with limited resources. Travel was also more difficult for Black players, as the existence of "sundown towns" (communities with by-laws or informal practices requiring Black people to leave by a certain time) in Ontario and racist restaurant and hotel owners meant Black people never knew if they could find a place to stay or eat.[1] The Chatham Coloured All-Stars experienced this first-hand as they ventured into places where they had never been. As well, the Chatham Coloured All-Stars had to navigate OBAA politics, and interact with officials and umpires (all white) whom they had never met. As Black men, they were disadvantaged in those interactions, and several of the players later spoke about controversies and conflict they experienced. Finally, representing Chatham in the OBAA playoffs put the All-Stars under a bigger spotlight, watched closely by hometown spectators and the local press. What they felt about that pressure is unknown, but their performances were uneven during the four regional playoff series. They won some games easily, but lost others by wide margins. While it is difficult to say what causes a sports team to win and lose games, the All-Stars encountered pressures and problems that a white team would not have faced. Playing baseball could never entirely be separated from the world that created it.

Despite those challenges, the Chatham Coloured All-Stars won the 1934 OBAA Intermediate B championship. At a time of deep racial division, they moved into the "white space" of organized amateur baseball and brought public attention to a group of Black men from Chatham. In the years since that historic win, it has become a central part of the collective memory about the Chatham Coloured All-Stars, and was a focus of oral history interviews conducted in the 1970s and 1980s. In recounting that championship season, the former players remembered the controversies, the tension, and the racism they experienced, as well as the fun times with their teammates. Family members and others who witnessed the series were more likely to talk about what it meant to see a Black team from their East End neighbourhood win a title and be celebrated by the entire city. Clearly, the 1934 OBAA championship continued to mean something to them, decades later.

While the All-Stars easily made the OBAA playoffs in 1934, one of the more immediate problems they faced was finding money to pay for it. Although these were amateur leagues, players were expected to raise money to cover their equipment, uniforms, and travel. As Black men, the low-paying jobs they could find did not leave much for supporting a baseball club. And unlike some of the white teams in the league, the All-Stars did not have a main corporate sponsor.[2] As noted earlier, the All-Stars raised money by playing exhibition games, travelling up the highways of southwestern Ontario. Even getting to these games was a challenge, as the players did not have cars. Boomer Harding recalled sometimes people with cars would drive them, and other times "we just borrow them [cars] off the lot and we'd get there."[3] Harding said they would cram six people into a car, so crowded that "when one would move in the car the other two would have to move because you're so cramped up."[4] Other times, he said, they all rode in the back of a flour truck from a local mill. He explained, "We'd go anywhere, anytime, for a ball game…and a dollar or two."[5] In fact, after qualifying for the OBAA playoffs and before starting their first series, the All-Stars squeezed in numerous exhibition games, likely trying to earn enough money to cover the expenses to come.

One expense the team had for the playoffs was new uniforms. Playing in the city league for two years, as King Terrell recalled, they just had an odd assortment of uniforms, with nothing matching.[6] As they headed off to the OBAA playoffs representing the city, however, they needed matching uniforms. These were a considerable expense—Terrell thought they cost about twenty-five to thirty dollars each. The team managed by asking various businesses in town to pay for one or two, in return for letting them put their company names on the back. Terrell claimed he convinced his boss at the William Pitt Hotel to pay for uniforms for him and Len and Boomer Harding, who also worked there. He said, "He [the boss] was going on holidays that day at noon and I asked him in the morning." Besides catching the boss in a good mood, Terrell remembered holding dances at the Taylor Community Centre to raise money. Playing in competitive OBAA baseball cost money, which may be why other Black teams in the region played in city leagues only.

Playoff Series Against Sarnia, Welland, and Milton

The Chatham Coloured All-Stars began their playoff run in early September in a series against the Sarnia Red Sox, winners of the Lambton-Middlesex league.[7] The best-of-three series began strongly for the All-Stars, with an 8–3 win in Sarnia for the first game.[8] The All-Stars had played the Sarnia Red Sox in an exhibition game earlier in the season, so the team and the city were familiar to them. Chase pitched that first game, having recovered sufficiently from an arm injury he sustained during the season. He had twelve strikeouts (to his opponent's four), while the veteran Sarnia pitcher, "Smoky" Joe Allen, struggled. The series ended rather anticlimactically, however, when the Sarnia team failed to bring enough OBAA-registered players to their next game.[9] With that, Sarnia defaulted both the game and the series to Chatham.

After the shortened Sarnia series, the All-Stars moved on to play the Welland Terriers, Intermediate B winners of the Niagara region. The All-Stars faltered when they lost the opening game at home by a score of 17–7, their biggest loss of the season.[10] The *Chatham Daily News* called it a "weird game" for the All-Stars, as they were not accustomed to losing by such a wide margin. Chase was the starting pitcher, but as the *Chatham Daily News* reported, he "was far from his usual form. When this became apparent right at the start of the proceedings, the fact unnerved the local lads." Chase seemed to be struggling (and he had been nursing a sore arm for weeks), as batter after batter got hits. Terrell relieved him in the first inning, but he, too, had trouble staving off the opposing batters. Donise Washington finally replaced him in the second inning (with Len Harding taking over as catcher). The team's other relief pitchers, Donald Tabron and Ross Talbot, were not at that game, leaving Washington with few other choices. Although Welland scored thirteen runs in the first two innings, the All-Stars, with Washington pitching, finished the game and managed to score a few more runs of their own. Whether or not Chase's sore arm was the only reason for the uneven game, or if there were other factors, is difficult to say.

Despite a shaky start to the series, the All-Stars won their second game in Welland by a score of 4–2. Not only did the All-Stars win (with Terrell pitching), Flat Chase hit a home run that almost instantly became a legend in Chatham baseball. An article appearing in the *Chatham Daily News*, claimed, "'Flat' Chase, hard-hitting shortstop for the Stars, supplied the biggest thrill of the afternoon when he drove a mammoth drive far over the right field fence in the sixth for a home run. It was the longest drive in the history of the local park."[11] Decades later, Chase's home run in Welland had become part of the Chatham Coloured All-Stars' oral history. In oral history interviews, Terrell and Boomer Harding both spoke about it. While their accounts differ slightly, they both emphasized that Chase's home run was a big moment, and that people in Welland recognized and talked about it. Suggesting the story was important, both men remembered details about where they were when Chase hit the ball. Harding claimed, "It was one of my greatest moments because I was on first base when he hit it."[12] Likewise, Terrell remembered that he was pitching that day.[13] According to Harding, "The ball not only cleared the right field fence, it cleared a building way behind the fence. People in Welland later said the ball ended up downtown."[14] When Terrell told the story, his details were slightly different, with the ball clearing a tree behind centre field rather than a building. Whether it was a tree or a building, the point was that it sailed very, very far. And both men claimed that people from Welland were impressed by it. Terrell claimed, "we talked to different people there and they had seen baseball games there and said they'd never seen a ball hit that far or that hard in their lives before."[15] Harding also spoke about the impression the home run made: "If you were in Welland today and told anybody you were from Chatham, the first thing they would tell you would be about the home run Flat hit there one day."[16] According to Chase's son Horace, people in Welland were still speaking about it, years later, when he went to visit. He said, "one time we went to Welland to see the locks and an old fellow asked me my name and when I told him Chase he asked me if I was related to Flat Chase. I told the fellow Flat was my dad and he started telling me about the home run Dad hit there one day."[17]

Although Chase's "mammoth" home run has overshadowed the game in which it took place, it did propel the All-Stars into the third and deciding game in the series. The OBAA announced it would take place in London, a location agreed upon because it was roughly halfway between Chatham and Welland.[18] Before a small crowd in London's Tecumseh Park (now Labatt Park), the All-Stars won the game 11–7.[19] Tabron was back with the team and he pitched the winning game. The team's strengths as batters were on display, outhitting the Welland team 14 to 8. Although Chase did not score another home run, he, Tabron, and Gouy Ladd each got three-base hits (hitting the ball and getting as far as third base). Jack Calder, in his "Analyzing Sport" column, declared, "Chatham's high-riding Stars seem well on their way to an O.B.A.A. championship."[20]

While the All-Stars advanced to the next playoff round, they encountered more financial problems. After defeating Welland, the All-Stars moved on to play the winner of the OBAA's eastern division. At the time, the eastern division playoffs were underway, with Milton, Ontario playing against Peterborough.[21] The All-Stars were faced with either travelling at least 150 miles (Milton) or possibly 260 miles (Peterborough) for their next series in the OBAA championship. As the OBAA did not provide full travel costs, particularly when it was not a final championship series, the organization expected teams to pay most of their own travel expenses. As previously stated, the All-Stars relied primarily on what they earned from their share of the amount collected for tickets at games. Calder noted in his "Analyzing Sport" column that the team's earnings from their sparsely-attended game in London, when they defeated Welland, was just five dollars.[22] In fact, a *Chatham Daily News* article in early October suggested that "supporters of the team were doubtful" that the team would be able to continue with the OBAA playoffs if they were not able to find a sponsor.[23]

Finances became even more pressing when the All-Stars learned that they would need to play one more series than they were expecting if they wanted to win the provincial championship. Milton won the eastern division, and normally they would have met the All-Stars to decide the Intermediate B title.[24] That year, however, two other teams in the eastern division, Meaford and Penetanguishene, had launched an appeal with the OBAA over officiating in their playoff series.[25] The OBAA allowed the disputed game to be replayed, and in doing so, they also allowed the winner to play the winner of the Chatham-Milton series for the provincial title. The *Chatham Daily News* remarked that "followers of the Stars said it seemed hardly fair that the Chatham team should have to travel to the far east twice in order to win an O.B.A.A. title."[26] An extra series meant more expenses for the All-Stars to cover.

Eventually, a local white garage owner, Peter (Pete) Gilbert offered to help cover some of the All-Stars' travel costs. The *Chatham Daily News* referred to him as an "enthusiastic baseball fan," who provided three cars (and gas) for the team to get to their games.[27] In oral history interviews, Terrell, Boomer Harding, and Ferguson Jenkins Sr. all spoke about Gilbert.[28] Harding recalled, "he helped us on a few trips because he was—sometimes he'd go to the games—a lot of times he'd go to the games."[29] He told a story about Gilbert offering Flat Chase his coat for a home run. "He'd offer Flat a coat—the coat he was wearing if he'd hit a home run. Flat would hit the home run and he'd give him the coat off his back or something like that [laughing]."[30] Terrell also recalled that besides transportation, Gilbert supplied uniforms and equipment for the team.[31] Competing in an OBAA-affiliated league cost money, and the farther they advanced, the more money it cost. Clearly, there was a price for playing at an elite level, and it was a major barrier for Black teams.

As the All-Stars moved through the playoff rounds, they continued to play strongly in some games while struggling in others. As they began their next series against Milton, they won their first game at home. The game featured strong batting from Chase, who had two home runs, including "one of the longest—if not the longest—drive ever poled on the Queen Street grounds."[32] When he batted in the final game-winning run, sending Boomer Harding across the plate, Chase "was almost mobbed by his team mates" who were excited about their first (and only) win at home during the OBAA playoffs. That momentum, however, did not last as the All-Stars lost their next game by a score of 21–4, their largest loss of the season (and perhaps ever). The newspaper article gave few details, but suggested that Milton's pitcher, Barney Marsh, "curve artist," had "baffled the Stars."[33] While the All-Stars were having trouble connecting to the ball, their pitchers were also faltering. In fact, the All-Stars went through five pitchers, as one by one, Chase, Terrell, Tabron, and Talbot went to the mound and were quickly relieved. Washington finally took the ball and pitched the rest of the game.

While it is not clear what caused the shaky start, Calder noted in a column that the players had blamed poor umpiring.[34] Although he had not been at the game,[35] Calder dismissed that complaint, claiming the All-Stars faltered because they never had to "fight" in their previous games. Despite

Calder's skepticism, the All-Stars may very well have had problems with an umpire. The game write-up, supplied by a wire service, was brief, so it is difficult to gain much insight from that source. In their oral history interviews, however, both Boomer Harding and Jenkins spoke about their encounters with racist and unfair umpires while playing ball. They did not refer to that game specifically, but they indicated that being treated unfairly by game officials was a common experience for them. That the All-Stars came back to Milton a few days later and won by a score of 8–7, taking the series, suggests that they did not lose the earlier game for lack of talent. The same pitcher was on the mound for Milton in both games.[36]

For their third game, the All-Stars ending up playing in Milton again, instead of following the normal OBAA practice of picking a spot halfway between the two communities. According to Boomer Harding, they did it for financial reasons. He explained, "after they beat us 21–4, we didn't have any money, you know. We didn't mind travelling. And they offered us $200.00."[37] Harding explained that while they had lots of supporters in Chatham, they often did not pay the admission price at the home ball games. He said, "we let them have the third game because we'd have drawn more people away from home than we could—we'd get a lot of people here, but they wouldn't pay. They'd watch it for nothing or put in a quarter or something. And we'd took the chance of going up there and beating them on their own home diamond. And they'd come through."[38] For a Black team with little money, sometimes they had to forego playing closer to home.

OBAA Final Series with Penetanguishene

After a long playoff season, the Chatham Coloured All-Stars finally advanced to the provincial Intermediate B finals against the Penetanguishene Foundry Rangers, the winners of the Penetanguishene-Meaford series.[39] It was mid-October, late for baseball, and the weather was getting cold. As well, the 250-mile distance between Chatham and Penetanguishene added to the time spent on the road, and the costs. The OBAA covered some travel expenses in the final series, but long distances meant more time off work and wages lost.

For the Chatham Coloured All-Stars, however, one of the first problems they encountered as the first game approached was simply finding a place to stay for the night in Penetanguishene. The *Chatham Daily News* reported that the team had driven north for their first game in the series on October 15, and stayed overnight in Midland, a few miles away from

Penetanguishene.[40] The newspaper said nothing about why they did not stay in Penetanguishene, where the series would take place. Years later, however, several of the former players, including Boomer Harding and Donald Tabron, explained that the Penetanguishene hotel manager had turned them away, saying the hotel was full. In describing the incident, however, both men were skeptical about the excuse. As Black men, they were regularly barred from many restaurants and hotels in southwestern Ontario (including hotels in Chatham), so they had good reason to doubt the hotel manager's claim. In a 1978 newspaper interview, Harding concluded, "They wouldn't allow us to stay overnight in Penetang because we were colored."[41] King Terrell also remembered the manager turning them away.[42] He said they got back into their cars and headed to nearby Midland, Ontario, where they found a hotel that accepted them.

Several features of this story, recounted in the oral histories, suggest the emotional impact of the incident on the players. When recalling this experience, Terrell, Harding, and Tabron all added specific details to give the listener a sense of how they felt when it happened. Tabron remembered that it was cold, while Terrell remarked that they arrived late, after eleven at night.[43] Harding remembered that it was raining when they pulled up to the hotel. He recalled, "we arrived there late on a rainy night. We had driven from Chatham thirty-five miles per hour and it was a long trip."[44] It was late, cold, and raining, all details setting the stage for the rejection to come. Harding's son, Blake, recalled his father talking about the experience, saying, "And I would just listen to them and hear the anxiety in the retelling of the story about getting to play in this game, which would put them ahead in the OBA championship. And then see some of the disappointment, or hear some of the disappointment when they were saying they finally got a place to stay, they got some sleep, and they were anxious about playing."[45] Decades after it happened, the story still evoked the emotions, and the anxiety, of that experience.

Despite the rejection, however, the former players claimed they were welcomed when they got to Midland. Terrell remembered the hotel manager in Midland welcoming them: "'Bring them all down here,'" Terrell recalled the hotel manager saying to them.[46] Likewise, Harding said, "so we went to Midland and they gladly accepted us. Then the next day they come over and cheered us on to try and help us win the game."[47] Tabron claimed that the next day, "half of Midland went back with us to watch the game…There was between 50 and 100 cars going to Penetang. It was just like a parade."[48]

Terrell also described in great detail the hospitality they received in both Midland and Penetanguishene after the game was over.[49] He claimed people in Penetanguishene took them out for beer after the game, while the hotel in Midland hosted a dinner and dance for them. Although the players spoke positively about the more welcoming treatment they later received, it does reflect the conditional acceptance afforded Black athletes. At the beginning, they were turned away; only after they "proved themselves" through their strong ball playing were they more fully welcomed. That experience, and the way the former All-Stars remembered it, is also a reminder of the perils Black people faced while travelling in unfamiliar places.

The encounter at the Penetanguishene hotel also suggests that the OBAA was not prepared, or they had no knowledge of the way racism could affect Black teams taking part in playoffs. According to Jack Calder, the OBAA had offered the All-Stars money to play the entire series in Penetanguishene before it began.[50] The All-Stars reportedly turned down the offer, saying their fans would want to see them play in Chatham. If the OBAA did make that offer, it suggests the OBAA and the Penetanguishene management expected the team would stay in Penetanguishene for several days. Either the OBAA executive and Penetanguishene team managers did not check with the local hotel, or they simply had no idea the team might have problems finding a place to stay. Even if the hotel was full (although that seems unlikely in Penetanguishene in mid-October), that information was clearly not given to the All-Stars. This incident, however, reveals the challenges the Chatham Coloured All-Stars faced in playing at the OBAA level, and the organization's lack of awareness of the problems they might encounter.

Despite the problems finding a place to stay in Penetanguishene, the All-Stars won their first game 4–2 in ten innings.[51] With the score tied in the tenth inning, one of the Harding brothers (the wire service article did not indicate which one) got a hit that sent two runners on base across the plate, winning the game. The article also noted the All-Stars' strong fielding, including a "marvelous throw" from Stanton Robbins that the author called the "best fielding play" of the game. Indeed, the strong defensive work helped, as the All-Stars faced a very effective Penetanguishene pitcher, Philip (Phil) Marchildon. In that game, Marchildon struck out nineteen Chatham batters and kept the team to seven hits and two walks. Born in 1913, Marchildon would later have a major league career with the Philadelphia Athletics (1940–42; 1945–49) and the Boston Red Sox (1950).[52] He was also inducted into the Canadian Baseball Hall of Fame.[53] In his memoir, Marchildon recalled his series with the Chatham Coloured All-Stars, remarking, "Ferguson Jenkins' [*sic*] home town was producing some pretty fair ball players even back then."[54] He also recalled how cold it was in October, and that he was glad when the series, and the long season, finally ended.

Indeed, accounts suggest that the second game in the series was affected both by cold weather and growing tensions between the teams and the spectators.[55] Played at Athletic Park in Chatham, the second game drew 1,600 fans who, according to Calder, huddled under blankets and built fires to keep warm.[56] The game was close throughout, with Marchildon and Tabron pitching (Terrell started, but Tabron replaced him). In the ninth inning, with the All-Stars behind 10–9, an umpire made a call that led Chatham fans to run onto the field in protest. According to the *Border Cities Star*, Tabron stole third base and the umpire called him "safe."[57] The third base bag, however, was loose, and Tabron, immediately slid off it, leaving him vulnerable to a Penetanguishene player who tagged him. The umpire then called him out. After that reversed call, according to the *Border Cities Star*, "players swarmed [the umpire] in arguing fashion and three hundred fans crowded on to the field." After a few minutes of arguing, the umpire once again reversed his decision, declaring Tabron safe once again. Meanwhile, according to the *Border Cities Star* report, the Penetanguishene team started packing up, assuming the game was over. After the umpire had called Tabron safe for the second time, the Penetanguishene team initially refused to come back to the field. Eventually they returned, but declared they were playing under protest. A few minutes later, a Penetanguishene player tagged Tabron who was trying to steal home, and the All-Stars lost the game, 10–9. The closeness of the game, as well as the tensions and conflict, had characterized the series. The *Chatham Daily News* called it a "one of the weirdest chapters in Chatham's sports history."[58]

By the third game, played in Guelph, Ontario, both Chatham and Penetanguishene were showing their fatigue in what the *Chatham Daily News* called a "gruelling" series after a "long season of baseball."[59] The newspaper's article gave a sense of the fatigue: "the chilly weather and dull skies made conditions miserable but a tight battle was served up and both sides had several chances to win, but muffed them."[60] Marchildon pitched, once again, while Chase pitched for Chatham. Both Marchildon and Chase struck out a good number (eighteen for Marchildon, twelve for Chase) but fewer Penetanguishene players got hits off Chase. The score was tied late in the game, and it remained so through the end of the tenth inning.

At the top of the eleventh inning, Chatham scored a run, giving them a 3–2 edge.[61] Before they could finish the inning, however, one umpire declared it was too dark to continue, and stopped the game. It would have been about four thirty in the afternoon.[62] As the eleventh inning had not completed, the officials erased the All-Stars' last run, reverting the score to a 2–2 tie. According to a *Border Cities Star* report on the game, "Supporters of the Chatham squad objected and a lengthy conference was held but the only decision was to have a replay held."[63] Decades later, Boomer Harding said he was suspicious about the umpires' decision to call the game. He said, "It was 4:30 in the afternoon and the sun was shining brightly. We had the bases loaded and none out—and the umpires called the game. The plate ump just said 'too dark' to continue and ran off the field."[64] Harding elaborated in a 1980 oral history interview, suggesting the umpires did not stick around to explain their decision: "they had a prearranged signal I guess 'cause they just took right out running. There was no talking to them. They just took to running and jumped in the car and gone."[65] As a Black man who had experienced racism all his life, he had plenty of reasons to believe that the umpires were motivated by reasons other than fading afternoon light.

When the umpires stopped the game, the Chatham Coloured All-Stars and the Foundry Rangers had to negotiate with the OBAA about where and when to resume it. A small note in the *Chatham Daily News* claimed the teams stayed overnight in Guelph and they would play that day to avoid extra expenses. Years later, however, both Harding and Terrell recalled some tense discussions among the different parties in deciding the terms of the resumed game. Harding remarked, "There was a lot of internal fighting with the OBA [*sic*] at the time over when the deciding game would be played. Penetang wanted it delayed one week so that Marchildon could pitch again."[66] Marchildon had pitched for the entire series and wanted a rest. Harding claimed the All-Stars, with several reliable pitchers, wanted to resume the game the next day. Harding asserted, "We told the OBA [*sic*] Penetang could have the title if we didn't play the next day," he said in a 1984 interview.[67] Harding also claimed that during the back and forth, Archie Stirling got involved, calling the OBAA executive members to ensure the final game was not delayed. "Archie got on the phone to the OBA [*sic*] in Toronto to pull for us,"[68] he said. Terrell also spoke about Stirling speaking up for the team, calling the OBAA head office and asking that the umpires who had stopped the game the previous day be replaced.[69]

Whatever happened during the back-and-forth discussions between the OBAA and the two teams' representatives, the game resumed the next day. While it is not known which arguments swayed the decision, both Harding and Terrell's comments about Stirling helping them negotiate with the OBAA are important. In their experience as a team, the All-Stars never had to interact with the provincial baseball organization until they reached the 1934 playoffs. As well, as Alan Metcalfe notes, the OBAA executive was an insular body with little turnover in this period, with just a small number of white men filling the roles.[70] W.J. Snyder, for example, who was the secretary of the OBAA in 1934 and remained in that position through the 1930s, was on the executive for nineteen years. Considering the "old boys' network" that characterized the OBAA leadership, having someone like Stirling who could intervene on the team's behalf clearly mattered to the players.

When the last game finally resumed the next day in Guelph, Flat Chase and Phil Marchildon pitched for their respective teams. After a fraught series, the Chatham Coloured All-Stars won by a score of 13–7. The newspaper reporter covering the game argued the All-Stars' pitching carried them to the championships: "Chatham won the title because of the fact that the ace hurler of the club, Flatfoot Chase, was able to do a successful comeback inside twenty four hours, whereas young Marchildon of Penetang, who was suffering from a sore arm, could not equal his great effort of Monday."[71] Although the reporter remarked on Marchildon's youth, the Penetanguishene pitcher was actually the same age as Chase (and Chase also had a sore arm).[72] Marchildon got a few more strikeouts than Chase, but the Penetanguishene batters had a harder time connecting to Chase's pitches. In a 1984 newspaper interview, Donald Tabron also credited Chase's pitching, saying, "Marchildon didn't have much of a team behind him and he was dead tired by the end of the first game. Chase was strong in both games for us."[73] Although defeated, it was Marchildon, not Chase, who went on to have a professional baseball career.

Meanwhile in Chatham, fans began celebrating and waited for the team's return from Guelph.[74] Throughout the game, *Chatham Daily News* sports desk staff posted score updates after each inning to fans gathering outside their office. Once the final score was announced, more people made their way to the city centre. When the members of the team drove into town around ten thirty that night, about 2,000 people waited to greet them. The

DR. VERN KINZIE NAMED PRESIDENT OF KIWANIS CLUB

Page of Comics Every Day

The Chatham Daily News

YOU CAN SELL IT WITH A NEWS CLASSIFIED ADVT.

PRICE THREE CENTS | CHATHAM, ONT., WEDNESDAY, OCTOBER 24, 1934. | ESTABLISHED 1862

CROWDS ACCLAIM VICTORIOUS CHATHAM TEAM

Chatham Stars Given Great Reception On Return To The City

Tremendous Crowd Greets O. B. A. A. Champions—Enthusiastic Parade, Headed by Band and City Officials, is Staged as a Preliminary to Speech-making—Players Congratulated on Their Achievement

SCHOOL GRANTS ARE HIGHER

KINZIE WILL TAKE OFFICE IN JANUARY

Elected President of Kiwanis Club by Acclamation

A GOOD WORKER

James S. Byrne is Named as Vice President

AMERICA'S PRETTIEST

REDUCTION OF ONLY TEN PER CENT IS MADE THIS YEAR BY THE DEPARTMENT

U. S. Postoffice To War On Lotteries

Grant Receivable, However, Smaller from Salary Cuts.

CHEQUE RECEIVED

Grants for C. C. I. and Vocational School to be Less.

FALL PLOWING IS HAMPERED BY

LUCKY AGAIN

Fig. 6.1 ▪ Front page of the *Chatham Daily News*, October 24, 1934, after the All-Stars won the OBAA Intermediate B championship. Photo credit: *Chatham Daily News*, October 21, 1934, 1.

Kilties Band, a Scottish marching band, led a parade, followed by the players riding along in cars. The *Chatham Daily News* reported that "Enthusiastic supporters yanked players out of the cars and gave them a rough handling in demonstrating their admiration. Among those carried shoulder height were Chase, Washington, Terrell and Harding."

Friends and family members of the team who were there that day remembered the crowds and the excitement. As Bruce Kidd, Russell Field, and others have argued, sports spectators often have deep emotional connections to their teams.[75] For the family members of the team who also experienced racial discrimination themselves, seeing the All-Stars return from Guelph after their win made a deep impression that remained with them many decades later. Wanda Milburn recalled, "I can remember where we all stood on the Fifth Street Bridge, and the horns tooted and the parade came in."[76] In a 2017 interview, Pauline Parker Miller, daughter of All-Stars' manager Joseph Parker, also remembered the noise: "Well, they were clapping, so, you know? On King Street, you know, coming down King Street? And making so much racket. I thought people went to extremes. But they were so happy."[77] John Olbey, younger brother of All-Stars player Cliff Olbey, remembered the players and the crowds as they celebrated the win:

> When they won the series, the last series, and they came into town they were riding on the sides of the cars and everything and the whole town was jammed at King and Fifth Street to meet them. And they just hollered and cheered them because nothing like that had ever happened in Chatham before and they had all kinds of white fans, coloured fans...They were all Ontario winners and everybody jumped on the bandwagon [laughs].[78]

Nothing like that had happened in Chatham, a point emphasized in a short piece on the All-Stars' championship win that appeared in an early November edition of the *Chicago Defender*. A prominent Black-owned newspaper, the *Chicago Defender* regularly featured community news submitted by local correspondents from across North America.[79] In 1934, Dorothy L. Binga was the Chatham correspondent for the paper, and throughout the 1934 baseball season she had included short items on the progress of the Chatham Coloured All-Stars.[80] After the All-Stars won the championship, the *Chicago Defender*'s Chatham news section included a note reflecting on the historic achievement of a Black team winning the title: "Never before in the history of Canada has there been a baseball team of color to win an O.B.A.A. pennant and in performing this feat the Chatham Stars were the first to bring this great honor to Kent County and Chatham."[81] Unlike the *Chatham Daily News*, the piece in the *Chicago Defender* remarked on the historic "first" for a Black team.[82]

Family members of the All-Stars, reflecting on the win many years later, spoke about why the team's achievement mattered to them. John Olbey explained:

> They could get together and do something because they were unwanted on the other teams in Chatham. There's lots of ball teams that flourished around here but there was no coloured team and when it was formed, it became a unit that was well known. And I know they all had pride in their accomplishments. I think it left a legacy that lasted for quite a while anyway, until the boys were gone.[83]

Pauline Williams, niece of All-Stars players Stanton and Hyle Robbins, was very young when they won the championship, but she had clearly heard the stories, saying, "When they came back and when they did win, they came back into Chatham and they had a big to do with them when they got here, didn't they? They had something in Chatham for them. It was a happy time. Yeah, it was a big, big, big thing."[84] Blake Harding, who also grew up hearing stories about his father's team, reflected on what the win would have meant in the community at the time:

> It was a real turning of time, because before that there was very little acceptance, you know, of Blacks at the time. They went to church, or they did menial jobs. Now they were celebrities that had brought respect, through sport, to Chatham. And so, when they played ball on Sundays and Saturdays, the ball park was filled with everybody. And a lot of people were out to cheer the boys on. A lot of them were relatives, but it was something that gave them hope.[85]

For these family members of the team, the win represented hope, and the promise of respect and recognition.

While the family members of the players saw the Chatham Coloured All-Stars' win as significant for the Black community, Chatham city officials and those involved with local baseball saw the All-Star's OBAA championship more in terms of the glory it brought to the city. Jack Calder saw their win as a boon for local baseball, a chance to rebuild the game in the community.[86] In his "Analyzing Sport" column after the win, Calder invoked the city's white baseball heritage, rhyming off the names of well-known white players from decades past. Absent was any reference to the Chatham Colored Giants or the Black players who had provided models and support for the 1934 OBAA champions. At a brief reception outside the William Pitt Hotel, Mayor Isaac Davis proclaimed that the "boys had brought distinction to their native city."[87] Likewise, several aldermen congratulated them, saying they had "proved worthy representatives of the city." Even in victory, the Chatham Coloured All-Stars were being judged, as if it had remained uncertain until that point that they were fit to represent Chatham.

While the *Chatham Daily News* reported on the round of speeches the mayor and other city and baseball officials gave at the short reception for the team the night they won the OBAA championship, it did not record what any of the All-Stars players said or thought about their win.[88] According to the newspaper, each of the players spoke briefly at the event that was being broadcast by a local radio station, but the news article recorded just a few words from manager Joseph Parker, thanking the mayor and the public for their support. Neither Jack Calder nor any of the other reporters asked the players about what they thought (or if they did, they did not include it in any reporting). Indeed, the newspaper reporting on the celebrations is yet again another reminder of the unequal power relationships in a racialized environment. In the *Chatham Daily News*'s coverage of the victory, the All-Stars were standing on the sidelines.

Whatever the former players thought about their OBAA title at the time, in oral history and newspaper interviews in the late 1970s and early 1980s, they were more interested in reflecting on the overall experience of being on the team than they were about winning the championship itself. When asked questions about the 1934 championship, they gave a lot of details about the games, the players, the controversies including officiating, and getting turned away from the hotel in Penetanguishene. They said relatively little, however, about how they felt about winning the OBAA title or the celebrations held in their honour. Boomer Harding mentioned the banquet the city organized, and some windbreaker jackets given to the team (he said he gave his away).[89] He claimed when their manager, Joseph Parker got up to thank the city for the banquet, he pointedly said, "Now give the boys some jobs." Harding noted a few got better jobs eventually, but it took a long time before opportunities opened more fully to Black people in Chatham.

Instead, the former All-Stars' strongest and warmest reactions in the various interviews came when talking about the friendships and the baseball. Art Cartier, a sports journalist who covered the All-Stars in the *Border Cities Star*, and later the *Chatham Daily News*, observed years later about the team: "There was a real friendship among them. They made as much noise playing ball as anyone else—they were chattering all the time—but it was all part of the game."[90] Harding described some of those good times, whether it was relaxing around the piano in a hotel after a game, or making the most of long, crowded, car rides to games. He recalled on one trip, "King Terrell, from here to Owen Sound, he told jokes, and all the way back he told jokes, and no two of them were the same. At any time he'd just kept us in stitches [laughs]."[91] Harding's sister Wanda remembered Flat Chase as being the centre of the team's social life, saying, "I think Flat had a lot to do with keeping the boys up in those days." Harding replied, saying,

"Very much so. It was a lot of fun."[92] Donald Tabron, likewise, spoke about the broader experience of his time in Chatham: "That year was one of the most memorable times in my life. I was 18 and away from home for the first time but the memories are most pleasant. I always had fond memories of that year in Chatham."[93] In their memories, titles were less important than the friendships and the baseball.

7

New Opportunities and Continued Racial Conflict in the 1935 Season

Winning the OBAA Intermediate B championship in 1934 made life easier for the Chatham Coloured All-Stars, at least in some ways. In their first two years as a team, they struggled to find enough money to cover the costs of uniforms and travel. When they won the OBAA title, however, they attracted a new group of sponsors and local baseball officials who offered to help. While the support was welcomed for a financially-strapped team, both local and regional amateur baseball organizations also hoped to gain from the relationship. As the Chatham Coloured All-Stars won over crowds with their fresh style and talented ball players, local and regional baseball organizers saw this Black team as an opportunity to promote the game in southern Ontario, and perhaps win back supporters lost to softball in the previous decade. In 1935, the Western Counties Baseball Association (WCBA), comprised of OBAA-affiliated leagues in Lambton and Middlesex Counties invited the Chatham Coloured All-Stars to join their top Intermediate A circuit.[1] Leaving the Chatham City Baseball League, the All-Stars began playing in "the Big Six," as the Intermediate A group in the WCBA was known, and competed against top teams from southwestern Ontario, including London, Strathroy, and Sarnia. These new arrangements, however, also put greater demands and expectations on the Chatham Coloured All-Stars as they continued to navigate their way through a white-dominated baseball environment.

Indeed, despite the higher profile and playing in a new league, the Chatham Coloured All-Stars continued to face the challenges of being a Black team. Although they had gained many new fans and supporters, the All-Stars still faced racism in various forms. After some racist incidents (and newspaper coverage that was racist and insensitive to racial issues) early in the season, someone close to the team (or perhaps one of the team members themselves) wrote a letter to the editor of the *Chatham Daily News*. The author spoke frankly about the racism and called on the public for understanding and support. In making these appeals, the letter's author reflected ideas and language employed by Black activists in both local and North American Black organizations.

Marketing the Chatham Coloured All-Stars

As local Chatham baseball organizers began planning for the 1935 season, they knew that the All-Stars would be in demand and could be asked to play in a league outside Chatham. With their reputation for drawing large crowds, the All-Stars were an attractive commodity for southern Ontario baseball leagues needing a financial boost. Initially, *Chatham Daily News* columnist Jack Calder reported that the nearby Lambton baseball league was "anxious to have a Chatham team—and preferably the Stars—in that circuit."[2] Even before the All-Stars' season plans were settled, Chatham baseball officials began looking for more financial support for the team. If the All-Stars were to move into a regional league, their travel expenses would increase. Before the 1935 baseball season started, Calder reported that new funding had been secured through a group of "Chatham sportsmen of long standing" and "businessmen." As he noted, with secure financial backing the Stars would "be in a very definite place in Ontario's baseball picture during the next few years."[3]

Besides financial support, local baseball organizers also arranged for a new manager for the All-Stars. Just before the baseball season started, the *Chatham Daily News* announced Leslie Hyatt was taking over from Joseph Parker as the team's manager. Hyatt was white, and a member of the city's baseball league executive.[4] While these local organizers may have genuinely wanted to support the team, taking charge in that manner suggests they thought the team could not succeed on their own. In his sports column, Calder approved the move, saying that if the All-Stars' "matters financial and managerial can be straightened out properly…they should do even bigger things."[5] In a later column, Calder again noted that the All-Stars "have been taken under the wings of men experienced in baseball and accustomed to dealing with baseball executives."[6] Moreover, he claimed that the new manager would bring discipline and consistency: "Les Hyatt will have them playing ball." "Dealing with baseball executives," however, was a valid concern for the All-Stars, as they had had to rely on Archie Stirling for help during their 1934 playoff run. The All-Stars were still relatively new to organized amateur baseball in Ontario, a space dominated entirely by a small group of white men.[7] Having people to help them deal with league politics was useful, particularly considering the unequal power dynamics of a Black team trying to advocate for themselves in a racialized environment. On the other hand, installing a new manager suggested the local baseball leaders felt the All-Stars needed some outside leadership.

While the *Chatham Daily News* reported on these management changes for the All-Stars' 1935 baseball season, it is not clear what the team members thought about them. In talking about their managers, they spoke more often about Joseph Parker, as well as Donise Washington and Len Harding.[8] King Terrell claimed Washington "practically run the ball club," but added that everyone volunteered to keep it going.[9] Len Harding also helped organize the team from the beginning and assumed formal management duties later in the 1930s.[10] Whatever the former members felt about the local, white, baseball organizers' impact on the team, they either did not consider them significant, or did not feel comfortable talking about it. As Boomer Harding noted, they were largely a self-coached team, with most of their guidance coming from the more experienced players.[11]

As the 1935 baseball season approached, the All-Stars announced they were joining the "Big Six," organized by the WCBA and involving teams from Kent, Lambton, and Middlesex Counties.[12] The league had recently expanded and was in building mode. For the All-Stars, this was a more competitive circuit than what they had been accustomed to in the Intermediate B-level Chatham City League. Teams playing in Intermediate A groups tended to be more experienced, and they had to apply directly to the OBAA executive to be accepted.[13] The other teams in the Big Six were from strong baseball towns—London, Strathroy, Sarnia, Wallaceburg, and West Lorne. In his "Analyzing Sport" column, Calder observed, "The grouping looks like one of the most attractive ever arranged for a club representing this city and interest should run high as a consequence."[14] While competition was strong, he claimed the All-Stars were "stronger than last year by a considerable degree" and would have a good chance at making the league playoffs.

Even before the 1935 season started, the WCBA leadership signalled they were counting on the Chatham Coloured All-Stars to generate interest in the Big Six. According to Calder, the new WCBA president, D.L. Graham, had identified the Strathroy Colonials and the Chatham Coloured All-Stars as southern Ontario's "top draws."[15] Clearly Graham saw getting Chatham into the grouping as a financial boon to the newly expanded league. Calder confirmed the benefits of bringing the All-Stars into the league, observing the team would attract large crowds in London. Later, he assured everyone that "Chatham's far-famed Stars will be packing them in around the Western Ontario Baseball Association."[16] Toward the end of the season, Calder noted that both the All-Stars and the Strathroy Colonials were the undisputed "money teams" of the WCBA, underscoring the transactional relationship at the heart of organized amateur baseball.[17] While having the attention of WCBA leaders may have been beneficial for the All-Stars, it also meant there were pressures on them to perform and support the league.

Returning Players, New Players

One of the reasons Calder was so hopeful about the 1935 All-Stars is that the team had kept many of their strongest players from their 1934 championship season. Brothers Len and Boomer Harding, Flat Chase, King Terrell, Ross Talbot, Stanton Robbins, and Gouy Ladd all played regularly throughout the 1935 season and playoffs. The two Americans, Donise Washington and Donald Tabron, also came back to play in Chatham in 1935. Several other players, however, had moved away and were no longer with the team, including Hyle Robbins and Sagasta Harding, who had both moved to Michigan. Robbins worked in a factory and Harding for the Ford Motor Company.[18] Cliff Olbey had moved to Windsor, Ontario, and worked at the Prince Edward Hotel.[19] Both Sagasta Harding and Olbey rejoined their teammates occasionally during the 1935 season when they were back home for visits. As well, the team's base coaches, Louis Pryor and Percy Parker, remained with the team.

The Chatham Coloured All-Stars replaced their departing teammates with a few new players. Ferguson Jenkins Sr. joined the All-Stars full time in 1935.[20] Born in Windsor, Jenkins grew up near Wigle Park, just down the street from Flat Chase.[21] Jenkins and Chase played baseball together for the Windsor Colored Stars in 1933.[22] The two also regularly travelled to Detroit to play baseball in the Black church leagues. Jenkins recalled playing for Bethel Church (likely Bethel African Methodist Episcopal Church), a Black congregation dating to the 1830s. Well-regarded by his fellow players, Jenkins normally played outfield. Terrell recalled, "I've seen him catch balls out in the outfield that you'd swear up and down that he would never even get close to."[23] By the end of the 1935 season, Jenkins's batting was so strong that he had been moved up to second in the batting order.[24]

Besides Jenkins, the Chatham Coloured All-Stars recruited a new pitcher, Wellington "Willie" Shognosh, an Anishinaabe man from Bkejwanong (Walpole Island First Nation).[25] In Bkejwanong, an unceded First Nations territory seventy-five miles from Chatham, people had been playing baseball since the early years of the twentieth century. In 1903, Elijah Edward Pinnance from Bkejwanong became one of the first Indigenous men to play in the major baseball leagues, pitching for the Philadelphia Athletics.[26] In a late 1970s oral history interview, Robert Kiyoshk, of Bkejwanong, recalled seeing Pinnance hit a home run at a baseball game held at Walpole Island's annual fair in 1921. He said, "that ball what he hit, hit the veranda roof on that house. And one of the spectators, they said that's even a longer drive than Babe Ruth with a home run."[27] Another member of the Walpole Island First Nation, Frances Miskokomon, recalled baseball being taught at their schools in the 1920s.[28] She also remembered people playing baseball in church leagues, as well as teams that travelled to surrounding towns to play.[29] Miskokomon herself played softball: "I played on the girls' softball team in Wallaceburg and Chatham, and other girls' teams would come in to play us."[30]

Shognosh, who grew up on Bkejwanong about the same time as Miskokomon, came from a family who farmed, like many others in the community.[31] He first came to the attention of baseball enthusiasts in Chatham in 1932, when he was a member of the Walpole Island Junior team which played in the same league as Chatham's Junior team.[32] One *Chatham Daily News* sports columnist observed in 1932, "when this boy Shagnosh [*sic*]...can travel nine innings hurling the brand of ball he did for six frames on Saturday, the Walpole lads are going to cause the other fellows a lot of trouble."[33] The same columnist also noted a week later that the young pitcher had "everything that goes to make a bang-up hurler."[34]

Although it is not known who or how the Chatham Coloured All-Stars approached Shognosh about joining their team, the All-Stars played against him frequently during the 1934 season. Bkejwanong teams came to the city to play exhibition games with various Chatham teams in 1932 and 1933, and in 1934, the Chatham Colored All-Stars called on them to play exhibition games as well.[35] In fact, the All-Stars played Bkejwanong teams at least five times during that season.[36] Most of those games took place in August, when the All-Stars were getting ready for the OBAA playoffs.

The *Chatham Daily News* sportswriters continued to praise Shognosh's pitching after he joined the Chatham Coloured All-Stars.[37] Calder credited Shognosh with strengthening the Stars' pitching roster, calling him the "brightest light in the constellation that is the 1935 edition of the Chatham Colored All-Stars."[38] In an extended discussion of Shognosh in his July 19 column, Calder remarked on his "coolness" while pitching, as well as his ability to hit home runs, including one that apparently flew out of Stirling Park and sailed between two houses on Park Street. Calder claimed Chase was a more dynamic pitcher ("a regular pitching typhoon"), but admiringly described Shognosh as a "cool workman."[39] By early August, Calder had proclaimed Shognosh the "best pitcher in the Western Counties League."[40]

While newspaper reporters and columnists praised Shognosh as a ball player, they frequently used racialized and racist terms when describing him. As Janice Forsyth, Bruce Kidd, and others have shown, racist coverage was common for Indigenous athletes.[41] While the *Chatham Daily News* sometimes noted Shognosh's origins, comparing him to Elijah Edward Pinnance, more often, Calder and other reporters drew on white-created stereotypes.[42] In various *Chatham Daily News* articles and columns, Shognosh was described as "smiling chief," "Medicine Man," "stony-countenanced," and someone from "the wilds of Waubuno and Walpole Island."[43] Even Calder's description of Shognosh as a "cool" pitcher may have been rooted in stereotypes about Indigenous people being unemotional and reserved. Calder clearly thought highly of Shognosh as a baseball player, but at the same time, he could never separate him from the racialized and racist constructions of Indigenous Peoples.

Shognosh's pitching skills attracted more than just local interest. In August 1937, *Chatham Daily News* sports columnist Art Cartier reported that Shognosh was having a tryout with the Detroit Tigers later that month.[44] Acknowledging that it was "a long and difficult jump from intermediate O.B.A.A. baseball to a spot in the Big Time," Cartier noted that Shognosh was among the "ablest amateurs in Ontario." He claimed that ever since Shognosh's debut as a Junior player, he had "been in demand throughout the district," whether supporting his home Walpole Island teams or playing on other Intermediate-level teams in southwestern Ontario. No further reporting indicated how Shognosh's tryout with the Tigers went, but he continued to play baseball in the southwestern Ontario baseball leagues until the end of the 1930s.[45]

In oral history interviews years later, Shognosh's former teammates offered insights on what he was like as a person. Terrell, Boomer Harding, and Ferguson Jenkins Sr. all remembered him as quiet, but friendly. Jenkins, who roomed with Shognosh in 1935, laughingly recalled their awkward first

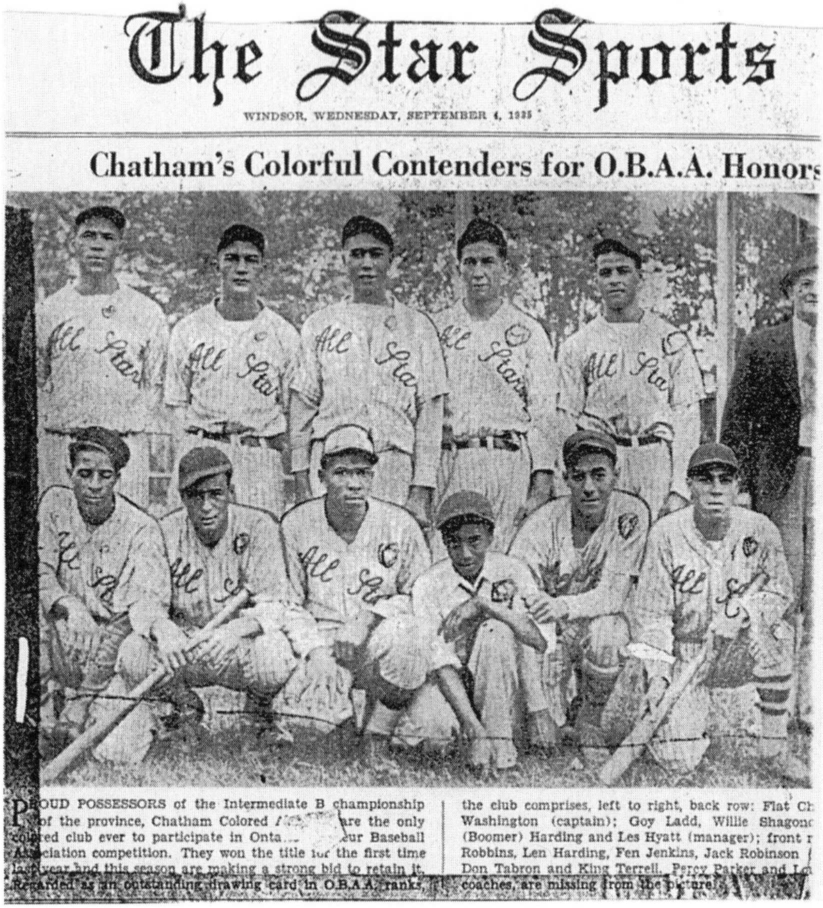

The Star Sports

WINDSOR, WEDNESDAY, SEPTEMBER 4, 1935

Chatham's Colorful Contenders for O.B.A.A. Honors

PROUD POSSESSORS of the Intermediate B championship of the province, Chatham Colored A... are the only colored club ever to participate in Onta... ...eur Baseball Association competition. They won the title for the first time last year and this season are making a strong bid to retain it. Regarded as an outstanding drawing card in O.B.A.A. ranks, the club comprises, left to right, back row: Flat Ch... Washington (captain); Goy Ladd, Willie Shagonc... (Boomer) Harding and Les Hyatt (manager); front r... Robbins, Len Harding, Fen Jenkins, Jack Robinson ... Don Tabron and King Terrell. Percy Parker and Lo... coaches, are missing from the picture.

Fig. 7. 1 ▪ Chatham Coloured All-Stars, team picture, 1935 season. The team members are wearing new uniforms. Back row, from left: Flat Chase, Donise Washington, Gouy Ladd, Willie Shognosh, Boomer Harding, manager Les Hyatt. Front row, from left: Stanton Robbins, Len Harding, Fergie Jenkins Sr., Jack Robinson, Don Tabron, King Terrell. A note indicates coaches Percy Parker and Louis Pryor were missing from the picture. Photo credit: Leddy Library Archives and Special Collections, F1033 (Wilfred "Boomer" Harding Collection), Scrapbook 1. Picture is from *Windsor Daily Star*, September 4, 1935, Second Section, 3.

meeting when they discovered that they would have to share the small flat's only bed.[46] Harding remembered that Shognosh and Jenkins got along well, remarking, "you'd see them any night walking the streets."[47] Harding and Terrell also remembered Shognosh's tryout with the Detroit Tigers, an opportunity they themselves would not have had.[48]

Continuing Racial Conflicts

With strong players such as Shognosh and Jenkins joining the team, the 1935 season was looking promising for the Chatham Coloured All-Stars. As they joined the Big Six of the Intermediate A circuit of the WCBA, however, they continued to face racist incidents and other conflicts. Although the WCBA leadership worked to get the All-Stars into the league, it is not clear how bringing a Black team into the circuit was received by the other teams or their communities. As the All-Stars came into the league with a high profile, it is possible some players, officials, or fans resented the attention paid to the Black team. There is no evidence this feeling was widespread—the players themselves never indicated this in their various oral history interviews. The former players did, however, comment on various racist incidents they encountered in communities where they played in the WCBA.

One of these incidents the former players described happened in Strathroy, a community about seventy-five miles northeast of Chatham early in their first season in the WCBA. The players spoke about arriving in Strathroy for their first game against the team and finding that someone had scrawled racist slogans on the sidewalks. *Chatham Daily News* sports columnist Bill Reddick, interviewing Ben Talbot in 1984, quoted him saying, "They wrote on the sidewalks, 'the n___ are coming' and the 'black clouds are moving in,'" adding, "That was the worst thing we ever came across."[49] Likewise, Ferguson Jenkins Sr. remembered sidewalk drawings featuring a caricature of Chase, showing him with an exaggerated nose.[50] Boomer Harding also recalled the sidewalk and added "they were out to beat us."[51] Whatever the specific details, the hostile comments and images on the sidewalks affected the players, who remembered and spoke about them nearly fifty years later.

Not only did the Chatham Coloured All-Stars encounter hostile writing on the sidewalks, they also learned of a racist write-up of the game that appeared a few days later in the *Strathroy Age Dispatch*.[52] Although the article's headline, "Baseball Crowd Sees Smart Game" suggested some positive coverage, the subheading, "Dark Days for the 'Darkies,'" set the tone for the piece. Drawing on prevailing racial stereotypes, the author portrayed the team as exotic entertainers, "boys from Dixie," rather than men who grew up just seventy-five miles from Strathroy. In the article, the All-Stars players came across as caricatures, rather than as competent baseball players. It called Don Tabron a "show man," claimed Donise Washington was "full of pep," and described Chase as the "colored Babe Ruth." In an attempt at humour that was profoundly racist, the article claimed the skin of one of the players got "blacker" when he was denied a home run.

The Black women, wives, girlfriends, and family members of the team who travelled to Strathroy for the game also drew attention from the Strathroy newspaper reporter. As Ornella Nzindukiyimana and Kevin Wamsley have argued, misogyny and racism affected Black women's experiences as spectators at public sports events.[53] Sitting in the stands of a largely white sports audience made Black women potential targets of racist and sexist verbal attacks. Sheldon Gillis, in his MA thesis on Black hockey leagues in late-nineteenth, early twentieth-century Maritimes, also observed the white press' portrayal of Black women sports spectators.[54] He notes that the local press described the women as loud and boisterous as they cheered for their teams, straying outside white middle-class expectations for female behaviour. The *Strathroy Age Dispatch* drew upon similar racist and classist assumptions about the Black women (the author used the term "colored girls") who attended the game in Strathroy. The author claimed the women had taken an interest in "our tall boys" on the Strathroy team, suggesting a looseness and possible racial transgression. Even their clothing came under scrutiny, as the author remarked that both the Chatham players and the women accompanying them were "smartly and fashionably dressed, as if they were going to the Dark Town Strutter's Ball."[55] By alluding to a Dixieland tune, the author invoked images of Black people as easy, loose, and exotic. As well, "Dark Town," a reference to an African American neighbourhood of Atlanta, was a reminder of the racialized, segregated world of 1930s North America.

While those incidents happened in Strathroy, it was only after the Strathroy team came to Chatham for a game that details of the earlier racist events became more widely known. After the second game in Chatham, the *Strathroy Age Dispatch* published another unflattering piece on the All-Stars, this time accusing them of physical roughness on the diamond. Calling them a "husky crew," and comparing them to football players, the author of the piece claimed the All-Stars were tackling Strathroy players as they approached the bases. The reporter remarked: "Our pitchers learned for the first time in their baseball careers that they should be football stars to play against their colored friends."[56] Emphasizing their race and physicality, the Strathroy reporter leaned into stereotypes of Black masculinity while condemning the Chatham players.

Although neither Calder's column nor the *Chatham Daily News's* coverage of that second Chatham-Strathroy meeting described any violence during the game, Calder raised the issue several days later. Calder reported in "Analyzing Sport" that readers had complained to him that the All-Stars had been particularly aggressive during their game with Strathroy.[57] Calder insisted he was "no believer in docile baseball," but claimed that the All-Stars were "creating an unfavorable impression when they knock opponents to the ground with stunning force three times in a single game." While criticizing the All-Stars for roughness, Calder also spoke about the relationship between the team and their fans, claiming that the All-Stars owed their fans a "clean" game. He said the All-Stars "provide colorful and highly pleasing entertainment," while the fans showed support by coming to their games. Calder's remark about "colorful and highly-pleasing entertainment" alludes to the expectations of white audiences—entertainment from Black athletes in return for support.

Several days after Calder's rebuke, someone calling themselves "A colored fan" wrote a letter to the editor of the *Chatham Daily News*, challenging the sportswriter's views.[58] While the letter was unsigned, the author of the "A colored fan" letter appeared to have attended the games in Strathroy and Chatham, as they remarked on details from both games. They were also clearly presenting the story from the perspective of the All-Stars, using the plural first-person ("we," "our," "us"), and referring to events the Black players themselves experienced. While the author is unknown, the perspective and views suggest that they were close to the team, perhaps a member of their club who travelled with them, or a family member.[59] The author may also have been one of the All-Stars themselves. Whatever the case, the letter described some of the players' direct experiences.

Whoever the author was, they countered Calder's remarks about the All-Stars being overly rough in their last game. While admitting that the game between the All-Stars and Strathroy the previous week "may have bordered on the rough side," the author explained the All-Stars were defending themselves against assaults from the other team.[60] The author explained that at the previous game in Strathroy, the Strathroy players made "cripples of no less than three (3) of the Chatham Stars by the friendly spike route." As mentioned earlier, Boomer Harding spoke about the violence that was sometimes part of the game, with balls aimed at their heads or spikes to the shin. In addition to describing physical attacks on the diamond, the author of the "A colored fan" letter commented on the behaviour of the

Strathroy spectators who, they claimed, spewed racist insults in "a tirade of embarrassing bandinage [*sic*]."

The "A colored fan" author also revealed that they had seen the racist coverage in the *Strathroy Age Dispatch*.[61] The author quoted several lines directly from the June 20 newspaper article, highlighting the blatant racism directed at the team. The article, they remarked, was "pregnant with such democratic sentences as 'Dark Days for the Darkies' and 'The Boys from Dixie,'" as well as "complimentary remarks about the hue of our flesh and the attire of our wives and girlfriends." By repeating those phrases, the author aimed to show the white readers of the *Chatham Daily News*, in stark terms, the racist abuses the All-Stars faced as Black men, as Black husbands, and as human beings.

The author of the "A colored fan" letter also addressed the relationship between the All-Stars and their fans.[62] While Calder had described the All-Stars as owing their fans a "clean game" in return for support, the author of the "A colored fan" letter envisioned a relationship that also included their fans recognizing and understanding the problems they faced as Black athletes. The All-Stars, the author assured the readers, were indeed grateful for the "kindness and reception tendered us in victory." The team, however, needed more than just friends in good times, but real support in the face of racist treatment. "We implore you," the letter asked, "to attempt to see the game as it is going on this summer from an unbiased sporting angle." Recognize the racism that we endure, they suggested, and we can build a relationship based on mutual understanding and respect. Reminding the fans of what the team gave to the city, the author said, "if our baseball means anything to sport and the community we ask only for Canadian sporting justice from a Canadian sporting town." Through support and understanding, the letter suggested, they could build a more meaningful bond.

The letter ended with an appeal to a common British citizenry, as well as community solidarity: "we are, after all, just so many more human, British subjects desirous of reciprocating in a world of give and take. We are conscientiously desirous of uplifting sports in Chatham. For the old Maple City—and for democracy—be with us."[63] Connecting with a British identity had long been a strategy for Black individuals and groups seeking rights and acceptance in Canada. As Melissa N. Shaw shows, Black people protesting their exclusion from military service early in World War I invoked a sense of "British imperial belonging" as they demanded a right to take part in Canada's war effort.[64] Sports also had strong connections to the imagery and symbolism of the British Empire. For example, Sheldon Gillis observes that several Black hockey teams in the Maritimes named their clubs in honour of Queen Victoria's Jubilee in 1897. Later, sports and British identity were married in the British Empire Games (later renamed the Commonwealth Games), held for the first time in Hamilton, Ontario in 1930. When the author of the "A colored fan" letter referred to a common British cultural heritage, they were looking to connect with the broader community and perhaps find acceptance.

The letter also reflected a broader quest for respectability and equality of opportunity found in organizations such as the NAACP and the United Negro Improvement Association that were influential in southwestern Ontario in the interwar years.[65] As Cheryl Thompson shows, the Black-owned *Dawn of Tomorrow* newspaper reflected similar values in this period, promoting "racial uplift, community advancement, civic engagement, and Black entrepreneurship."[66] In 1923, during the newspaper's first year of publication, the Chatham agent/correspondent was Beulah Harding, sister of Len and Boomer.[67] Similar messages of uplift and respectability were also featured in other Black institutions, including the Black churches and the Black Masonic Lodge chapters. They could also be heard in speeches at the annual Emancipation Day celebrations.[68] In nearby Windsor, Ontario, as historian Irene Moore Davis explains, a Black organization, the Central Citizens Association, was lobbying the city and private businesses to open up employment for Black people.[69] Although speaking about sports, the letter from "A colored fan" expressed the same aims found in the other organizations, suggesting the connection between sports and social justice.

The timing of the "A colored fan" letter is also important, appearing as it did in the 1935 baseball season. Racist treatment was nothing new for the Chatham Coloured All-Stars, as seen in their various encounters during the 1934 season and the OBAA playoff runs. What had perhaps changed by 1935, however, was that the All-Stars were in a much more secure position in Chatham baseball. Initially, they were an unknown Black team, and only gained traction with the wider public once they reached the OBAA playoffs in 1934 and won the Intermediate B title. They moved into a more competitive circuit in 1935, playing against the top baseball teams from southwestern Ontario. At that point in the season they were doing well in the new grouping, challenging Strathroy for first place.[70] A position of strength builds confidence and makes it easier to ask for some respect.

"A colored fan's" plea for understanding and support appeared to have resonated at the *Chatham Daily News*. Less than two weeks after the letter appeared, the paper published an editorial acknowledging that the All-Stars had been victims of racism. The editorial, titled "Value of a Smile," had no byline, suggesting it was written by the editorial team, and it is not clear if Calder was one of the authors.[71] The detailed information about the All-Stars and their most recent game in Strathroy suggests, however, that Calder may have contributed or been consulted. The editorial began with qualified praise for the All-Stars, calling them "a clever aggregation of colored athletes." Although it did not refer to "A colored fan's" letter, the editorial admitted that the All-Stars had been having "a somewhat difficult experience" with the Strathroy team and its fans (although it said nothing about Calder's column criticizing the All-Stars for rough play). The team, the piece acknowledged, "have been compelled to put up with stinging insults, largely because of their racial characteristics." While still understating the issue, this was the first time the paper openly addressed racism and the Chatham Coloured All-Stars. Using the term "clever" was also likely deliberate, as it went against prevailing ideas about the intelligence of Black athletes. Whether the editors felt chastened by "A colored fan's" letter or whether they were trying to mollify the paper's Black readership (perhaps both), the piece was a departure from how they usually covered the All-Stars.

Although racism was addressed, the editorial still relied on older ideas about dealing with racial conflict. They claimed that at the most recent game with Strathroy, team captain Donise Washington had urged the All-Stars not to react, but rather to "take it smiling—and play ball."[72] According to the editorial authors, the All-Stars ignored the racist insults and umpires' decisions that went against them, and either smiled or laughed in response. Moreover, according to the authors, Washington charmed the hostile crowd, laughingly announcing when he reached first base that "he would steal two bases—and he did." By the time Flat Chase hit a record-setting home run in the park, the editorial noted the Strathroy fans were appreciative and respectful. They credited Washington for his leadership, proclaiming him "a philosopher and a diplomat. He knows the value of a smile."

Whether or not the experience on the field and in the stands was as conciliatory as the authors of "The Value of a Smile" portrayed, the editorial at least acknowledged the racism. At the same time, however, the editorial implied that the victims of the racism, the Black men on the field, were ultimately responsible for ignoring the bad behaviour. Just like

Jackie Robinson, who joined the Brooklyn Dodgers more than a decade later, the All-Stars were expected to ignore or tolerate the poor treatment. The editorial did not call out the white perpetrators or demand they stop. Instead, they suggested that racism and racist taunts were a regrettable, but enduring fact of life. The editors' approval of the All-Stars "smiling" their way through the racist taunts also reminds us of the daily choices that Black people in a racist and racialized world faced. Deciding whether to push back or keep the peace was part of everyday existence, and this editorial raises the question of the price that Black people paid by having to make that choice.

While some of the former Chatham Coloured All-Stars remembered the racism they encountered in Strathroy (including an incident Jenkins recalled, where they had to "get out of Strathroy and flying" after a Chatham player hit one of the Strathroy players with the ball[73]), they also spoke about happy times spent in the town. Harding recalled how enthusiastic people in Strathroy were about baseball.[74] He claimed when the All-Stars came to play, the Strathroy merchants would close their stores and people would leave work early to see the games. He said, "they were out to beat us, but they attracted big crowds." Ben Talbot claimed he did not believe that everyone in Strathroy was racist, and they mostly got along with the team and fans.[75] Washington, who later moved to Strathroy to manage a baseball team there, recalled the incident in a 1984 newspaper interview: "I remember the streets being painted but when I lived there everybody treated me well."[76] He stayed in Strathroy for two years before returning to Detroit. Both Harding and Jenkins also spoke about relaxing at a hotel in Strathroy after the games. Harding said, "King Terrell would get on the piano and Flat Chase would do the dancing. Win or lose, and we had a real good time and relieved all our tears and woes."[77] Likewise Jenkins remembered the "best meals," they ate at the hotel, all paid for by their sponsors that year.[78] Considering that they could not eat at many restaurants or hotels in Chatham, their own home city, being able to eat at the hotel in Strathroy was a novelty. While the former players remembered the racist incidents, they also found Strathroy a welcoming place, at least sometimes. The openly racist treatment, however, is a reminder that Canada was not necessarily a haven for Black athletes, as the mythology around Jackie Robinson's experiences in Montreal in the 1940s sometimes suggests.[79]

Apart from the blatant racism experienced at Strathroy, the All-Stars had other tension-filled games with their opponents in the WCBA in the 1935 season. Just weeks after the incidents in Strathroy, the All-Stars faced a particularly difficult game against the London team at Stirling Park.[80] A lot was at stake, as the two teams were vying for second place in the WCBA standings. As examined earlier, newspaper reports on baseball game conflicts rarely mentioned racial tensions. In face-offs between a Black team and a white team, race was always part of the encounter, whether overt racist incidents occurred or not. The All-Stars controlled the game, winning it 13–0. Shognosh was pitching, and according to the *Chatham Daily News* reporter, he gave "one of the best hurling displays fans of this city have ever seen." The rest of the team was hitting well, with most of the roster earning at least one run. While the news report was cryptic, they suggested that tensions were brewing throughout the game. They said "arguments slowed up the progress of the tilt. Both clubs protested umpires' decisions and argued back and forth and gave signs of fistic outbreaks." As well, Len Harding was ejected from the game for "talking back" to an umpire, and Jenkins was hit by the ball three times (he also earned the most runs of any player in the game). While the reporter seemed impatient with the players, suggesting only Jenkins had any reason to feel aggrieved, clearly something was happening to fuel those tensions. Harding's encounter with the umpire was also unusual, as the Chatham player was not known for getting into arguments with umpires. While it is hard to identify the source of the tension, such conflicts continued to be part of the Chatham Coloured All-Stars' experience as a Black team.

King Terrell and Ben Talbot also spoke about an unnerving experience the All-Stars had in West Lorne, another of the Big Six teams in the WCBA Intermediate A circuit. It is not clear which year the incident happened, as the All-Stars regularly played in West Lorne from 1935 through 1938. The details of the stories vary, but both Terrell and Talbot recalled having to leave town quickly after angering the West Lorne fans.[81] Talbot remarked that they "caused a small riot" when the spectators became angry after Boomer Harding collided with the other team's catcher as he was heading toward home plate. Terrell did not mention a specific incident, but he remembered the West Lorne fans were upset about losing. Both Talbot and Terrell recalled the spectators grabbing makeshift weapons—Talbot claimed they "snatched boards off the fence," while Terrell remembered them having clubs and rakes. Terrell said, "We got everything all packed up before the game was over because we knew there was something going to happen." Both men described the menace and the threat of angry spectators. While racist incidents would have happened to the All-Stars while they were playing at home too, threating events at away games were more dangerous. By joining the WCBA, and playing away from home every week or every other week, they faced these risks more often.

The WCBA and OBAA Playoffs

Despite the ongoing racism and challenges of adjusting to the WCBA Intermediate A circuit, the Chatham Coloured All-Stars impressed many with their baseball playing. In fact, they ended the 1935 season tied for first place with Sarnia, ahead of experienced teams from Strathroy, London, and Wallaceburg. Although they began their season shakily, the All-Stars grew as a team over the summer. Calder argued the All-Stars became more consistent in both pitching and fielding skills.[82] Although Chase was not able to pitch for much of the 1935 season, Shognosh, along with "curve ball hurler" Tabron, carried mound duties.[83] Despite his earlier praise for the new managers who were supposedly bringing "discipline" to the team, Calder ultimately credited catcher Donise Washington with bringing the players together and improving their fielding skills. He noted, "Don Washington proved himself a master of his art in the way he handled the team."[84] As he had in the past, Calder continued to emphasize Washington's intelligence, calling him the "smart and inspirational catcher,"[85] as well as the team's "professor."[86] Overall, Calder concluded that the team was more well-rounded, more consistent, and more skilled than the one that had won the Intermediate B championship the year before. Calder noted,

> The Stars are an entirely different team to what they were last season when they won the provincial intermediate B-1 title. In 1934 they had to depend on great clubbing rallies to carry them through important games. This year they have added consistent hitting and fielding to their fortes and their games are many times more interesting to watch.

Art Cartier, who was covering sports for the *Windsor Daily Star* in 1935, also remarked on the improved fielding skills of the All-Stars compared to their 1934 season.[87] Noting that the 1934 All-Stars had attracted a lot of fans with their style and "showmanship," Cartier pointed out that in 1935, the more consistent pitching and "defence support accorded by Captain Don Washington and Wilf Harding" made them a stronger team.

During the WCBA playoffs, the All-Stars' more consistent play, strong pitching, and fielding helped them advance. They reached the WCBA title semi-final series against Wallaceburg, losing the first game but winning the next two.[88] Shognosh pitched both winning games, in 2–1 and 6–1 victories. The newspaper report on the game claimed that Shognosh had "courage, a willing right arm, a team behind him, and above all, a smart and inspirational catcher in Don Washington."[89] After the series with Wallaceburg, the All-Stars faced the Strathroy Colonials in the final series for the WCBA championship. Chase, whose arm had recovered, pitched the first game. According to Calder, he "made a headline-hitting return to form."[90] Calder claimed Chase was instrumental in the win; he not only pitched the 2–1 victory, but he also "batted in the tying run, scored the winning run and secured four of the club's seven hits."[91] Indeed, Calder was effusive in describing Chase as the "hero his teammates needed," while also emphasizing his physicality (the "broad-shouldered fence-flattener" and "pitching typhoon in the flesh"),[92] as he tended to do with the Black players. Shognosh, who pitched the second game, was a little unsteady as he was just getting over an illness.[93] Strathroy's star pitcher, former US minor league player Art Fidler, was not pitching, and their team made a few errors.[94] The All-Stars won the game, 4–2, and with that, they won their first-ever WCBA league championship in the Intermediate A class.

The Chatham Coloured All-Stars' WCBA win was as significant, if not more so, than winning the 1934 OBAA Intermediate B title. Although the public memory of the 1935 WCBA championship title has faded in comparison with the 1934 win, the All-Stars' 1935 victory was made at the more competitive Intermediate A level, against some of the strongest teams in southwestern Ontario. A *Chatham Daily News* article (possibly written by Calder, but not attributed to him) claimed that while the All-Stars were undoubtedly the best team in the 1934 OBAA Intermediate B playoffs and deserved to win, the overall competition that year was not strong.[95] The article continued, arguing that the field in 1935 was more advanced, and that "the Stars and their opponents gave some of the most brilliant and polished exhibitions Chatham fans have ever witnessed. And the Stars won out because they were the very best among four very good Intermediate A teams."[96] Cartier acknowledged that in 1934, the All-Stars "overcame all sorts of odds" to win the OBAA championship.[97] The next year, he noted, the All-Stars had "stepped up a notch and played in the Big Six against more experienced teams like Strathroy, Wallaceburg, Sarnia and West Lorne. They surprised quite a few by taking the group title." The All-Stars' 1934 title win was important because it put a Black team in the spotlight, and family members of the team continued to think about that moment throughout their lives. That the All-Stars continued to grow as a team, defeating some of the strongest teams in southern Ontario the following year, suggests the larger impact they made on regional baseball.

After winning the WCBA title, the All-Stars moved forward to the provincial OBAA playoffs. Their run was cut short, however, when they lost the OBAA semi-final series against Sandwich (now part of Windsor, Ontario) of the Essex County Baseball League. Although Calder claimed the All-Stars should have beaten the other team easily, they lost the series in three straight games.[98] Calder blamed errors and a lack of focus, but the newspaper reporting also suggests conflict and tension among the players and with the officiating.[99] Racial tension was always part of conflict and violence at baseball games involving Black players, given the heavily racialized and racist environments of 1930s southern Ontario. In the second game, tensions erupted as Chase and a Sandwich player got into a fist fight, which soon spread to the stands. It began when a Sandwich player running bases knocked Chase to the ground. As the two men began fighting, "Players and spectators rushed toward the melee and Chase clinched as umpires broke through the mob." Officials ejected both Chase and the Sandwich player from the match. Later in the same game, the Chatham Coloured All-Stars protested an umpire's call. According to the *Chatham Daily News*, a Sandwich player waiting his turn at bat stepped in front of Washington at home plate while the catcher was throwing the ball. With his throw blocked, an opposing player was able to steal a base, leading to the Sandwich team's game-winning run. Claiming interference, the Stars protested, "but Umpire Star Mason refused to listen." In the final game, the All-Stars were stronger but still lost 5–4.[100] Decades later, Ferguson Jenkins Sr. still recalled the tension-filled games with Sandwich, and he described something he had seen one of the umpires do as "very shady."[101] While Jenkins did not give details about what he saw, his comments reflect the suspicions that the former All-Stars often expressed about officiating in games.

During the 1935 playoffs, there were signs that the Chatham Coloured All-Stars players may have been feeling the strains of a long season in the new league. During the playoff series with Sandwich, Calder wrote two columns chiding the All-Stars for not working hard enough and not making time for practice.[102] Calder interpreted their problems as a lack of discipline, and not adopting the right "frame of mind." He did not consider how difficult it may have been for the Black players to find time for practices and games. Most worked in low-paying service or manual labour jobs, and taking time off meant not getting paid. Years later, King Terrell and Wanda Milburn spoke about how difficult it was to field a team. Terrell claimed, "you were lucky if you got nine guys to play baseball through the week."[103] Milburn, prompting him, said "maybe the reason why they missed some ball games is because if they had a day's work, they had to work," and Terrell agreed with her. Boomer Harding, in an interview he did in 1980, also said it was hard to take time off work, and most could not afford to lose wages.[104] In the 1935 season, the work issue was compounded because the team had to travel more often. In 1933 and 1934, the All-Stars played their regular season games in the Chatham city league, and only travelled when they were playing exhibition games and when they made the OBAA playoffs. When the All-Stars joined the WCBA in 1935, they travelled regularly to Wallaceburg, Sarnia, Strathroy, West Lorne, and London, all communities located thirty to eighty miles away from Chatham. While the local businesses covered the All-Stars' travel expenses, they did not pay the players for lost wages. While Calder was generally supportive of the team, his lack of awareness of the difficulties the players faced as Black men trying to earn a living reflected the larger patterns in the way the white press covered Black athletes.

One of Calder's remarks also suggests that the All-Stars' players had been complaining about their treatment in the Sandwich series. Calder said, "The Stars may talk as they like about bad breaks, umpires' decisions and conspiracies to beat them."[105] Although Calder dismissed those complaints, saying the team simply was not working hard enough, his report suggests that the players may well have been talking about racial discrimination (as Jenkins implied in his 1980 interview). Moreover, Calder claimed that during the series with Sandwich, "the heart has gone out of Don Washington." While he attributed the catcher's apparent loss of spirit to the team not working hard, Calder, as we have seen, was not sensitive to the other reasons why Washington may have been discouraged.

Finally, Calder's end-of-season columns are also a reminder of the pressures that the Chatham Coloured All-Stars faced to "deliver" as the premier team of the city. In discussing the All-Stars' discouraging performances in the OBAA playoffs, Calder mentioned that "a good deal of plugging on the Stars' behalf has been done this season by men interested in baseball; the city's fans have turned out remarkably well."[106] In saying that, Calder underscored the All-Stars' implied obligations to perform for those who provided financing, and the fans who supported them. He followed by saying, "The Stars owe to Chatham, then, the best ball they can provide." As Colin Howell reminds us, amateur sport was embedded in capitalism, and Calder's comments reflect the transactional nature of the relationship between the players, the financial backers, and the fans.[107] Despite "A colored fan's" letter asking white audiences for understanding and awareness of racism earlier in the season, Calder was not able to look more broadly at the fuller experiences of the players' lives.

Although it has not received the attention that the 1934 championship season did, the Chatham Coloured All-Stars' 1935 season was no less significant. Joining the more competitive Intermediate A circuit in the newly-expanded WCBA gave the All-Stars a higher profile in the region by playing experienced teams in strong baseball towns like Strathroy, London, and Sarnia. After some initial difficulties, the All-Stars not only adjusted to the higher level of play, but won the WCBA championship against the strongest teams in southwestern Ontario. These new opportunities (and the new sponsors and financial backers that came with it) also led to greater demands and expectations on the team. When baseball league organizers hoped to regain fans lost to softball in the interwar years, they wanted the All-Stars to create new interest in the game. Despite the high profile and attention (or perhaps, because of it), the Chatham Coloured All-Stars continued to face racism both on and off the field. In 1935, however, someone close to the team (or one of the team members themselves) wrote a letter to the editor of the *Chatham Daily News*, identifying and condemning the racism the team experienced. Like other groups and individuals organizing for civil rights in the period, the letter's author appealed to a wider sense of citizenship and justice in the context of sport. It was just one gesture, but it would not be the last time that the Chatham Coloured All-Stars would demand "sporting justice."

8

"All we ask is a fair break"

Baseball and Sporting Justice in the Chatham Coloured All-Stars' Later Years

For the Chatham Coloured All-Stars, the 1939 baseball season was one of their most successful, yet also one of their most tumultuous. After several uneven years, by 1939 the All-Stars were back to full strength, with Flat Chase and Willie Shognosh pitching for them. With renewed energy, they had their sights set on another OBA (the OBAA shortened its name in 1939) Intermediate A title run. Still, it was never easy being a Black team in Ontario's primarily white, amateur baseball organization in the 1930s. Financially, they were having a hard time, as the crowds were thinner and the sponsors fewer than they had been in the wake of their 1934 and 1935 championships. They also played fewer exhibition games to earn cash, and while the reasons for that are unknown, most of the players were in their late 20s, many were married, and it would have been harder for them to spare the extra time. Despite the difficulties, however, the All-Stars were more experienced and confident, and that showed in the way they responded to conflicts and controversies involving both the local and provincial amateur baseball bodies. By 1939, the All-Stars had become more outspoken, taking their complaints over unfair treatment to the public. Led by their manager, Len Harding, the All-Stars openly challenged both the local city league and the OBA in disputes over their treatment that season. When negotiations with the baseball organizations failed, the team took their complaints about unfair and inequitable treatment to the local press, and appealed to the public for support. While the disputes did not always end the way they hoped, the resistance they showed and their strategic use of the local press mirrored the actions of other Black individuals and groups in the region organizing for change. Through baseball, the Chatham Coloured All-Stars claimed a right to be heard and to be taken seriously.

Getting Organized for the 1939 Season

In the years since their 1935 debut in the Big Six Intermediate A circuit of the WCBA, the Chatham Coloured All-Stars shifted leagues several times. After winning the WCBA Intermediate A title in 1935, the All-Stars returned to the Big Six for another season, reaching the finals but losing the title to Strathroy.[1] According to the *Chatham Daily News*, by 1937 the high costs of travelling to regular games in London, Sarnia, and Strathroy (all located between one and two hours away from Chatham) led the All-Stars to leave the Big Six for a league closer to home.[2] They found it in the Intermediate B circuit of the Kent County Baseball League (the league had no Intermediate A grouping that year), where travel times and costs were considerably less. Besides, the team may have needed to rebuild. At the start of the 1937 season, the All-Stars lost their catcher, Donise Washington, when the baseball organizers in Strathroy recruited him to play and manage their Intermediate A team. *Chatham Daily News* sports columnist Art Cartier remarked that Washington's loss "was the big reason why the All-Stars found it necessary to play a slightly lower class of baseball this season."[3] The All-Stars spent two years playing Intermediate B baseball in Kent County. In their first year, they reached the league playoffs but lost in the quarter finals. In 1938, they made the league playoff finals but lost to a team from Tilbury, a small community about sixteen miles from Chatham.[4]

In 1939, the Chatham Coloured All-Stars decided to return to Intermediate A baseball. That year, both the Chatham Coloured All-Stars and the Tilbury Motors (winners of the 1937 and 1938 Kent County Baseball League Intermediate B titles), applied to the OBA to play at the Intermediate A level.[5] The OBA approved both teams, but Chatham and Tilbury were the only two teams in the district to apply. They were not able to rejoin the Big Six, as several of those teams had joined a cross-border, Michigan-Ontario league.[6] With only two teams signed up for Intermediate A ball in Kent County, they could not run a regular season. Instead, the OBA agreed to let Chatham and Tilbury hold a five-game series in August to determine which of them would advance to the OBA playoffs. With that agreement in place, the All-Stars decided to spend the summer playing in Chatham's Industrial Baseball League, a four-team baseball group that was not affiliated with the OBA at the time.[7]

Although the All-Stars' roster changed over the years, the team kept a core group of players who had been with them since 1933. Len and Boomer Harding

C[illegible]THAM ALL-STARS need a victory over Blenheim Thurs[illegible] [illegible]r Walpole Island a wee[illegible]nce to gain a playoff bert[illegible] in th[illegible] Intermediate "B" Baseball League. Here they ar[illegible]

nga (coach), Stanton Robbins, Gordon Ladd, Wilfred Hard-
, Gerald Browning, William Crosby, Leslie Crosby and Joe
annyll Parker (manager). Front row: Andrew Hardin, Earl

Fig. 8.1 (previous spread) ▪ The Chatham Coloured All-Stars in 1937. With Donise Washington's departure, the team called on Joe "Happy" Parker to be their manager one last time. Back row, from left: Bethune Binga Sr. (coach and team secretary), Stanton Robbins, Gouy Ladd, Boomer Harding, Gerald Browning, William Crosby, Leslie Crosby, Joseph Parker. Front row, from left: Andy Harding, Flat Chase, Len Harding, King Terrell, Ben Talbot. Willie Shognosh played for the Walpole Island team that year, and both Walpole Island and the All-Stars played in the Kent County Intermediate B League. Photo credit: Leddy Library Archives and Special Collections, F1033 (Wilfred "Boomer" Harding Collection), Scrapbook 1. Original source: *Chatham Daily News*, n.d., c. August 1937.

returned, with Len reclaiming the catching role he had relinquished to Donise Washington while the American was on the team. As well, Flat Chase, King Terrell, Gouy Ladd, Ross Talbot, and occasionally his brother Ben all played with the All-Stars in the 1939 season.[8] Willie Shognosh, who had spent a couple of years playing with the Walpole Island team in the Kent County Baseball League rejoined the All-Stars for the 1938 and 1939 seasons.[9] Several others from the 1934 All-Stars also left in the intervening years, including Don Tabron who left after the 1935 season. Stanton Robbins, an outfielder who also pitched for the team in later years, last played for the All-Stars in 1938.[10] Ferguson Jenkins Sr., who had not played regularly with the All-Stars since 1935, rejoined them for the 1939 OBA playoffs. As well, younger Harding brother Andy was also playing for the team. He had been batboy for the All-Stars in 1935 and played occasionally through the later 1930s. The younger Harding was known for his speed, and like his two older brothers, he was a high school track and field champion.[11] Harding's nephew, Blake Harding, said his Uncle Andy "could run like a deer."[12] Other players who were with the All-Stars in the 1937–1938 period include William and Leslie Crosby.

The Chatham Coloured All-Stars also filled out their roster with help from a new Black Junior (under 20 years) baseball team, the Red Sox. Despite years of the All-Stars' success, local amateur baseball in Chatham remained largely racially segregated. While some young Black players were finding spots on youth teams, Black participation in organized baseball was not strong.[13] Perhaps to provide a place for younger Black players, the Talbots founded and managed the Red Sox.[14] The 1939 team included Ken Milburn, Andy Harding, Bill Henson, Albert "Abie" Scott, and Gerald and Harold Browning, who all occasionally played for the All-Stars that season. Many of those Red Sox players would also later play for the Taylor AC in the 1940s.[15] As Art Cartier noted in one of his newspaper columns, the All-Stars had trouble getting enough players out for games, but they were able to call on members of the Red Sox.[16]

One Red Sox player, fourteen-year-old Abie Scott, reportedly "stole the show" one day when the All-Stars asked him to fill a last-minute gap in their lineup.[17] According to the *Chatham Daily News*, Scott "fielded three chances perfectly," including providing "the finishing touch to a thrilling rundown play between third and home in the sixth inning." Boomer Harding explained years later, "Oh he was their bat boy, but a lot of games they'd put him in and my brother would tell him to wait for a walk and he'd slam the ball out. He'd just—he couldn't have been over fifteen, or fourteen. He was a child [laughs]."[18] Harding recalled that he was an outstanding all-around athlete, excelling at not only baseball, but also lacrosse, swimming, and diving.[19] He remembered Scott diving at the Stirling Park pool, saying, "he could dive off of the roof and he'd hardly make a ripple."

While the Chatham Colored All-Stars remained a primarily Black team, over the years they relied on local white players, usually from the other city teams, to fill temporary gaps in the lineup. One of these white players was Alvin "Dutch" or "Dutchy" Scott, who grew up in Chatham's East End. Scott had played with the All-Stars occasionally since the team was formed in 1933.[20] In 1939, Scott joined the All-Stars full-time for the OBA playoff rounds. Years later, several of the former Chatham Coloured All-Stars players, including Harding and Jenkins, described Scott as "one of the boys."[21] Harding recalled Scott telling them that he "would rather play with us than against us."[22] Jenkins remembered Scott cheering loudly from the sidelines when he played for them, saying, "he raised more Cain on the bench...He'd keep everybody's spirits up."[23] He also recalled that the "fans didn't understand," or were at least surprised to see a white man leading the cheering for a Black baseball team. Scott's ties to the All-Stars suggests that although sports remained largely segregated in 1930s Chatham, baseball created a few cross-racial, neighbourhood connections.

The All-Stars also changed managers several times in the 1930s. Washington helped manage the team while he was there, and after he left in 1937, Joseph "Happy" Parker returned to the team for a year.[24] In 1938, Ross Talbot and his brother, Ben, managed the team, and they continued in that role for the first half of the 1939 season. By early August, Len Harding had taken over as manager for the All-Stars, perhaps because the Talbots were also managing and coaching the Red Sox.[25] Len was well-liked by the former players.[26] Boomer Harding recalled his brother's time as manager, saying "He did a wonderful job. He kept the boys cool and everything."[27] With the constant harassment a Black team faced, keeping the "boys cool" would have been a significant part of the manager's job. Pauline Parker Miller said something similar about her father, Joseph Parker. She claimed he "had a time keeping the boys under control" when the team members got angry over racist treatment.[28] Harding worked with Parker as a barber in the older man's shop, and he would have had the opportunity to get advice from someone who had been connected to baseball in the community since the early years of the twentieth century.[29]

The *Chatham Daily News* continued to cover the All-Stars as closely as they had in the past, but with different reporters and columnists. In 1937, Jack Calder, who wrote about the All-Stars in columns and articles, left for a job with the Canadian Press.[30] Replacing him was Art Cartier, another local young white man, the son of a contractor.[31] In the mid-1930s, while barely out of his teens, Cartier covered Chatham sports stories for the *Border Cities Star/Windsor Daily Star*.[32] When he moved to the *Chatham Daily News,* Cartier started his own column, "Sport Talk," replacing Calder's "Analyzing Sport." In his reporting style, Cartier differed from Calder in how he got input on the games he covered. Calder had been an enthusiastic observer of community baseball, but as was common in sports reporting at that time, he did not often speak to the players themselves or include their views in his columns. During the 1939 season, however, Cartier was speaking directly to the players, particularly to manager Len Harding about conflicts and controversies that arose. Whether this closer relationship between the reporter and the All-Stars represented a difference of journalistic style or the All-Stars' growing comfort with speaking to the press (or perhaps both) is not clear. Cartier was also the *Chatham Daily News* sports editor, and when Len Harding took various complaints to the paper during the 1939 season, he took them to Cartier. While their voices were still filtered through a white journalist, the press became an important vehicle for the All-Stars as they dealt with conflict and controversial issues in their later years.

Playing in Chatham's Industrial Baseball League

The All-Stars had a disappointing start to their 1939 Industrial Baseball League season, losing all their games in June. Scores were close in those games, but they struggled with pitching as Chase had some injuries and Shognosh was not able to attend all games.[33] A *Chatham Daily News* article later in the season noted that many of the All-Stars had trouble getting off work during the week (a point Terrell also made in his oral history interview).[34] Despite this unevenness, Cartier claimed the All-Stars were a good draw, and seeing Flat Chase play was still "worth the price of admission alone."[35] He observed that Chase was batting over .300, and in fact, by late June, Chase and four of his teammates were ranked among the top twelve batters in the city league.[36] Six members of the All-Stars were batting over .300, with two (Gouy Ladd and Andy Harding) over .400. The All-Stars' slump ended in early July after Shognosh's return to the pitcher's mound which, according to Cartier, "did much to steady the team."[37] Later in July, Cartier noted that the All-Stars, were "looking better right now than they have all season."[38]

Not long after recovering from their slump, however, the All-Stars became embroiled in some controversies with the Industrial Baseball League. The first involved a conflict with the Kent Bridge team that began with a disputed "safe" call, but soon escalated into physical fighting among both players and fans. According to the newspaper account of the game, the All-Stars had complained that a Kent Bridge player running from third base to home had strayed far outside the baseline to avoid being tagged.[39] Both officials at the game, however, upheld the original call. The reporter covering the game claimed that after the call, "Menacing gestures came from several quarters, wild words were tossed with apparent abandon." Whether or not those "wild words" included overt racial insults, any kind of physical or verbal conflict involving Black and white players was affected by the dynamics of power and race in that environment. During the heat of the verbal exchange, according to the report, Chase "made a move at a Kent Bridge coach." According to the newspaper report, at that point both players and spectators rushed onto the field. The report noted that a (white) spectator started arguing with a young Black boy, and the two began to fight. Their conflict ended, however, with "the appearance of a colored lady who directed the youth off the field." While the reporter appeared to take that particular incident lightly, the woman's concern about the fighting underlines the dangers for Black youth in getting caught up in violence, even at a baseball game. Play resumed after about twenty minutes, but officials ejected Chase from the game.

While dealing with verbal and physical conflict on the diamond was nothing new for the All-Stars, the executive of the Industrial Baseball League thought it was serious enough to call a meeting to discuss it.[40] The *Chatham Daily News* spoke to the teams' managers before the meeting, and each accused the other team of being physically rough during the game itself. Bert Williams of Kent Bridge claimed that members of the All-Stars deliberately hit a Kent Bridge batter and catcher in the head during the ninth inning.[41] Furthermore, he claimed, on account of the roughness, the Kent Bridge team had decided they would never play the All-Stars again. Len Harding, in turn, alluded to violent actions from Kent Bridge, saying "We will play the same kind of ball against Kent Bridge as they play against us. All we ask is a fair deal and hope we get it at the meet Tuesday." As Boomer Harding explained years later in an oral history interview, the All-Stars had many "rough" games where they felt they had to push back to defend themselves.[42] Len Harding asking for a "fair deal," however, also signalled they wanted to participate in the decision-making process and wanted to be heard. After the Industrial Baseball League executive meeting, the organization released a statement condemning "rowdyism" at games, but they did not issue any further player suspensions.[43]

Whether or not the All-Stars and Kent Bridge came to a truce during that meeting about the game violence is unknown. A week later the All-Stars formally withdrew from the Industrial Baseball League. Their withdrawal was related to a dispute the All-Stars had with the Industrial Baseball League executive over the way it handled a complaint the team had made about a game that took place on August 12, 1939.[44] Rain had delayed the start of the game, and after umpire Fred Peardon arrived, he claimed the All-Stars did not have enough players on the field and declared the game forfeited. He then said the teams would play a seven-inning exhibition game instead. The All-Stars, who disputed the forfeit, refused to play an exhibition game, and said they would play the game under protest (meaning they planned to challenge the ruling). The game went ahead, and the All-Stars won 2–0. When the Industrial Baseball League executive met, they decided not to review the case, instead siding with Peardon's original call that the All-Stars should forfeit the game.[45] The All-Stars, upset that the Industrial Baseball League Executive refused to let them present their case, formally withdrew from the league.

In the August 18 edition of the *Chatham Daily News*, Len Harding presented the All-Stars' position in a letter to the sports editor.[46] Taking a measured, formal tone, Harding explained, "The management of the All Stars feel that baseball fans of the city should be informed of the circumstances which resulted in a decision of the team to withdraw from the City League." Harding began by sharing some background on what had happened at that game, information he said the league executive had not considered when making their decision. First, he said, there was confusion over the start time, as the *Chatham Daily News* had given the incorrect start time for the All-Stars' game.[47] Moreover, Harding continued, it was raining at the start time, at a quarter to two, and the players did not know if the game was going ahead. No game officials had shown up and the field was not ready for play. He said officials finally arrived at the park at 2:05, and indicated the game would go ahead. The umpire, claimed Harding, called the game as forfeited at 2:20, without first calling "play ball" or checking to see if the All-Stars were ready to play. Harding insisted that by 2:20 they had enough players to take the field. The All-Stars' manager claimed, however, that they were less upset with the original call than they were by the process. The city league executive, he said, simply took the word of the umpire without letting the All-Stars explain why they disputed the call. Considering that the umpire had admitted that he allowed the game to continue under protest, Harding felt they had a right to a hearing. Harding concluded by saying that their decision to leave the Industrial Baseball League was the result of "the culmination of a series of unfavorable decisions and incidents towards the Star [*sic*] ball team." Harding's last remark suggests that perhaps other issues, including their earlier conflict with the Kent Bridge team, may have played a role.

Besides explaining the team's withdrawal from the league, Len Harding's letter also suggested the way the All-Stars were using formal rules and process to seek redress. Harding had clearly prepared a set of arguments about why they felt the call was wrong, and was upset that he was not given a chance to make them. As Rob Ruck argues, sport, unlike other areas of life, "presupposed conditions of equality on the playing fields. Although these conditions of fairness were often violated, there was, nonetheless, the feeling that the rules applied evenly to black and white alike."[48] Len Harding's letter to the sports editor assumed that fair play was possible, and he felt justified in protesting when it fell short. At the same time, however, Harding's letter also revealed a strategy of using the local press to speak directly to the public. He could have sent his letter to the Industrial Baseball League executive alone but he wanted, as he said in his letter, to reach "baseball fans of the city." Using the newspaper in this way allowed the team to direct the narrative, and perhaps dispel any ill will or rumours about them. This was a change from their first years in organized baseball, when they did not speak to the press about controversies or conflicts.

While Harding's letter was about baseball, the strategy and sentiments mirrored those of other Black individuals and groups working toward greater racial justice. In fact, just weeks before Harding and the All-Stars addressed the public through the *Chatham Daily News*, Black community leaders at the annual Emancipation Day celebration in the city encouraged Black people to work together to achieve social and economic rights in society. The event held at Chatham's Tecumseh Park also included a baseball game featuring the Red Sox and a musical program with the choir from the First Baptist Institutional Church from Hamtramck, Michigan.[49] The day's speakers, including ministers from the North Buxton BME Church and the First Baptist Institutional Church, emphasized liberal citizenship and solidarity for Black people. Rev. F.O. Stewart of the North Buxton BME Church told the crowd that Black people "must realize they must band together, and march forward together, toward a common goal of greater economic liberty and a better status of citizenship."[50] Likewise, Rev. Benjamin H. Wright, the Jamaican-born pastor of First Baptist Institutional Church in Hamtramck, a city east of Detroit, told the crowd that the "Demand of the colored man today is for justice."[51] Emphasizing self-improvement, Wright argued that justice was necessary "so that he [the Black person] may take the station in life of which he is capable." These speeches reflected the ideas of liberal self-improvement, respectability, and justice that were being expressed by larger Black organizations in North America, including the NAACP and the United Negro Improvement Association. While it is unknown if Len Harding or any of the All-Stars were at the park that day, the Emancipation Day speeches give insights into the ideas and words circulating in the local Black churches. If they were in the churches, they were likely in the wider community.

Len Harding would have had some exposure to those ideas in his own household. Describing her growing up years, Harding's older sister Beulah Cuzzens claimed their father, Andrew, wanted his children to connect to the world outside Chatham.[52] She explained one of the reasons they attended the local African Methodist Episcopal Church was that it often hosted visiting bishops and ministers from the United States.[53] She said their father "thought this would be pretty good for us to hear from the outside world."[54] Cuzzens remembered speakers from Kansas City, Detroit, and Cleveland, and chances were that at least some were expressing ideas similar to those in the 1939 Emancipation Day speeches. Blake Harding claimed his grandmother Sarah also valued education, encouraging her children "to get through at least high school."[55] As noted earlier, both the older Harding daughters had professional careers and social networks that intersected with those advocating for civil rights. Beulah had been the local agent for the *Dawn of Tomorrow* in the mid-1920s. Georgina worked for a Detroit law firm where one of the partners had become the first Black state senator in Michigan, and another partner became the first Black judge in the state.[56] Whatever inspired Len Harding to begin speaking publicly about how his team was treated, he had plenty of people within and connected to his family that were challenging prevailing racial stereotypes.

Challenging the Ontario Baseball Association

Despite the setbacks with the Chatham Industrial Baseball League, the All-Stars gained new energy as they turned to the OBA playoffs. In late August, they met Tilbury Motors for their five-game series to decide which team would advance to the OBA playoff round. An article in the *Chatham Daily News* claimed that the All-Stars were playing better than they had all season.[57] The All-Stars' series with Tilbury was well-matched. The series went to five games, with the All-Stars finally taking the Kent County Baseball League Intermediate A championship.[58] As the All-Stars advanced to the OBA playoffs, the author of a *Chatham Daily News* article on the team was optimistic about their chances, claiming that "the Stars have been playing smart baseball lately and deserve encouragement in their effort to go places along the O.B.A. championship trail."[59] When the All-Stars entered the OBA playoffs, they quickly defeated Leamington and LaSalle in two games straight.[60] As the playoffs advanced, both Shognosh and Chase performed well on the mound. Cartier remarked after a game with LaSalle, "If Shaugnosh [*sic*] can toss a few more games like he did Sunday and if Chase can remain anywhere close to recent form, the Stars' chances in O.B.A. will rocket to a new high..."[61]

When the All-Stars reached the OBA semi-finals with Aylmer, Ontario, they faced what could have been their biggest challenge of the playoffs. The Aylmer Laundrymen were the defending Intermediate A champions, and anticipation was high. Len Harding, however, was confident when he spoke to the press before the series, saying he was starting Chase on the mound.[62] He claimed, "The big fellow has been plenty hot in our recent playoffs and we're sure he can take care of Aylmer. All the boys are in good condition and ready for their toughest opponents of the season." The All-Stars ended up taking the series in two close games. In the first, which the All-Stars took 7–6, the reporter covering the game commended Chase for "pitching his

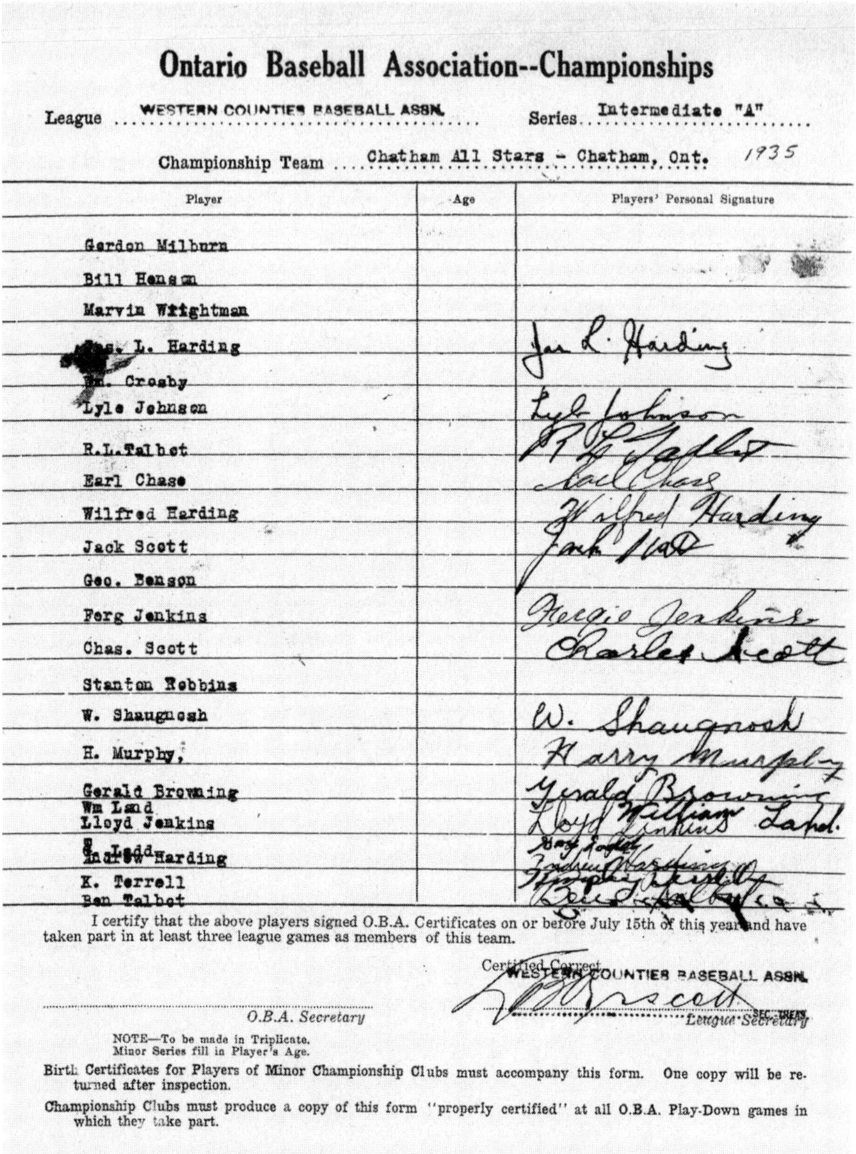

Ontario Baseball Association--Championships

League WESTERN COUNTIES BASEBALL ASSN. Series Intermediate "A"

Championship Team Chatham All Stars - Chatham, Ont. 1935

Player	Age	Players' Personal Signature
Gordon Milburn		
Bill Henson		
Marvin Wrightman		
Jas. L. Harding		Jas L. Harding
Wm. Crosby		
Lyle Johnson		Lyle Johnson
R.L. Talbot		R. L. Talbot
Earl Chase		Earl Chase
Wilfred Harding		Wilfred Harding
Jack Scott		Jack Scott
Geo. Benson		
Ferg Jenkins		Fergie Jenkins
Chas. Scott		Charles Scott
Stanton Robbins		
W. Shaugnosh		W. Shaugnosh
H. Murphy		Harry Murphy
Gerald Browning Wm Ladd Lloyd Jenkins		Gerald Browning William Ladd Lloyd Jenkins
E. Ladd Andrew Harding		Andrew Harding
K. Terrell Ben Talbot		Ben Talbot

I certify that the above players signed O.B.A. Certificates on or before July 15th of this year and have taken part in at least three league games as members of this team.

Certified Correct
WESTERN COUNTIES BASEBALL ASSN.

O.B.A. Secretary

SEC.-TREAS. League Secretary

NOTE—To be made in Triplicate.
Minor Series fill in Player's Age.

Birth Certificates for Players of Minor Championship Clubs must accompany this form. One copy will be returned after inspection.

Championship Clubs must produce a copy of this form "properly certified" at all O.B.A. Play-Down games in which they take part.

Fig. 8.2 ▪ The registration sheet for the OBA playoffs for 1939 (note: "1935" was written on the document, but the list is for 1939). All teams entering the OBA playoffs had to get names and signatures of players who would take part in the playoffs. Not all players on the list would attend every game, but they had to be on the list to be eligible to play. Several players on this list, including Bill Henson, Andy Harding, and Gerald Browning were also members of the Junior team, the Red Sox. Note that the team's name is given as the "Chatham All Stars," not Chatham Coloured All-Stars, as they were generally known. Photo credit: Leddy Library Archives and Special Collections, F1033 (Wilfred "Boomer" Harding Collection), Scrapbook 1.

head off" and getting the game's first home run.[63] In the second game with Aylmer, the *Chatham Daily News* claimed, "Something heroic happened in practically every inning."[64] The reporter was speaking to the umpires who claimed the game was "the classiest Intermediate A baseball performance they had seen in years." The All-Stars were looking strong as they prepared for their final series against the Meaford Knights. In fact, Cartier predicted the All-Stars would ultimately take the championship as, "Few rate the Northern representatives as strong as Aylmer."[65]

Before the final Intermediate A series could begin, however, tragedy struck the Meaford team. Meaford's coach, George Bell, along with several players, had driven down to Aylmer to watch the All-Stars and the Laundrymen play in the semifinal game.[66] Knowing they would play the winner of the series, they wanted to get a sense of their competition. Driving back to Meaford, near Georgian Bay, their car collided with a train at a level crossing. Bell was killed and two of the players were injured. The team decided they would go ahead with their series against Chatham, which was slated to begin days later. The Chatham Coloured All-Stars sent the Meaford team flowers which, according to Art Cartier, was well-received in the community.

Within days of Bell's funeral, the All-Stars arrived in Meaford to play. Rain, however, stopped the first game, so the All-Stars stayed overnight, hoping they could play the next day.[67] When it was still too soggy the next morning, their hosts took the Chatham players fishing instead.[68] Years later, Ferguson Jenkins Sr. recalled that visit fondly, saying, "we were treated like kings."[69] He remembered people from Meaford coming out with their boats to take them fishing. Jenkins laughingly claimed he was the only one who caught any fish large enough to keep. Art Cartier, who had travelled to Meaford for the game, also reported that the All-Stars enjoyed the fishing trip.[70] He said the players were in good spirits, joking about their fishing skills (or lack thereof). One player claimed he would have brought his fish back home with him but "the car in which he was riding was already too crowded." The team went back to Chatham without playing a game.

The first two games in the championship series finally happened on October 12 in Chatham and in Meaford on October 19; each team claimed a win. In the first game in Chatham, the All-Stars prevailed by a score of 13–5.[71] All but one of the Chatham players scored at least one run, with King Terrell getting three. Chase pitched the full game, and according to the reporter covering the game, was "his usual dashing self on the mound."

In the second game (delayed for a few days because of rain), the Knights' pitcher, Elmer Goldsmith, led Meaford to a 9–1 victory.[72] Shognosh was pitching for Chatham, but was relieved in the eighth inning by seventeen-year-old Jack Scott, who had occasionally filled in for the team during the season. The Meaford team then scored six runs, taking the game.

In that second game in Meaford, an incident occurred suggesting some tension was building between the teams. In the eighth inning, Boomer Harding was ejected from the game for either pushing or arguing with the base umpire. Cartier, covering the game, later spoke to Harding who claimed that the umpire had been taunting him, saying such things as "You're lucky to be still in there."[73] Cartier suggested that the umpire was referring to an incident earlier in the game when Harding, playing first base, was accused of tagging a runner too hard. Cartier noted that the umpire had said other things to Harding, but did not provide details. Whatever the official said, it was serious enough that, according to a wire service article, the All-Stars considered making a formal complaint about the umpire's behaviour.[74] Harding, like his brother, was not known for getting into fights with officials or other players on the diamond. Both Cartier's report and the wire service article indicated that Harding's ejection from the game upset and unsettled the players.[75] The wire service article suggested players (they did not identify from which team) "milled about and struck a few light blows" but that no one was injured. Nevertheless, someone called the police, ostensibly to restore order. Indeed, the newspaper had downplayed the violence, raising questions about whether or not assumptions about Black male criminality contributed to the decision to call the police.

Although the second game was tense (particularly with the appearance of the police) the Chatham Coloured All-Stars faced more conflict once the game was over. The question arose immediately about where and when they would play the next game. Customarily, when ball teams were playing a series, they traded off home games and then if a deciding game were needed, the teams would often choose a neutral location amenable to both. If there were considerable distance between the two home communities, they might choose a mid-way point, such as when the All-Stars played Penetanguishene in the Intermediate B championship (they played the final game in Guelph, halfway between the two towns). The OBA provided some travel costs, approximately one dollar per mile travelled, but teams would often need extra funding to cover all expenses.[76] While Chatham and Meaford had not talked about a location for the third game beforehand, the All-Stars were already concerned about travel expenses.[77] Meaford was approximately 220 miles from Chatham, and the All-Stars had already driven north twice, once for the game that was rained out and again for the second game. Long trips also meant having to travel the night before the game and taking yet more time off work. The players appear to have spoken to Cartier about their concerns, as he commented on their financial issues in several of his columns.[78] In an article before the game against Meaford in Chatham, Cartier observed that the All-Stars "were in dire need of a big gate" at their home game to cover travel costs.[79] That game was on a cold Thursday afternoon and it drew only 200 spectators, hardly enough to cover their travel costs.[80] In a later column, Cartier remarked that the Stars had taken in less than $300.00 in gate revenue all season.[81]

Rather than waiting to discuss the location for the third game with the All-Stars, however, the Meaford management went ahead with plans of their own. According to Cartier, who had accompanied the team to Meaford, just as the game ended someone announced over a loudspeaker that the third game would be held on the following Saturday (October 21) at Hanover, Ontario.[82] Hanover is less than sixty miles from Meaford, but over 150 miles from Chatham. Alarmed at the announcement—and the prospect of taking yet another long trip north— Len Harding headed over to speak to Meaford management. Harding later said he told them Hanover was too far for them and suggested they just stay in Meaford and then play in nearby Owen Sound the next day to save on travel.[83] None of his suggestions were acceptable to the Meaford group, however, and Cartier, who claimed he witnessed the exchange, said that "after fifteen minutes of argument which went exactly nowhere," Harding left, but told them he would be contacting the secretary of the OBA, W.J. Snyder.[84] The All-Stars knew Snyder, a long-time member of the OBAA/OBA executive, since their first run at the championship in 1934. Within a few minutes, Cartier reported, Harding was speaking on the phone to Snyder who seemed to be sympathetic and suggested Harding look into Clinton, Ontario as a possible site, halfway between Chatham and Meaford.[85]

As Len Harding was trying to negotiate a new game site, he had to speak to J.C. McDonald, the vice-president of the OBA and chair of the subcommittee that oversaw the playoffs. After returning to Chatham, Harding phoned both McDonald and Snyder. Through those conversations, Harding got the impression that McDonald, rather than the Meaford management, was leading the push to hold the third game at Hanover.[86]

McDonald lived in Chesley, Ontario, where his father had owned and published the local newspaper, the *Chesley Enterprise*.[87] Chesley is less than sixty miles from Meaford and only a dozen miles from Hanover. McDonald had been at the third game in Meaford and was there when Harding was arguing with the Meaford representatives about playing in Hanover.[88] After speaking with OBA representatives in Clinton to see if it were possible to play there, Harding reportedly called McDonald with the proposal.[89] McDonald, however, would not agree to holding the game in Clinton, claiming their gate revenues would be higher in Hanover than Clinton. Harding also claimed McDonald dismissed his concerns, telling him he "should not kick" as the All-Stars would get their mileage. Harding then claimed that when he pressed McDonald about whether they would guarantee they would receive the full mileage owed to them, the OBA Vice-President hung up on him. Whether or not those exact words were used, the exchange suggests McDonald was not willing to negotiate and expected the All-Stars to accept his decision.

According to Boomer Harding, the All-Stars normally had an easier time arranging compensation for travel, which would help explain why Len Harding was bothered by McDonald's unwillingness to guarantee they would get their money. Harding explained that when they were in playoffs, opposing teams sometimes offered the All-Stars money to play the third game in the opposing team's community rather than finding a neutral location. Harding explained, "Well, if we tied our series, we would get an offer of 300 or 500 [dollars] to have the game played in the city we were going to play against. Our business managers would say, 'That's a wonderful deal because we might not have two or three thousand people out and they will.' We'd go there and usually win the game and win the money too."[90] As noted earlier, Harding claimed the All-Stars had played their third game in their 1934 OBA playoffs against Milton in Milton because the team had offered them $200.00 to do so.[91] If that were the case, McDonald and Meaford were operating out of the norm, at least from the All-Stars' perspective. For Len Harding, and the All-Stars, accepting the offer to play in Hanover for a share of the gate (but not a guaranteed share) would have been risky. It was, after all, the third week in October, and taking a trip north without a guarantee was a much bigger risk than it would have been in August or early September.

While Art Cartier and another *Chatham Daily News* columnist, A. Roustabouter, speculated that favouritism for a local team led McDonald to push for the Hanover location, McDonald's motivation is uncertain.[92] Whether it was local favouritism, racism, or both, McDonald could pressure the All-Stars because of who he was—a white man with power. The power differential between McDonald, a white, middle-class man, and Vice-President of the OBA, and Len Harding, a twenty-six-year-old Black man who worked as a barber, was significant.[93] McDonald felt secure enough to exert his authority and (white) privilege against a Black team from Chatham, but he would likely have had a more difficult time pressuring white teams with more power and influence. As well, unlike the Meaford Knights, who were owned and managed by well-known furniture manufacturers, the Knight family, the Chatham Coloured All-Stars had no major sponsors who may have had some pull.[94] Ultimately, McDonald prevailed. On Friday morning, October 20, Archie Stirling received a telegram from W.J. Snyder of the OBA, telling them the third game would take place on Saturday, October 21, in Hanover.[95]

Len Harding remained in close touch with Cartier and the *Chatham Daily News* throughout this period, as he had shared information on his negotiations with OBA officials. On hearing the news about the OBA's decision to hold the game in Hanover, Harding once again spoke to the press, and an article summarizing the team's concerns appeared that same day, in the afternoon edition.[96] This article outlined the All-Stars' case, arguing that the team had been left out of the decision-making process and that holding the game in Hanover was unfair and financially burdensome to the All-Stars. It also appealed directly to the public for support. It began by asserting that the All-Stars had no say in where the third game would be played, saying the decision to hold the game in Hanover was "made strictly without the consent of Chatham management." The article then explained why the team felt it was unfair to ask them to travel to Hanover, pointing out that Meaford was just sixty miles from Hanover, while the All-Stars would have to travel "nearly three times that distance." The All-Stars, the article claimed, felt they should play at a point halfway between the two communities, such as Clinton, Ontario, a location which the article claimed that OBA Secretary Snyder had suggested.

Once the article laid out the All-Stars' case against going to Hanover, it then turned to the reader, asking for input. The article revealed that "The Stars, while feeling that under existing circumstances it would be most unfair to make the trip to Hanover, are content to let the decision rest with the Chatham fans. Fan opinion and fan opinion alone will decide whether they make the trip tomorrow."[97] To that end, the newspaper invited people to call and tell the team if they thought they should go to Hanover or not. The article advised people to call either the *Chatham Daily News* sports desk, or Joseph Parker's barber shop, where Len Harding worked. The article ended with perhaps one of the more persuasive arguments, particularly for cash-strapped people in the 1930s—going to Hanover would be a huge financial burden to the All-Stars. It explained,

> The Chatham boys have lost considerable time from work on account of this series for trips to Meaford and district necessitate leaving the night before. It has cost the boys plenty so far as O.B.A. allowances do not completely take care of travelling when a game is postponed [the last comment referring to the first game in Meaford that was rained out].

Sealing the deal, the article outlined clearly that the team felt that not only was the process unfair to them, going to Hanover would cost them money they did not have and threaten their livelihoods.

While Cartier and Harding would likely have collaborated on making this proposal (particularly as it required the cooperation of the *Chatham Daily News* sports desk to answer phone calls), this effort revealed the All-Stars' growing comfort with using the local press to speak to the public. The All-Star's gamble that the public would back them seemed to have worked. While it is unknown how many people called Joseph Parker's barber shop, Cartier claimed that at the *Chatham Daily News* sports desk, the "calls poured in from all parts of the city and county. Practically all of them suggested that the boys stay home and see what happens."[98] The paper printed transcripts from ten calls, and while the race of the callers is unknown, differences in how the callers viewed the conflict are apparent. Some attributed the dispute to regional favouritism, with the OBA supporting the northern district over Chatham in the province's southwest. Others, however, implied race was a factor, such as the person who said "If the O.B.A. doesn't want the Chatham boys to be provincial champions why do they invite them in their organization in the first place?" Someone else was concerned about the financial hardship that taking another long trip north would have on the players, saying they should stay home and "look after their jobs." Overall, the callers urged the All-Stars not to go to the final game as scheduled. One person declared they would have liked to see the team win an OBA championship, "But not if they have to go to Hanover."

Another caller simply said, "Brother, I vote no on the question and so does everybody else at our house."

Later that evening, the All-Stars met and decided not to take the trip to Hanover. Len Harding told the *Chatham Daily News*, "Our team wanted the opinion of the fans before they made up their minds on the matter. And from the calls received, we know we are doing the correct thing in refusing to make the trip to Hanover."[99] Validated with the fan support, Harding explained, "All we ask is a fair break and everyone knows that we would gladly travel as far as the other fellows, perhaps a little farther. But Hanover, only sixty miles from Meaford, is out of the question." They were willing to be flexible, but they would not travel without guarantee of fair compensation.

Len Harding was not known to be involved in any civil rights groups at the time, and he never specifically referenced race in his appeals to the public. He was, nevertheless, a Black man speaking out in public, asking for a "fair break," the right to be treated equitably. A simple but powerful gesture, Harding was able to use it to make a claim on equity. He was also able to make the claim from a position of strength that playing on a successful baseball team gave him. The All-Stars had a strong reputation in the city. They won Chatham's first provincial championship, they made a big impression in regional baseball through the WCBA, and were at that point on the verge of possibly winning an Intermediate A-level OBA title. That strength made it possible, made it easier, for a Black man to speak to a largely white public in that way. As Rob Ruck explained, sport had a strong symbolic power. He noted, "Through competition with whites in a variety of contests, sport provided the black community...with its most visible heroes and its most tangible elements of a new self-esteem."[100] In this way, we can see the connections between sport and the movement for social justice. It also mirrored the community-based activism taking place in southern Ontario in the 1930s. While the Chatham Coloured All-Stars were not actively organizing for greater civil rights, their willingness to put themselves into the public sphere came at a time when other Black people in the region were articulating those aims.

After informing the OBA head office on October 21 that they would not be going to Hanover, the team waited for word on the status of the series. According to the *Chatham Daily News*, the team still hoped a new game could be rescheduled.[101] Several days later, they got some news, not from the OBA directly, but through the *Owen Sound Daily Sun Times*, which reported on October 25 that J.C. McDonald had announced the Meaford Knights had won the OBA Intermediate A title by default.[102] Moreover, McDonald claimed there was "a distinct possibility that the O.B.A. will take drastic action in suspending the Chatham club for several seasons."[103] Making a threat publicly like that was a power move, made by someone with privilege based on his race, class, and position, trying to intimidate a much less powerful Black team. Indeed, it is hard to imagine McDonald treating a white team, particularly one from the region's influential baseball communities such as London and Strathroy, in the same way. That difference in treatment marks this episode in amateur baseball politics as a racist act.

While the *Owen Sound Daily Sun Times* took McDonald at his word about Meaford winning the championship, several clues in their article suggested that he may have been speaking without the authority of the OBA. McDonald made his announcement from his home in Chesley, Ontario, and the only people attending the meeting were McDonald and representatives from the Meaford team. Snyder usually issued official OBA news from the organization's head office in Hamilton. In fact, columnist Art Cartier remarked on the oddness of having a meeting to decide the fate of the series attended by only McDonald and three people from the Meaford team. Furthermore, as both Cartier and fellow sports columnist Roustabouter observed, no one from the OBA head office had contacted either local OBA representative Archie Stirling or Len Harding about the status of the series.[104] Days went by after McDonald's announcement, with no confirmation, or denial, from the OBA. Both Cartier and Roustabouter speculated on the possible meaning of the silence, suggesting there were internal divisions within the OBA executive.[105] Cartier wondered if McDonald had "overstepped his bounds" by declaring the Meaford team the winner, noting that "Secretary W.J. Snyder and president J.W. Scott have been strangely silent on the whole thing."

Meanwhile, newspaper sports columnists from around southern Ontario had picked up on the Chatham-Meaford story, having seen both McDonald's announcement and coverage of the Chatham Coloured All-Stars protests.[106] While the columnists varied on whether they supported Chatham's position, they criticized the way the OBA was handling the situation. For example, Nels Whitmore, sportswriter with the *St. Thomas Times-Journal*, said, "From this angle, it will seem that the Chatham All-Stars have a grievance against the O.B.A. and it may not do the parent organization much good."[107] While supporting Meaford's claim to the title, *Owen Sound Daily Sun Times* sportswriter Dick Payne noted "We have more than a little sympathy with Chatham's claim that Hanover should not have been selected for the third game."[108] As well, Red Taylor, sports columnist for the *Woodstock Sentinel-Review*, observed, "Chatham appears to have a good cause for complaint."[109] A reporter with the *London Free Press* also criticized the OBA and the Meaford management for not accepting the Chatham team's offer to stay overnight in Meaford and play the next day, noting that "this way of deciding titles is expensive."[110]

The *London Free Press* reporter was not the only one to criticize the amateur baseball organization over finances. Whitmore argued the conflict with Chatham would not have happened if the OBA had been more forthcoming with financial support for team travel. He said, "Either cough up some of the travel expenses or stage one game on a neutral field half-way."[111] Whitmore also claimed the OBA had a "well-filled treasury" and should not insist on taking a large cut from the money collected for admissions at championship games. Meanwhile, he said, teams struggled to cover their costs during playoff runs. He remarked, "No doubt the Chatham ball club is bankrupt or close to it following trips of over 200 miles each way to Meaford and only one game at home." Whether or not Whitmore's characterization of the OBA's finances was accurate, his public comments lent support to the All-Stars' grievance. Indeed, in a later column, Whitmore acknowledged that the All-Stars "had good reason to stand their ground."[112]

In the days after McDonald declared Meaford the OBA champions, Len Harding continued to speak out about the All-Stars' treatment. In a press interview he gave that was picked up by the wire service Canadian Press and reprinted in several southern Ontario newspapers, Harding confirmed that the team had taken a financial loss in their last trip to Meaford.[113] Citing the OBA constitution, Harding noted that the All-Stars should have received $200.00 in travel compensation. Instead, he claimed the Meaford management had given them just $90.00 from money collected at the gate. Taking a parting shot at J.C. McDonald, Harding surmised that if the OBA Vice-President "had been as anxious to see that the Stars got a square deal regarding finances as he was to have a championship in his own district, the Chathamites might have made their third trip into the north country." While clearly concerned about finances, Harding's pointed remarks about McDonald also suggest he was not afraid to challenge those at the highest level of the provincial baseball body. It also shows how differently the team was handling baseball politics compared to their early years when they relied more heavily on Archie Stirling to smooth the way for them.

With the growing public criticism, OBA Secretary Snyder finally spoke out about the Chatham-Meaford conflict, a full five days after McDonald had declared Meaford the winners, and nine days after the All-Stars informed the OBA they would not play in Hanover.[114] While not directly naming McDonald, he claimed, "I have seen statements that Meaford has been awarded the championship. This is not correct." He went on to explain that Chatham had not necessarily forfeited the championship when they refused to go to Hanover. He claimed that the OBA executive would meet to decide the fate of the championship series. On reporting on Snyder's remarks, Cartier surmised that "Province wide newspaper comment on the situation undoubtedly had something to do with yesterday's statement just eight days late."[115] Cartier noted that at least nine sports columnists wrote about the Intermediate A series in the previous week.[116] Cartier added, "Wonder how many of those were read by secretary Snyder and vice-president McDonald?"[117]

The public criticism they received from Harding and the various newspaper sportswriters may well have led Snyder to distance the OBA from McDonald's actions. As Bruce Kidd and Alan Metcalfe argue, the interwar period was formative for Canadian amateur sports organizations as they tried to establish legitimacy and grow support and influence.[118] Any questioning or challenges could be a threat to their stability. Metcalfe notes that membership in the OBA rose and fell throughout the 1930s, with leagues joining and leaving.[119] A wider debate in the pages of southern Ontario newspapers about the policies and practices of the OBA could be concerning for an organization that already had challenges holding on to their membership. A columnist from the *Peterborough Examiner*, who claimed "the case is hardly fair to Chatham," recounted grievances that a Peterborough team had the year before with the OBA over travel during the playoff season.[120] In Chatham, some local baseball organizers and politicians had been speaking about possibly withdrawing from the OBA, based in part on the All-Stars' treatment.[121]

On hearing the OBA would be meeting to discuss the fate of the Intermediate A championship, Harding claimed his team was still willing to play the third game. He said they would play Meaford "in any kind of weather. We can beat Meaford and bring the championship where it belongs."[122] Cartier observed, as well, that Flat Chase was "throwing a few each day to keep the old arm in condition" in case they got a chance to finish the series.[123] When the *Owen Sound Daily Sun Times* reported that a

Meaford player said the team still wanted to play the final game, Harding reached out to the Knights' manager.[124] In a phone call that Archie Stirling helped set up, Harding asked the Meaford manager if they were serious about the offer.[125] The manager reportedly replied they were but they wanted the All-Stars to pay for the Meaford team's expenses to Hanover for the day they travelled there expecting a game. When Harding asked what his expenses were, the manager reportedly replied, "two hundred and fifty dollars." Hearing such a high price demanded for travelling just sixty miles, Harding replied, "That means that I am to take your answer as a direct refusal to play." With that, the call ended, as well as any hope that Meaford wanted to finish the series.

Despite Harding's efforts, the Intermediate A championship series was decided in "a committee room," rather than on the field.[126] The OBA held a meeting and invited representatives from both Chatham and Meaford teams to present their cases. After a long meeting, the OBA subcommittee that oversaw championships announced that the 1939 title would remain "open," with no winner or loser declared.[127] The OBA also declined to suspend or penalize the Chatham team for not going to Hanover, suggesting that on that point the other members overruled McDonald. With no surviving records of that meeting, it is unknown how or why they came to that decision, and whose influence and arguments held sway. What is known is that McDonald's initial position was at least partially reversed, perhaps only to mitigate the negative publicity circulating through the sports pages of southwestern Ontario newspapers.

While it was not the outcome the Chatham Coloured All-Stars wanted, the team's protests nevertheless forced the OBA to backtrack and at least acknowledge that the team had some grounds for grievance. Len Harding's ease with the media, and the way he told the team's story and got the public and sports journalists engaged helped ensure their complaints reached the OBA, forcing them to listen to a Black team who demanded a "fair break." Their bold and very public resistance suggests they were no longer willing to play baseball at any cost. Being treated fairly (and being fairly compensated for travel) mattered more to the All-Stars than any prize the OBA could give them.

This affair also showed the players, particularly Harding, out front and managing the conflict themselves. Earlier they had relied more heavily on Archie Stirling to deal with problems, such as during the 1934 championship series. Although Stirling was apparently still advising them, it was Len

Fig. 8.3 ▪ Although the OBA declared no official winner for the 1939 season, members of the Chatham Coloured All-Stars were given championship cups, with "Chatham All-Stars 1939" inscribed on one side and the player's name on the other. It is not clear who had these cups made, as the OBA normally gave a single cup to the team and individual medals to team members. Several of these cups still exist in the community, including two at the Chatham-Kent Black Historical Society and Black Mecca Museum. Photo credit: Leddy Library Archives and Special Collections, F1033 (Wilfred "Boomer" Harding Collection), Scrapbook 1. Original source: photo taken by Bryce Shreves.

Harding, not Stirling, at the front of the story. Harding also had developed a relationship with *Chatham Daily News* sports editor and columnist Art Cartier, and he used that connection to get his messages to the public and around southwestern Ontario. Whatever their personal relationship, the newspaper would also have benefited from covering a lively, controversial story that got traction throughout the region. Both Cartier and Roustabouter devoted many columns to the All-Stars' conflict with the OBA, as well as other grievances against the organization.

The wider publicity generated by the All-Stars' conflict with the OBA led to a major shakeup in regional baseball. After the end of the 1939 season, the entire WCBA withdrew from the OBA, deciding to play independently of the provincial organization. While not the only reason, the All-Stars' conflict with the provincial body in 1939 was a factor. During the controversy, *Chatham Daily News* columnists and Chatham municipal politicians had proposed that Chatham should leave the OBA, and perhaps set up a rival organization.[128] Roustabouter, for example, remarked that "it looks like the entire district is disgusted with the O.B.A."[129] Cartier noted that other factors besides the All-Stars' treatment over the championship title also contributed to the WCBA withdrawal, including frustration over the OBA's handling of finances and scheduling.[130] Nevertheless, the withdrawal suggests how successful the All-Stars were at garnering support, not just from their Black fans, but from the wider amateur baseball leadership. The WCBA did not return to the OBA until 1944.

Sadly, Len Harding, who led the team through the crisis with the OBA, died suddenly in 1942, from complications from minor surgery on his nose. His younger brother Boomer said it was "something that never should have happened."[131] He said the operation went well, but immediately after the surgery he was left alone without anyone monitoring him. While in recovery, a medical complication arose and he died. He was twenty-nine years old. When asked about the impact of his brother's death, Boomer said, "Ah, that's a sticker. We have a very close family and he was—it's hard to put into words. He was the greatest as far as I was concerned." In an obituary, Art Cartier argued that Len Harding had been the heart of the Chatham Coloured All-Stars from its beginning, and that it was he who, "more than anyone else who kept the All-Stars intact through many lean years."[132] The obituary also quoted others in the baseball community, including Archie Stirling and Jim Millman, president of the WCBA, praising his baseball playing and character. "He was a real star on the All-Stars," said Stirling, "A fine young man." As seen during the 1939 baseball season, however, Len Harding also envisioned a world where he and his team could expect and demand "a fair break." At a time when "a fair break" was not guaranteed to Black people, Harding's leadership during that tumultuous 1939 season offers insights into the many different ways that Black people were working to create that world.

9

After the All-Stars

Racial Integration and the Next Generation of Black Baseball, 1940–1958

After eight years together, the Chatham Coloured All-Stars had changed Chatham baseball. They were the first Black team to play in the Chatham City Baseball League and compete for an OBAA title. After winning an Intermediate B title in 1934, they moved into the more competitive Intermediate A circuit with the WCBA, playing among the top teams of southwestern Ontario. Along the way, the All-Stars also found a public voice, asserting themselves in conflicts with both local organized baseball and the OBA, at a time when Black individuals and groups in the region were organizing for greater civil rights. Although the All-Stars disbanded after the 1940 baseball season, the former team members continued to influence local baseball by joining white teams. When Flat Chase, Boomer Harding, King Terrell, Gouy Ladd, and others took to the field with their white teammates, there was no question that baseball in Chatham was different than it had been a decade earlier. The former All-Stars' influence deepened after they helped their teams bring home an unprecedented number of regional and provincial baseball titles for Chatham through the 1940s. In doing so, they continued to keep Black baseball players in the public eye.

While the former members of the Chatham Coloured All-Stars helped integrate Chatham baseball, few other Black men found spots on the rosters of white baseball teams. In 1946, however, younger Black men had the chance to join a new Black baseball team, founded by Harding, Chase, and other former members of the All-Stars. Playing out of the Taylor Athletic Club in the East End, the new Taylor AC baseball team provided a venue for both the former All-Stars and the younger players, many of them former members of the Red Sox Juniors. This new Black team, later renamed the Panthers, played through the 1950s and inspired the next generation of ball players.

As the former members of the Chatham Coloured All-Stars were moving onto white baseball teams, other Black community members were organizing for greater civil rights. Racial barriers in Chatham and southwestern Ontario of the 1940s and early 1950s were nearly as entrenched as they had been in the 1930s. Although the war opened up some areas of employment, Chatham restaurants and hotels regularly refused service to Black people.[1] In 1948, Black people from Dresden, North Buxton, and Chatham founded the National Unity Association (NUA) to organize for greater civil rights and access to employment.[2] In 1950, the NUA joined with other civil rights and labour groups in Ontario which pressed the Ontario government to pass the Fair Employment Practices Act (1951) and the Fair Accommodation Practices Act (1954). As well, NUA co-founder Alvin Ladd (first cousin of Chatham Coloured All-Stars player Gouy Ladd[3]) filed a high-profile complaint against the Liquor Licence Board of Ontario in 1953 after being denied service at Chatham's William Pitt Hotel. Clearly, the baseball diamond was not the only place where Black people were effecting change.

Chatham Coloured All-Stars and the Limited Integration of Chatham Baseball, 1940s

While little is known about the details of racial integration in sports in southwestern Ontario during the first half of the twentieth century, evidence suggests it happened slowly, with just a few Black players on white teams in the 1920s. In Chatham, Carl Harding and King Terrell had played on the primarily white Stirling-Imperial Juniors in the 1920s, but the sport continued to be segregated throughout the 1930s. As long as the Chatham Coloured All-Stars were together, any new Black players joined them, not the white teams. Whether or not any Black players would have been welcomed on the white teams (or whether they would have wanted to join them) in the 1930s is uncertain. In any case, it was the All-Stars themselves who welcomed non-Black people onto their team first, when they recruited an Indigenous man, Willie Shognosh, to join them in 1935. As well, from time to time, they asked other white men, such as Alvin "Dutch" Scott, to fill in gaps in their roster.

In 1940, the All-Stars (or, the Chatham Stars, as they were known that year) continued that trend, bringing several white players into their lineup.

Returning in 1940 for what would be the team's last year together were Len Harding, who continued as manager, his younger brothers Boomer and Andy, King Terrell, Ross Talbot, Ben Talbot, and Ferguson Jenkins Sr.[4] Gouy Ladd played, as did Lyle Johnson and William Crosby, who had both occasionally played with the team in previous years. A couple of younger Black players from the Junior Red Sox, Gerald Browning and Frank Brown, also joined them. Additionally, several white men became regular players, instead of just "filling in" as they had in the past. One of the white players was pitcher Wilfred Belanger. Belanger and his older brother Leo, also a pitcher, were born to a large, Roman Catholic family in the East End.[5] In the mid-1920s, they played on the Stirling-Imperial Juniors with Carl Harding and King Terrell.[6] In 1933, both brothers played with the Duns in the Chatham City Baseball League where they played regularly against the Chatham Stars.[7] The brothers continued to be a part of community baseball through the 1930s.[8] Another East End resident with French Canadian roots, Wilfrid "Buck" Boyer played with the Stars until he broke his arm late in the season.[9] As well, their catcher that year was another white man, Albert "Abie" Mason. He was possibly the same Mason who played with Carl Harding and Terrell on the Stirling-Imperial Juniors in 1926.[10] As well, Dutch Scott and a few other white men joined the Stars occasionally.

As the Stars began their last season, playing in the Kent County Senior Baseball League (affiliated with the WCBA), they did so without Flat Chase. In 1940, the seasoned player had joined the CYO (Catholic Youth Organization), another Senior team also playing in the Kent County league.[11] *Chatham Daily News* columnist Art Cartier claimed that a "combination of circumstances" led to the switch.[12] As Cartier pointed out, the CYO was a relatively young team, and it is possible Chatham baseball organizers wanted one or two more experienced players to round out the roster. Whatever the reason for the move, both Chase and the Chatham Stars had a difficult start to the 1940 season. By the end of July, however, reports suggest Chase had regained his form, and the CYO, was the leading team in the Kent County Senior Baseball League.[13] Cartier observed that Chase remained a draw, noting that he "was the biggest single reason why anyone in these parts went to a ball game."[14]

After a slow start, the Chatham Stars also regrouped. Although they finished the regular season in fourth place, they made the Kent County Senior Baseball League playoffs and advanced to the finals against the CYO.[15] The Stars lost the first two games of the best-of-five series, but were unable to complete it. Throughout the final series, reports suggested both teams

Fig. 9.1 ▪ 1940 Chatham Stars. In their last year together, the team included several white players on the regular roster. From left: Fergie Jenkins Sr., Ross Talbot, Boomer Harding, King Terrell, Frank Brown, Gerald Browning, Wilf Belanger, Len Harding, Andy Harding, Ben Talbot, "Deac" Barron. Photo credit: *Chatham Daily News*, August 22, 1940, Second Section, 1.

were having trouble filling their rosters. According to the *Chatham Daily News*, "some of the boys are holding down jobs that are difficult to leave."[16] Finally, after one postponement, Len Harding announced the Stars could not finish the series. Work demands, he explained, prevented them from continuing. He issued a statement to the *Chatham Daily News*, saying, "The Stars always want to give the fans their very best and owing to employment conditions it is hardly possible to finish the series."[17] Taking time off work had long been a problem for the Chatham Coloured All-Stars, and the more intensified demands (and opportunities) created by the war would have compounded that issue. Harding ended his press statement optimistically, saying "We'll be back next year."[18]

Despite Harding's optimism, the Stars did not come back in 1941. As the year's baseball season approached, the *Chatham Daily News* reported that neither the Chatham Stars nor the CYO could get enough players together to form a team.[19] Instead, some of the remaining players from both teams formed a single Senior team, the Crystals, which played in the Kent County

Baseball League. Len Harding, Boomer Harding, Flat Chase, and King Terrell all moved to the Crystals, along with half a dozen white men.[20] Boomer Harding was elected president of the new club and Chase became captain. Through the rest of the 1940s, members of the former Chatham Coloured All-Stars continued to play on the city's representative team in the Kent County Baseball League (sometimes playing in the Senior division and other times playing Intermediate). These teams were in contention for the WCBA title; and once the WCBA returned to the OBA in 1944, they were eligible for a province-wide title. Chase's son, Earl Chase Jr., recalled the years when his father played on those teams. He claimed that Archie Stirling helped put them together, saying Stirling, "started mixing teams, you know, white ball players...there was maybe two or three guys [former members of the All-Stars] on the white ball teams. That started already in '40."[21] While Stirling's actions may have contributed to the racial integration of Chatham baseball teams, it was the Black men themselves who played those games and formed relationships with the other players. They endured the day-to-day struggle of integrating white spaces.

Indeed, the former All-Stars reinforced their positions within Chatham baseball as they helped their teams bring a series of WCBA and OBA championships to the city. In 1942, Flat Chase, Boomer Harding, and King Terrell, playing for the Chatham Shermans (also known as the Sherman's-Arcades) featured prominently in the team's WCBA Intermediate A championship. In the last game of the final series against a team from London, the three former All-Stars scored four of the Shermans' nine runs.[22] A local fan penned a tribute poem featuring a few lines on each of the team's players, including Harding, Terrell, and "our invincible Flat Chase."[23] While being memorialized in a poem of dubious quality was hardly a high honour, it represented a greater visibility in white spaces for the Black players.

As World War II continued, the sports programs offered to enlisted people through the No. 12 Basic Training Centre (BTC) in Chatham also contributed to racial integration in sports. Part of a Canada-wide movement to encourage physical fitness, the BTC organized sports activities, including track and field, softball, and baseball. In 1943, Boomer and Andy Harding, who had both enlisted with the Canadian Armed Forces, participated in these sports. That season, the No. 12. BTC baseball team, which played regularly in Chatham, featured four Black players, including the Harding brothers. Playing alongside the Hardings were Black players from southwestern Ontario, pitcher and infielder Harry Morgan, of Windsor,

Fig 9.2 ▪ Three generations of baseball, featuring a former member of the Chatham Colored Giants (Percy Parker), former members of the Chatham Coloured All-Stars, and Abie Scott, who would play for the Taylor AC/Panthers. As several of the players are wearing Shermans-Arcades uniforms, the picture was likely taken in 1942, when Flat Chase, Boomer Harding, and King Terrell all played on that team. Back row, from left: Louis Pryor, Percy Parker, Boomer Harding, King Terrell, Ross Talbot, Flat Chase. Front row, from left: Albert "Abie" Scott, Fergie Jenkins Sr., Gouy Ladd, Ben Talbot, Andy Harding. Photo credit: Leddy Library Archives and Special Collections, F1033 (Wilfred "Boomer" Harding Collection), Scrapbook 1. This photograph is also in a scrapbook owned by the family of Earl "Flat" Chase.

and George McCurdy, of Amherstburg, Ontario. Morgan had played with the Windsor Colored Stars (Chase's former team) in the late 1930s.[24] Their BTC teammate George McCurdy was from a well-known Black family with a history of civil rights advocacy.[25]

As members of the Kent County Baseball League, the No. 12 BTC baseball team regularly faced off against the Chatham Shermans, which featured three of the Harding brothers' former teammates: Flat Chase, King Terrell, and Abie Scott. Reporting in the *Chatham Daily News* suggests that the Shermans and the No. 12 BTC teams attracted large crowds whenever they played each other in Chatham. A *Chatham Daily News* sports columnist, Doug Scurr, remarked on the rivalry between the two teams, but suggested the fans were flocking to the games because "the brand of baseball dished up is by no means the poorest."[26] A reporter described one mid-July game between the Shermans and the No. 12 BTC as "one of the wildest tussles seen here this year."[27] The reporter went on to say that the game had "everything from wild pitches, smart pitching, good base-running, lots of hits and arguments…all rolled into the tilt and fans enjoyed themselves thoroughly." Later that month, a reporter claimed that a large crowd of spectators at a Shermans-No. 12 BTC game were treated to a "fine performance."[28] Adding interest to these games were two white players with the No. 12 BTC, Hank Biasatti and Tommy White, who had both played for the London Majors with the Intercounty Baseball League. As the two teams competed for the Kent County Baseball League championship in early September, Scurr declared that White, Biasatti, and Chase added "glitter" to the game.[29] Besides the exciting baseball, two teams with well-known Black players on both would have been a draw for the Chatham Black community. As connections among the Black communities in the Chatham-Windsor area were strong, chances are that some people in Chatham either knew the players from Windsor and Amherstburg or knew their families.

At the end of the 1943 baseball season, the No. 12 BTC ultimately prevailed, defeating the Shermans for the Kent County Baseball League title. No. 12 BTC took the best-of-five final series in three games. The reporter covering the last game credited catcher Boomer Harding with "snuffing out a promising Sherman's-Arcades rally in the sixth with a smart double play."[30] In that same game, the reporter remarked on Terrell's "sparkling" unassisted double play, where he apparently grabbed a ball Morgan hit just before it reached the ground. Terrell then tagged out Biasatti who was running to third base. The army team continued through the WCBA playoffs, reaching the finals against a team from London.[31] For that final series, the Harding brothers brought 18-year-old Abie Scott along to help fill the roster. The army team won the best of three series easily, with the Harding brothers and Scott each scoring a run in the final game.

After the WCBA returned to the OBA in 1944, former Chatham Coloured All-Stars players were members of teams that brought home provincial titles. In 1944, Chase, Terrell, and Gouy Ladd, playing for the Chatham Arcades, defeated a team from Toronto to win the Intermediate A OBA championship, the city's first Intermediate OBA championship since 1934.[32] It was a busy year for Chase, as he also played for the London Majors of the Intercounty Baseball League, helping them win the Canadian Sandlot Championship.[33] Two of his teammates on the Majors were former No. 12 BTC baseball team members Biasatti and White, whom he had played against the year previously (and who were likely involved in inviting Chase to the team). Another former Chatham Coloured All-Star at the Canadian Sandlot Championship was Boomer Harding. Stationed in the Canadian Forces base at Kingston in the summer of 1944, he was playing for the Kingston Ponies, a Senior A team which had reached the Sandlot Championship finals.[34] In 1947, Chase and Abie Scott played for the Chatham Shermans, who won the OBA Intermediate A title. They defeated a team from Batawa, in eastern Ontario.[35] Harding was not playing with the Shermans that year, but he did play on a Legion soccer team which won a provincial championship.[36] The following year, Chase and Harding were once again playing together when their team, the Chatham Hadleys, won the OBA Intermediate A title against a team from Napanee.[37] While Chase and Harding were with the Hadleys, several other former members of the Chatham Coloured All-Stars played with a primarily white Senior team. King Terrell, Gouy Ladd, William Crosby, and Ken Milburn all played on the Chatham Maple Leafs who won the WCBA Senior title in 1948.[38]

Flat Chase's son Horace recalled his father's time with those teams in the 1940s. In a 2016 interview, Chase spoke about the Shermans and Hadleys, where both white and Black men played together. He noted that "they were a good defensive and good hitting teams. You know, they could hold their own with any team in the area. I remember riding with my dad, going to Sarnia. We'd been to Toronto…I think they were all competitive ball players on those teams, they were really good."[39] Chase also remembered the teams were popular, saying, "they used to crowd Stirling Park, sometimes get as many as 400 people coming out to watch the game. And sometimes, mostly on the Sunday, that they would crowd it. So, they had a good following here when they played ball, I'll say that much." Judging by their success in the OBA Intermediate A circuit in the 1940s, these were indeed strong ball players, and their collective achievements helped keep the former Chatham Coloured All-Stars players in the community spotlight. Boomer Harding also spent several years in the late 1940s playing community softball, which also brought him and several other Black players he recruited to the game to wider public attention.[40]

Fig. 9.3 ▪ OBA Intermediate A championship badge for 1948. The Chatham Hadleys, a primarily white team, plus Flat Chase and Boomer Harding, won the Intermediate A provincial title in 1948. Photo credit: Leddy Library Archives and Special Collections, F1033 (Wilfred "Boomer" Harding Collection), Scrapbook 1.

By staying in the public spotlight, these former All-Stars players also attracted interest from the local members of the press, who began commemorating members of the Black team from the 1930s. Newspaper sportswriters focused on Flat Chase especially, describing him as a legendary, "larger-than-life" figure. A 1947 column by *Chatham Daily News* columnist Matt Dennis described him as big, smiling, and of indeterminate age (he was in his mid-thirties).[41] Chase, Dennis declared, would "go into the record books as one of the greatest figures ever produced in the Maple City." Observing Chase signing autographs for "numerous youngsters," the columnist exclaimed that the ball player's following "consists of every baseball enthusiast in Chatham." The article also described Chase supporting younger players, saying he "instilled a confidence in the young players who benefited greatly during the season." While the sportswriters clearly admired Chase and the other Black players, their depictions of them remained one-dimensional, and they ignored the racism, exclusion, and economic marginalization that continued to affect them.

In fact, the years when the former Chatham Coloured All-Stars began playing on local white baseball teams were a period of both advancement and continued limitations for Black people in employment. The war had been the biggest factor in opening up employment for both Black men and women in areas beyond service and manual labour. With labour shortages caused by the war, and new demands for products, more jobs in factories and skilled trades became available.[42] In the war years and the decade following, many of the former Chatham Coloured All-Stars obtained jobs their fathers would not have been able to get a generation earlier. After Boomer Harding returned from the war, he became a mail carrier in Chatham, the only Black mail carrier in the city at the time.[43] His brother Andy became the city's first Black police officer.[44] Several other former members of the All-Stars, including Chase and Gouy Ladd, got jobs with the city's sanitation department.[45] Still, in reflecting on the changes, Ken Milburn, a member of the Taylor AC who was married to Boomer and Andy's sister, Wanda, suggested that there were still some barriers to employment for Black people.[46] He explained that while the war had created employment opportunities, "we knew there were certain jobs maybe that you couldn't get." In 1950, Milburn applied for, and got, a job as a Chatham firefighter—the first Black firefighter in the city. Aware that getting the job could be a challenge, he recalled that when he applied he contacted several people he knew, including a city councillor, who might be able to support his application. While he got the job, he acknowledged that he remained the only Black firefighter in Chatham during his long career.

The Return of Black Baseball Teams to Chatham, 1946-1958

While former members of the Chatham Coloured All-Stars played on primarily white teams throughout the 1940s, they were largely the exceptions. As Nzindukiyimana and Wamsley explain, "integration of Black athletes, either amateur or professional, was partial and conditional."[47] High-profile Black players such as Flat Chase, Boomer Harding, and King Terrell were known quantities, and had proven themselves in the community over the previous decades. By the mid-1940s, however, the only younger Black player who had played with the Intermediate A Chatham teams was Abie Scott. Others who had played on the Black Junior teams, including Pete Browning, John Olbey, and Ken Milburn, were not playing on these primarily white teams.[48] Chatham amateur baseball was becoming racially integrated through the former All-Stars, but the path for younger white players was easier than it was for Black players overall.

Perhaps thinking about the younger players, Boomer Harding formed a new Black team when he came back from the war. According to *Chatham*

Daily News sportswriter Doug Scurr, when Harding "received his discharge from the army, he got to work organizing a ball club."[49] The new team that Harding, Chase, and others created was known as the Taylor Athletic Club (Taylor AC) after the J.G. Taylor Community Centre in the East End which sponsored them. The Taylor AC featured former Chatham Coloured All-Stars, including Harding, Chase, Andy Harding, King Terrell, Gouy Ladd, and Stanton Robbins, but also included younger Black players, many of whom had been playing on the Junior teams in the late 1930s and early 1940s.

It is not surprising that the former All-Stars looked to the Taylor Community Centre to help with the new team.[50] Located on the site of the former Woodstock Industrial School on King Street in Chatham's East End, the Taylor Community Centre (named after J.G. Taylor, a leader in the Black community and one of the trustees of the Woodstock School) had operated as a community centre since 1927. Catering largely to the East End's Black population, the Taylor Community Centre provided a range of programs including sports, youth activities, and social events for adults. People who grew up in the East End in the 1940s and 1950s recalled the Taylor Community Centre as a welcoming space for young people at a time when racism limited access to public places. Jean Simmons, who moved to Chatham following her marriage in the early 1950s, said, "during the time when there's the prejudice, it was a wonderful thing for the getting together of the young people, the teenagers, and the adults."[51] Rosetta Alliet, who also grew up in the East End, remembered the centre's Saturday night dances, when bands from Detroit came to play. She recalled, "people enjoyed it so much that I would see some people standing on the chairs, dancing, standing on the desk, dancing. It was hilarious and absolutely fun."[52] Ken Milburn also spoke about the bands and dances at the centre.[53] Besides sponsoring local recreation, the Taylor Community Centre also provided a home for a boxing program, wrestling, and the women's softball team, the Taylorettes.[54]

Creating a new Black baseball team through the Taylor Community Centre may have been particularly attractive to Boomer Harding, who had spent several years in the largely white environment of the Canadian military. Apart from his time at the No. 12 BTC, Harding would have been surrounded by non-Black people for the first time in his life. Harding's experience playing hockey with the Canadian military is an example. An avid hockey player from his high school days, Harding was invited to play for Canadian military hockey teams in London, Kingston, and then in the United Kingdom. In all cases, he was most certainly the only Black player. As

Black hockey pioneers including Herb Carnegie, Willie O'Ree, and others have argued, hockey was (and continues to be) a difficult and often racist environment for non-white players.[55] Harding's son, Blake, heard from his father how hard it was being the only Black player on the ice. "I get the sense, when I used to listen to him, that it was pretty lonely," he recalled.[56] Harding remembered his father telling him "It's hard to hide a Black man on white ice."[57] Besides being a visible target for opposing players, Harding also had to earn the trust of his own teammates. Unlike his time on the Chatham Coloured All-Stars, when, as Blake noted, "they were like brothers, a band of brothers," with hockey he often had to win over members of his own team who were wary of a Black teammate. Blake remarked, "Before he could earn the respect of teams he was playing against, he had to earn the respect of the guys he was playing with, and he had to narrow that down to the guys on the same line as him. He had to earn their respect." He said his father loved the game, he loved the speed and power and he used it "as a tool," to channel his energies and to connect with his teammates. He claimed his father did it by "just going out every day and playing the hardest he could."

Harding's hockey skills earned him spots on a couple of Canadian army hockey teams during the war. He began playing for the London, Ontario team in the winter of 1943 while he was still at No. 12 BTC in Chatham. Harding explained in a 1988 interview, "I signed up at Chatham, but some major from the London regiment saw my name, and soon I was playing hockey in London on an army team."[58] That year, his team won the regional league championship and moved into the Ontario Hockey Association (the provincial amateur hockey league) playoffs.[59] The following year, while stationed in Kingston, Ontario, Harding played with the Vimy Signals, which was part of a city Senior hockey league comprised of several military teams and a team from Queen's University. Recalling his time playing hockey in Kingston, Harding exclaimed, "I loved it," noting they often played six nights a week.[60] *Kingston Whig-Standard* sports columnist Michael J. Rodden claimed Harding was "one of the most popular athletes who has ever appeared here."[61] Remarking on his impact on area sports including baseball and track and field, Rodden also claimed Harding was "one of the best players on the Vimy hockey team." Another reporter described Harding as "generally in command as he patrolled that mid-ice territory with the wisdom and effectiveness of a veteran."[62] Considering this league included several former and future National Hockey League (NHL) players, the press attention Harding received is notable.[63] In fact, it

Fig. 9.4 ▪ London Army Hockey Team, 1943 regional OHA champions, featuring Boomer Harding (back row, third from left). Harding was stationed at No. 12 Basic Training Centre in Chatham, but he was recruited to play hockey for the London team. He later played with the Vimy Signals, another army team while stationed in Kingston, Ontario in 1944–45. He also played on a touring exhibition hockey team in the UK in 1945. Photo credit: Leddy Library Archives and Special Collections, F1033 (Wilfred "Boomer" Harding Collection), Scrapbook 2.

was through an NHL player, Adam Brown, that Harding came to play for a Detroit Red Wings farm team for a season when he returned from the war.[64]

Harding eventually went overseas where he was part of the Canadian military's occupation force in the Netherlands. When he was back in the United Kingdom in December 1945, he spent a few weeks playing with a hand-picked Canadian Forces hockey team.[65] The Canadian military had formed a half dozen teams representing the army, navy, and air force, and sent them on tours throughout the United Kingdom. These were high-profile teams, and they featured several former and future NHL players including Sid Abel (Detroit Red Wings), Johnny Mowers (Detroit Red Wings), and Buck Jones (Detroit Red Wings, Toronto Maple Leafs). That Harding was invited to join suggests he was considered a strong player. Black hockey players accepted into that environment would have to be exceptional, as it seems unlikely a Black athlete of average ability would have been chosen to represent the Canadian military to the British public.

A letter Harding wrote to his sister Beulah while he was on a hockey tour in Scotland suggests he enjoyed the experience, but he also missed home.[66] Writing from Glasgow, he told his sister that he and his fellow hockey players had been treated well during the tour. He said the food was decent, and he joked they all expected to gain about thirteen pounds by the end of the tour. Harding clearly missed home, however, and he asked his sister about local news and their family. He mentioned their father's recent birthday party that his sister had attended, and he lamented not being able to find a nice present for his wife, Joy, without ration coupons. Harding ended by saying "give my regards to all the folks, and keep writing." After spending several years in a largely white environment (and particularly so while he was playing hockey), perhaps the thought of coming home to Chatham, and experiencing the easy camaraderie of playing with friends and family members again, was appealing.

In the spring of 1946, as the Taylor AC baseball team began their first season in the Intermediate A circuit of the Kent County Baseball League, the local sports newspaper writers were clearly excited about seeing some of the former Chatham Coloured All-Stars playing together again. As noted earlier, the press had already started building the Chatham Coloured All-Stars legend. They clearly admired the All-Stars and spoke reverentially about them. One columnist, Doug Scurr, described the All-Stars as, "one of the finest ball teams in the district, and also one of the best drawing cards to ever play in the Western Counties and O.B.A. ranks."[67] Another article began "When the word baseball is mentioned around the Maple City one automatically thinks of the Colored All-Stars of yesteryear."[68] At the same time, however, the sportswriters revealed the white expectations and demands on Black baseball teams. They described what the All-Stars gave to the city—their first championship win and a revived interest in baseball during the Great Depression. They never acknowledged, and probably never understood, how hard it was for a Black team in a racist environment to provide that championship title. Only Archie Stirling, interviewed for Doug Scurr's article, hinted at the racism the team experienced by saying they were initially "worried that they may not be accepted because of their color."[69] Stirling concluded by suggesting that they were welcomed into the organization "once the O.B.A. heads found what drawing power they had." Again, referencing "drawing power" is a reminder of the demands and expectations on this Black team to attract audiences. Those same expectations, by implication, were being directed at the Taylor AC baseball team.

While the local press was most interested in seeing the former All-Stars back together again, Harding and others clearly hoped to promote younger players who did not have as many opportunities to play on premier baseball teams. Some of the younger players with the Taylor AC had played with the Red Sox, the Black Junior team coached by Ross and Ben Talbot in the late 1930s and by Bethune Binga Sr. in the early 1940s.[70] One of those former Junior players was Abie Scott, who also played with Flat Chase on the 1943 Chatham Shermans. A *Chatham Daily News* article commented that Scott had "blossomed into a real hustler and now hangs his hat at short [stop]."[71] Another former Juniors player, Ken Milburn, also joined the Taylor AC.[72] He spent his early years on his parents' farm in Chatham Township, but by his mid-teens he was working as a luggage carrier at the William Pitt Hotel.[73] Like a number of the Taylor AC players, Milburn was a war veteran, having enlisted in the Canadian military during World War II. Pete Browning, another former Junior player, joined the Taylor AC. According to Doug Scurr of the *Chatham Daily News*, Browning played for the No. 12 BTC baseball team during the war (although not the same year that Boomer and Andy Harding did).[74] Browning, along with Boomer Harding, was also a member of the community's Legion soccer team, which won a provincial championship in 1947. Browning was normally an outfielder, but during the 1946 season he often pitched, as the team's pitching staff was small. Other newcomers to the Taylor team included a pitcher, Charles Foster, Charles "Chuck" Cooper, a right-fielder, and Bill Henson, a catcher who had also played on the Black Junior teams.

John Olbey, younger brother of former Chatham Coloured All-Star Cliff Olbey, was another World War II veteran who played for the Taylor AC. Olbey had spent his childhood at Stirling Park, watching his older brother and his teammates play.[75] He recalled playing on a junior baseball team, the Pythagoreans, organized by a local Black branch of the Masonic Lodge. He also played with Abie Scott, Ken Milburn, and Pete Browning on the

Chatham Red Sox in 1940.[76] In 1942, Olbey enlisted with the Canadian Armed Forces, serving with the Fourth Canadian Armoured Brigade.[77] He was a tank crew member, then a tank driver, and then a crew commander while seeing action in France, Belgium, Holland, and Germany. When he returned to Chatham, job prospects were still limited for young Black men (even for decorated war veterans) and he worked in service jobs for a time until he was able to get training to become a millwright.[78] In the summer of 1946, however, just back from war, he got to play baseball with the players he admired as a young boy.

While the newspaper hype was about the former Chatham Coloured All-Stars, Boomer Harding informed the press that at the first game of the season in Dresden, the younger players would start.[79] Perhaps hoping to create a fan base and following for the new players, Harding had Bill Henson catching and Charles Foster pitching. He did the same for the Taylor AC's first home game in Stirling Park, where the former All-Stars "rode the bench to give younger players a chance to prove what they had."[80] Toward the end of that opening game, however, the senior players took their places on the field, perhaps as a nod to their fans who undoubtedly had come to see them play. Boomer Harding moved into the catcher's position, King Terrell took to third base, and Flat Chase went to the pitcher's mound and showed he still had "plenty of speed despite his age."

As with the Chatham Coloured All-Stars, the reporters covering the Taylor AC often remarked on the size and physical traits of the players. Janelle Joseph has noted white portrayals of Black athletes tended to focus on physical strength and power, rather than on intelligence or discipline.[81] Newspaper articles referring to the Taylor AC players featured images of speed, power, and energy. The reporters did not describe the white players or teams in the same way. In one article, the reporter claimed the Taylor AC was a "fast moving colored club," invoking expectations of how Black people played ball.[82] In another article, they were described as "powerful,"[83] and in another, a "fine lot of hustlers with much promise."[84] One reporter, commenting on the Taylor AC's come-from-behind win against the Chatham Seniors, claimed the Black players were like "greased lightning on the bases."[85] The reporters also used adjectives referring to the size of the Black players, such as when one reporter referred to pitcher Foster as a "sturdy hurler."[86] While the reporters were admiring the strength and athleticism of the ball players, they were also drawing on pervasive stereotypes and assumptions about Black men. The fact that they rarely commented about the bodies of white ball players suggests the way ideas about race continued to shape newspaper coverage.

Besides their racialized portrayals, this newspaper reporting also reflected the expectations of white audiences for a Black baseball team. One article suggested that the Taylor AC were "inheriting the popularity that was built by the Colored All-Stars" and were in demand as an exhibition team.[87] Noting that the AC were "known as a fine club of colored players as far as Kirkland Lake," a mining town in northern Ontario, the report claimed that a promoter from Sarnia was trying to arrange an exhibition tour of several days in the northern region. Harding, in a late 1970s interview, claimed they had received offers to do exhibition tours in northern Ontario but it never happened because "the money wasn't there."[88] White audiences may have been eager for the novelty of a Black team, but they were not willing to pay fair compensation for the time and effort. Harding noted that for them, the biggest challenge was taking time off work and losing those wages. As many were employed in low-wage occupations, taking time away from work was simply not possible. Harding said being asked to leave their jobs was unrealistic, as "we weren't making much at your job," adding, "you had to work."

While the exhibition tour never took place, the Taylor AC had a successful first year in the Kent County Baseball League Intermediate A circuit, despite a few challenges. The team lacked a large pitching squad, made even smaller when Chase broke his arm partway through the season.[89] To keep the team going, Boomer Harding, normally a catcher, took to the mound himself.[90] By mid-July of the regular season, the Taylor AC and the city's other entrant in the Kent County Baseball League, the Chatham Seniors, vied for top place.[91] Both teams reached the WCBA playoffs, with the winner advancing to the OBA championship.[92] The Taylor AC eventually lost the WCBA title to the Chatham Seniors in the semi-finals, and the Seniors eventually went on to win the provincial OBA Intermediate A title.[93]

Over the next dozen years, off and on, a Black team played baseball out of Stirling Park. Boomer Harding managed the team through 1947, but after that, the team took a break for a couple of years. They came back together in the early 1950s with a slightly changed name—the Taylor AC Panthers (later known simply as "the Panthers").[94] Harding was still managing the Taylor AC Panthers, but he juggled many sports activities in those years, including starting to work as a local sports referee and umpire.[95] He did this all while working full time as a mail carrier and raising a family. Harding's son, Blake, remembered how busy his father was in those years; as a young child, he often went along with his dad to the baseball diamond and hockey rink. He recalled, "I used to go from rink to rink with him."[96] In the mid-1950s, Ken Milburn, former Taylor AC player, lightened his brother-in-law's load by taking over as manager, although Harding continued to play for the team, serving as catcher and pitcher. Interviewed in 1999, Milburn claimed, "those were good times… Baseball was popular in every town and there were a lot of good players who came through Stirling Park."[97] By the late 1950s, Allan Wright, who had grown up in the East End in a family active in sports, had taken over as manager.[98] Wright's older cousin, Orville Wright, had been team scorekeeper and secretary for the Chatham Coloured All-Stars in the 1930s. As their younger sister Dorothy Wright Wallace explained, Wright took over the team to try to keep the traditions of the Black teams going.[99]

By the early 1950s, the Taylor AC Panthers' lineup had changed, with younger players replacing the former Chatham Coloured All-Stars as the core of the team.[100] Boomer Harding still played, and Flat Chase and Gouy Ladd stayed on as coaches, but the newer players took the spotlight. These included Charles Cooper, and Charles and Bob Gibson who had been part of the original Taylor AC group in 1946. Others who were part of the lineup in the 1950s included Charles Hurst, Mel Cross, Ron Williams, John Matthews, Allan and Art Wright, Glen Shreve, Tom Shadd, Bill Shelby, John Robinson, Hank White, and Lloyd Pryor (son of former Chatham Coloured All-Stars coach, Lou Pryor).[101] As well, Abie Scott was living in Windsor, but returned to Chatham for the Panthers' games.[102] Another Windsorite, Lorne Foster, also played for the Panthers in 1958.[103] By the end of the 1950s, a few white players had also joined the team, including a pitcher, Bob Wright, who was an Ontario Provincial Police officer with the local detachment,[104] as well as Dick Toward, Bob Provost, and Bruce Huff.[105]

While Flat Chase stopped playing for the Taylor AC Panthers in the early 1950s, by 1957, his sons Earl Jr. and Horace had joined the team. Following his father, Earl Jr. was a pitcher, while younger brother, Horace, played infield.[106] Earl Jr. remembered his father helping both he and his brother on the team. He said, "I played with Dad a couple, well I was about fifteen, fourteen. I was a pitcher, but I played other positions. Me and Dad played together and my brother, he played with the Taylor ACs for a couple years and after that...yes, like I say, he encouraged the ball playing."[107]

Fig. 9.5 ▪ The 1951 Taylor AC Panthers, when they were playing Intermediate C ball in the WCBA. Back row, from left: Chuck Cooper, Tom Shadd, Boomer Harding, John Matthews, Mel Cross, Lloyd Pryor, Gouy Ladd, Bill Milburn. Middle row, from left: Art Wright, Glen Shreve, Henry White, Bob Gibson, Chuck Hurst, Ron Williams, Alan White, Bill Selby. Seated, in front: Ralph Williams. Photo credit: Leddy Library Archives and Special Collections, F1033 (Wilfred "Boomer" Harding Collection), Scrapbook 1. Original credit: *Chatham Daily News*, August 16, 1951, 13.

The Panthers continued to attract new young players, and they remained competitive in the WCBA Intermediate circuit.[108] In 1951 they were playing Intermediate C baseball and reached the WCBA playoff finals.[109] By the late 1950s, the team was particularly strong. In 1957, they won the WCBA Intermediate A title and went on to defeat Sarnia, Strathroy, and Owen Sound in the OBA playoffs before losing to Corunna in the OBA finals.[110] The following year they once again reached the WCBA playoffs.[111] Former Panthers player (and newspaper sportswriter) Bruce Huff claimed the team "left an exacting imprint in the city's sports history."[112]

While the names and players changed, Boomer Harding's son, Blake, explained there was a strong thread between the Chatham Coloured All-Stars of the 1930s, the Taylor AC of the 1940s, and the Panthers of the 1950s. Harding, who was the Panthers' bat boy in the mid-1950s, explained that the All-Stars "evolved into the Taylor ACs and then the Chatham Panthers."[113]

Through the former members of the All-Stars, the newer Black teams were nurtured and supported. Blake Harding suggested that, in a way, his father never left the All-Stars: "he never really quit playing for them as long as they existed."[114] He noted his father was "still playing and he was playing strong. And, you know, maybe not back-to-back games like he did when he was younger, but he was still catching."[115] Indeed, the former All-Stars including Harding, Chase, Ladd, and others, had provided the same kind of support that former members of the Colored Giants had given to them when they began playing as the Chatham Stars in 1933.

Remembering the Taylor AC/Panthers

Going to a baseball game in Stirling Park was an event, a social outing for the neighbourhood. In oral history interviews, people who grew up in the East End in the 1940s and 1950s spoke about the excitement of the baseball games, and the crowds. Dorothy Wright Wallace recalled, "Everybody came out. And they did have crowds and they were good sized crowds."[116] These weekend ball games mattered because no one had a lot of money, but everyone could go to Stirling Park. The ways people remembered and spoke about watching the Panthers, however, provides larger insights into why these baseball clubs were so important. As noted in *Remembering Jim Crow*, memories and stories told in Black diasporic communities are a way of expressing and celebrating identity, as well as recognizing acts of resistance. On display, as well, were models of Black, heterosexual masculinity featuring values such as competence, respectability, and responsibility that countered negative stereotypes about Black people circulating in white society.[117]

Edward Wright, a former bat boy with the Panthers in the 1950s and younger brother of team manager Allan Wright, remembered the Panthers' signature moves and styles.[118] As Janelle Joseph and others have noted, Black athletes' cultivated styles were expressions of identity and a challenge to dominant (white) models of masculine behaviour.[119] Some of Wright's strongest memories of the team were about the unique traits they brought to the game. Wright explained, "everybody had style. The players were great and they played their positions and they had style and something that I always aspired to when I played."[120] One of Wright's favourites was Abie Scott, whom sports reporters had described as "flashy" since the 1940s.[121] Scott had spent a couple of years playing Intercounty Baseball with the Brantford Red Sox, and according to *Chatham Daily News* sports editor Matt Dennis, he had had a tryout with the Montreal Royals.[122] Besides Scott,

Wright remembered Mel Cross, a left-handed first-baseman nicknamed "Beef" because of his size. Said Wright, "he was big and he was strong and he could hit right. You go to Stirling's Park, that fence there, and he'd hit the ball over the right field fence into the oil refinery yard [laughs]."[123] Wright also admired centre-fielder Charles "Chuck" Cooper, who had started playing with the Taylor AC in the 1940s. According to Wright, Cooper "was like smooth, he played the game with the smooth style." And like many others, Wright was fascinated by King Terrell's left-handed third-base minding, saying "You really didn't see that." Besides the players from the Panthers, Wright also recalled a player from a Detroit team that came to Chatham whom he referred to as the "singing catcher." According to Wright, he "would be behind the plate and he'd say, 'come on baby, pitch that ball in here to me' [laughs]. I mean, it was kind of a distraction, you know, catchers can be distracting, and he was, it was quite a show." Wright also thought the Panthers looked sharp in their New York Yankees-style pinstripe uniforms, presenting well to the wider public. The Taylor AC Panthers made a deep impression on Wright, and he credited them and others for inspiring his own career in sports, coaching hockey and teaching at the State University of New York at Buffalo.[124] He explained, "it was an experience that was part of who I am today."[125]

The sons of Flat Chase, Earl Jr. and Horace, who grew up watching their father play and became members of the Chatham Panthers later in the 1950s, described the relationships at the heart of baseball, both with their father and other members of the baseball community. They both spoke about how their father shared his knowledge and love of the game with them. Horace recalled, "He always advised me when I started playing about how to be a good sport, and taught me how to pitch, and how to throw, and taught me the game."[126] Baseball was also a big part of their social lives. Earl Jr. remembered his father "enjoyed playing ball and sports, stuff like that, and the camaraderie with the different ball players."[127] Horace also spoke about the relationships among the players: "you knew the guys, you grew up with them, worked with them, ate with them, you know you socialize with them. So, to me it's also like one great big family. And I was the same way when I come along, with all the guys I played with."[128] As with their father's generation, sports continued to provide a strong social role in their lives.

Others, in describing the Panthers, highlighted specific characteristics they valued, features that were also admired in the community. Dorothy Wright Wallace liked what she saw as the Panthers' work ethic and their sacrifices to keep the club running.[129] Unlike many of the white baseball teams in town, the Panthers did not have dedicated business sponsors to help with the bills. Wallace claimed that because they did not have sponsors they had to work harder to keep the club going. She noted, "You look at them and say yeah, they succeeded, but they worked at it. It wasn't just handed to them. And I think that's what made them stand above." She suggested that people in the community could see the sacrifices they made. She said, "And if they were playing, it was something to go and sit in the bleachers and see them play ball. And yes, they would pass the hat around and what you had you put in there because they needed balls, they needed bats, and a lot of them bought their own gloves, would even buy their own bats." Wallace clearly valued that sense of mutual support between the players and their fans. Mutual support, whether it was for a baseball team or other aspects of life, was also vital for dealing with a challenging and racist environment.

Rosetta Alliet, like Wallace, grew up watching and playing sports in Chatham's East End in the 1940s and 1950s (she was a member of the Black women's softball team).[130] For her, the Taylor AC Panthers represented achievement, excellence, and unity. As Colin Howell has noted, sport in Black and other marginalized communities "encouraged racial pride and neighbourhood identity."[131] She insisted, "We were so proud of that Black men's baseball team. We knew everything, we read about them. They were really great."[132] She explained, "I don't remember ever seeing them lose. No. That's why I thought I was so impressed with them. I thought that they were as good as any professional team." A group of Black men showing their abilities and strengths in such a public place meant a lot to people who received constant reminders of racial inequalities in their world. Aside from their baseball skills, Alliet admired the way the team members related to each other. She said, "I know that they were very united. I know that...what else about them impressed me? It was like they were training each other. What one couldn't learn, they were being taught by each other." For Alliet, the Panthers represented excellence, achievement, and mutual support.

Edward Wright, when remembering the Panthers, also commended them for the time they gave to the Black community by playing in Stirling Park on the weekends.[133] He said his brother, Allan, kept the team going because their games were "an event for the older folks in the community. 'Hey, the Panthers are playing today over at Stirling Park, come on over and watch the game and see the neighbourhood boys playing.'" For Wright, the men themselves embodied respectability and responsibility. He said, "Some of them had kids, they were married and just the very, very successful men in the community who had jobs and worked every day. Went to work to provide for their families. And then on Saturday or Sundays they had a game that was their outing for the day." He clearly admired the successful family men, taking time out of their lives to connect with the community.

Jean Simmons's memories of the Panthers reflected another valued trait in Black diasporic communities—the way they also faced and resisted racism.[134] Simmons explained she did not spend a lot of time watching baseball, as she was busy with her home and other community activities, but she recalled hearing about racist incidents the Panthers experienced. She said she heard her husband "talking about when they would go to play, the names that they would call, you know. They got called the 'N' word." She claimed they wanted to play fair, but if they were treated badly, they would stand up for themselves. She recalled, "They were an excellent team, and they could play ball, and also they stood up for what they believed in." Everyone growing up in Chatham's Black community faced racist verbal attacks, and Simmons's memory of the team resisting such treatment is a reminder of the daily realities for racialized people, and helps explain why the team was so fondly remembered. Indeed, the various features they remembered about the Panthers—hard work, mutual support, expressing identity, resisting racist treatment—reveals as much about what they valued as it did the Panthers themselves.

While people's memories of the Panthers suggest they were a well-loved team, they did not last beyond the 1950s. The full reasons are not clear, but by that point, there were more sports opportunities for young Black people outside the activities run through the Taylor Community Centre. By the 1950s, the various service clubs in town, such as the Jaycees and the Optimists, were running baseball and other sports programs for young people. Horace and Earl Chase Jr. had both played with the Optimist program.[135] Edward Wright played baseball through the Jaycees, and a young Ferguson Jenkins Jr. also played baseball through the service clubs.[136] As well, other activities like roller skating became popular in the 1950s and 1960s. Wright recalls that Sunday nights roller skating at the local arena was a big draw for young Black people from Chatham, Windsor, and as far away as Detroit. By the 1960s, more Black people left the East End as opportunities opened up elsewhere. With that, the East End's Black baseball teams, reaching back to the late nineteenth century, faded into memory.

Chatham Daily News Tue. Sept 16, 1958 pg 10

PANTHERS AFTER SECOND WCBA CHAMPIONSHIP

g their second straight baseball crown are ent Panthers of Chatham. Seated are B. Harding, C. Hurst, K. Calvert, B. Wright, D. Toward, L. Foster, and E. Chase. Standing, M. Cross, R. Reaume, A. Scott, C. Cooper, B. Selby, H. Chase, D. Baldwin, B. Gibson and A. Wright (St

Fig. 9.6 ▪ Panthers, 1958, when they were competing in the WCBA Intermediate League. They had won the WCBA championship in the previous year, and reached the finals in 1958 before losing to a team from Corunna, Ontario. The men in this picture include former All-Stars player Boomer Harding and occasional All-Stars player Abie Scott, along with the sons of Earl "Flat" Chase, Earl Chase Jr. and Horace Chase. Photo credit: Leddy Library Archives and Special Collections, F1033 (Wilfred "Boomer" Harding Collection), Scrapbook 1. Original source, *Chatham Daily News*, September 16, 1958, 10.

When thinking about the larger impact of the Chatham Coloured All-Stars on sports and the Black community, we need to look beyond the 1930s. While the All-Stars gained widespread attention and built a strong fan base with their baseball achievements of the 1930s, their longer-term effects and influences are best seen in the decades that followed. In the 1940s, a core group of the Chatham Coloured All-Star players moved onto the formerly all-white local baseball teams. In doing so, they created greater visibility for Black athletes, particularly after their teams won an unprecedented number of regional and provincial baseball championships. Flat Chase, Boomer Harding, King Terrell, Gouy Ladd, and Abie Scott became well-known figures in the community, reaching a wider number of fans than they ever had while they were playing for the All-Stars. Harding was especially prominent in his community sports activities, including hockey, and perhaps most importantly, through sports officiating. This visibility was important as Black people moved into white spaces: the baseball teams, the hockey rinks, and the soccer pitches.

At the same time, the path for other Black athletes in the 1940s was less clear; few, apart from the former All-Stars, played on community teams. Harding, Chase, and other former members of the Chatham Coloured All-Stars clearly felt that the community needed another all-Black baseball team, so they founded the Taylor AC in 1946. This team became a showcase for a new generation of ball players who made a big impact on the Black people growing up in the 1940s and 1950s. Just as the Chatham Coloured All-Stars had in the 1930s, the Taylor AC/Panthers generated a new group of talented players like Abie Scott, Chuck Cooper, and others that people such as a young Edward Wright (and a young Ferguson Jenkins Jr.) grew up watching. More than simply a group of excellent players, for the people watching them, the Taylor AC Panthers also reflected and represented community values, and models of Black masculinity and resilience at a time when racism, and social and economic marginalization were still a reality.

10
Conclusion

Baseball and Memory—Reflecting on Race, Heroes, and the All-Stars Years

After the last glove had been hung up and the uniforms laundered and put away, the young men of the Chatham Coloured All-Stars moved on with their lives, earning a living and raising families. Some continued to be involved in sports while others were not. Over the years, some of the players began speaking publicly about their experiences with the team, talking to newspaper reporters and taking part in the MHSO oral history project. As they reflected on and made sense of their time with the All-Stars, they also offered insights about themselves, Black men living through difficult, yet changing, times. That former members of the team continued to get together at various events and reunions suggests that the experience of playing with the All-Stars continued to have meaning for them, many decades later.

While oral histories and newspaper interviews have been drawn on to explore the history of the team throughout the book, this last chapter will consider the ways that the former All-Stars shared memories of each other. More than just admiring baseball skills, the former players conveyed much richer images of their teammates, beyond the one-dimensional "sports hero" edits that appeared in local newspaper sports pages since the 1930s. They also reflected models of heterosexual Black masculinity, revealing confidence, competence, and a willingness to stand up for themselves. At the same time, the anecdotes remembered and shared also provide insights into what the editors of *Remembering Jim Crow* call "walking the tightrope," between pride in Black institutions and accomplishments, and the constant reminders of the racism that caused exclusion and pain.[1] While the former players clearly felt it was important to celebrate and remember who the Chatham Coloured All-Stars were and what they did, those memories were also tinged with a sense of loss, and how things may have been different if not for the racism that affected all areas of their lives.

The timing of when those oral history interviews with the former All-Stars took place is important. As Hodgkin and Radstone note, memories are filtered through the politics and culture of the present. Boomer Harding, King Terrell, and others all spoke to oral history interviewers and newspaper reporters between the late 1960s and early 1980s, just after the rise of the civil rights movement in North America. As the images of the marches and key figures, including Martin Luther King Jr., appeared on newspaper pages and television screens, discussions about race became more open. Both the interviewers and the respondents, as they spoke about racism and their baseball experiences, connected to much wider narratives and debates.

The former Chatham Coloured All-Stars players sharing their stories as Fergie Jenkins Jr.'s Major League Baseball career took off is also significant. Originally signed by the Philadelphia Phillies, Jenkins's career blossomed later in the 1960s when he moved to the Chicago Cubs and emerged as one of the league's top pitchers.[2] He received MLB's top honour for a pitcher, the Cy Young Award, in 1971, and his record of six consecutive twenty-win seasons (1967–72) has rarely been matched. His career lasted through the 1970s and early 1980s (playing for other teams including the Texas Rangers and Boston Red Sox), and he was inducted into the National Baseball Hall of Fame in 1991. As the former Chatham Coloured All-Stars were giving their interviews, the younger Jenkins's achievements came up frequently. Indeed, his accomplishments were proof that someone from Chatham, Ontario could have a professional baseball career given the right breaks and chances. The younger Jenkins's success was a sharp reminder of the opportunities his father's generation was denied. While it is impossible to say if any of the Chatham Coloured All-Stars' generation could have had a baseball career outside Chatham, the point is they never had a chance to succeed or fail, and that thought lingered in the oral histories of the team.

Remembering the All-Stars

While playing with the Chatham Coloured All-Stars gave the players a high profile in the community, for most of them, playing competitive baseball was a relatively brief period in their lives. Many of the players remained in the Chatham area after their playing days, working and raising families. As mentioned earlier, Boomer Harding became a well-known public figure,

Fig. 10.1 ▪ The City of Chatham declared October 21, 1967 "Fergie Jenkins Day." Fergie Jenkins Jr. came home to Chatham to celebrate his success as pitcher with the Chicago Cubs. Orville Wright, former secretary and scorekeeper for the Chatham Coloured All-Stars, told a *London Free Press* reporter that they planned to pay tribute to the 1930s team during the community dinner being held to honour Jenkins. Photo credit: Leddy Library Archives and Special Collections, F1033 (Wilfred "Boomer" Harding Collection), Scrapbook 1. Original source, *Chatham Daily News*, October 20, 1967, 18–19.

not only as a city mail carrier, but also as a fixture in the sports community, umpiring and refereeing for baseball, hockey, and soccer. His brother Andy was the first Black police officer in Chatham, after having served in World War II, like his brother. Gouy Ladd, formerly a truck driver, eventually worked for the city in the sanitation department. He continued to be involved with baseball, coaching a Senior A team to an OBA title in 1970.[3] Flat Chase also worked for the city, in sanitation. His son, Earl Jr., recalled his employers would let him take time off work to play ball, such was his stature in the wider Chatham baseball community.[4] King Terrell also remained in Chatham, and worked for the William Pitt Hotel, supervising other staff members in the guest services area.[5] Ross Talbot worked for years as a driver for a wealthy family before leaving to operate his own poultry business.[6] Ferguson Jenkins Sr. spent many years as a personal chef and driver for the Houson family, who owned and managed the sugar refinery in town.[7] Although his work frequently took him away from Chatham, his son, Ferguson Jenkins Jr., recalled he still had time to take him to ball games in Detroit.[8] Stanton Robbins, who played with the All-Stars until 1938, remained at the family home in North Buxton.[9] Likewise, the All-Stars' manager, Joseph Parker, and base coaches, Louis Pryor and Percy Parker, remained in Chatham. Pryor and Percy Parker continued to coach baseball for many years. Pryor served in World War II and then returned to the East End where he worked in a factory. Joseph Parker continued running his King Street barber shop.

Other members of the All-Stars left Chatham. Cliff Olbey moved to Windsor and spent many years working for hotels in the city.[10] Donise Washington eventually returned to Detroit and enlisted in the US Army during World War II.[11] In 1950, he was working as a porter at a Detroit department store. According to Harding, Washington later owned a bar on Detroit's east side.[12] Donald Tabron also returned to Detroit and found work at the Ford Motor Company in River Rouge, Michigan.[13] While at the plant he trained as an electrician and got his contracting certification. He later opened his own electrical businesses in a growing Black middle-class area in a north-western neighbourhood of Detroit. Hyle Robbins, who played for the All-Stars in 1934, moved to Michigan where he spent the rest of his life. He worked as an electrician in a radiator manufacturing plant.[14] His niece, Pauline Williams, recalled that he got injured on the job and had to retire early.[15] Like his teammate Robbins, Sagasta Harding also spent the rest of his life in Michigan, where he worked for the Ford Motor Company's plant at River Rouge.[16] Overall, the men's experiences reflected both the growth and continued limitations for Black men in the immediate postwar years. Some were able to move into better-paying jobs, while others did not. Most of the former players were married by the end of the 1930s and early 1940s, and most raised children.

Not all the former All-Stars lived long lives, however. As mentioned earlier, Len Harding died in 1942 from complications after minor surgery, greatly affecting his tight-knit family and leaving a leadership gap in local Black baseball. Former pitcher Stanton Robbins passed away while in his forties. His niece, Pauline Williams, recalled that he had poor health for much of his adult life.[17] In 1954, Earl Chase Sr. died unexpectedly in an accident, at the age of forty. Perhaps as a sign of the meaning of baseball in his life, his pallbearers were his former Chatham Coloured All-Stars teammates: Gouy Ladd, Ferguson Jenkins Sr., Boomer Harding, Ben Talbot, Ross Talbot, and King Terrell.[18] At the time that he died, he was involved in coaching baseball and helping his teenage sons learn the game.

For years Chatham newspaper reporters described Flat Chase as a legend, a local baseball hero, but only when he died did they acknowledge that his life might have been different if not for the racial barriers in baseball. As much as newspaper reporters had praised him earlier, they never speculated on whether or not he might have had a chance outside of local baseball, even after Jackie Robinson broke the colour barrier in the major league in 1947. In reporting on Chase's death in 1954, however, Bruce Huff, a sports columnist and local white ball player who also played with the Chatham Panthers team, spoke about the changes in baseball since Jackie Robinson and others joined major league teams.[19] He also described Chase's outsized impact on local baseball, claiming that "former players and fans" argued that if not for the racial barriers in the sport when Chase was younger, he could have written "his own 'ticket'" to any of America's professional baseball teams.

In the years that followed, those questions about "what might have been" came up a lot in both the oral histories Vivian Chavis and Wanda Milburn conducted, and in newspaper interviews. Rather than simply fond memories, however, talking about lost chances and opportunities was also a way to reflect on how racism had affected their lives, and the lives of their teammates. Baseball was a lens through which to process and remember it, for the players themselves, and friends and family members who also experienced it. Milburn spoke openly about the racism the All-Stars experienced and the way it prevented the men from moving outside Chatham baseball. At a point in her interview with King Terrell, she said, "We know they [the All-Stars] had problems with prejudice everywhere they went, even at home. And they were good; Flat was major league."[20] Milburn then asked Terrell to speak about which of his teammates might have been good enough to baseball professionally. She explained, "And I think there were a few others on there who could have made it. Can you enlighten me on that?" Terrell did, naming several of his fellow teammates, including Chase, Donald Tabron, Ferguson Jenkins Sr., and Donise Washington. He then proceeded to describe the traits that made each stand out, from Chase's batting, to Tabron's shortstop work, Jenkins's fielding and creative ball handling, and Washington's ability to throw from a crouched position. Of Washington, he added, "And you heard all over...it was too bad that he couldn't get into the major leagues." Milburn spoke about the racism more directly, saying, "He was the wrong colour at the time." Terrell assented, repeating her words, "He was the wrong colour at the time." Others repeated those claims in different interviews, drawing a direct line between racism and opportunities denied. Orville Wright, the All-Stars' scorekeeper and team secretary concluded in a 1967 newspaper interview, "There's no doubt in my mind Flat Chase could have played major league baseball if the opportunities then were like they are in baseball today."[21] Likewise, in a 1978 newspaper interview, Boomer Harding remarked, "Flat was the most gifted hitter I've ever seen. There's no question in anybody's mind who ever saw him that he would have been a major leaguer had it not been for the color barrier."[22] Their lives were affected by racism beyond baseball, but talking about baseball was just one way of acknowledging it.

Another reminder of the racism in baseball was Phil Marchildon, the Penetanguishene's pitcher for the 1934 OBAA Intermediate B finals, who went on to have a professional baseball career. Several of the former Chatham Coloured All-Stars spoke about him, reflecting on the chances that the white man had that they did not. While acknowledging Marchildon's talent, they also noted that ultimately their own pitchers bested him in those games. Wright remarked in his 1967 interview that "Chase outpitched Phil Marchildon in the final two games to ensure the Chatham victory."[23] Harding also pointed out that Flat Chase out-performed the Penetanguishene pitcher, saying, "He beat Marchildon too. Flat was a strong, strong man."[24] Tabron admitted that Marchildon was a good pitcher, but he still beat him.[25] Terrell pointed out that they beat Marchildon three times during that series.[26] Wanda Milburn said it most plainly: "He [Marchildon] was a white man and he made it to the big leagues. And Flat was better than he was." Marchildon clearly became part of the oral history of the Chatham Coloured All-Stars, and it continued into the next generation as two of the sons of the All-Stars also mentioned him (Earl Chase Jr. and Blake Harding). Marchildon became a stark reminder of the racism that allowed a white man from 1930s Ontario to become a major league ball player, but not a Black man.

Besides talking about chances lost and denied, the former members of the Chatham Coloured All-Stars also offered more nuanced and complex images of each other, offering clues to the values and traits they admired.

Fig. 10.2 ▪ Wilfred "Boomer" Harding continued to be involved in sports and competitions later in life, seen here c. 1975 with his doubles darts partner, Cliff Scott. Harding won numerous darts championships, mainly through the Canadian Legion leagues, in the 1970s. Besides his continued involvement in sports (he was still umpiring in this period), Harding shared his memories of the Chatham Coloured All-Stars with several newspaper sports reporters, and took part in the Multicultural History Society of Ontario oral history project in 1980. Photo credit: Leddy Library Archives and Special Collections, F1033 (Wilfred "Boomer" Harding Collection), Scrapbook 3.

Wright's stories about Chase, for example, contain descriptions of his baseball performances, as well as quirky, more human details about the man himself. Wright, like many others, described Chase's batting skills as almost magical, claiming "Flat hit one in Chatham I don't think they've found yet."[27] Wright talked about one of Chase's hits by describing how far the ball flew and which landmarks it bypassed, saying "It cleared the centre field fence at Stirling Park …went over the trees and houses on Park Street, cleared the road and the houses on the other side, and landed in a back yard on Wellington Street." More than just a super-human batter, however, Wright revealed other details he recalled about Chase, including his habit of smearing his pitching arm with liniment before a game. Wright explained,

"That stuff would take the skin off most men…it just made Flat warm." He also recalled the way Chase and catcher Washington used to spar over what type of ball Chase should pitch (a point Terrell and Jenkins also made in their interviews). Wright remarked, "[Donise] used to get so hot at Flat he'd throw the ball back a lot harder than Flat was throwing it in." These personal details, absent from 1930s newspaper accounts, appear in the oral histories of his teammates, offering a more nuanced image of the man.

While the former Chatham Coloured All-Stars praised each other's baseball skills, Harding and Terrell also spoke about another trait they admired—a willingness to resist and fight back against rough or unfair treatment. As the editors of *Remembering Jim Crow* note, stories of resistance were central to oral histories of marginalized Black American populations. Filling a need to provide a model and engender hope, oral histories reveal "the extraordinary resilience of black citizens, who, individually and collectively, found ways to endure, fight back, and occasionally define their own destinies."[28] In one interview, Harding described the way Chase asserted himself during the game.[29] He explained that while playing "up north," Chase sometimes had trouble with umpires not recognizing when he, at second base, had tagged a player out. Harding claimed that if Chase just lightly tapped the runner, the umpires often called the runner "safe." Harding claimed that to get the umpire's attention, he tagged the incoming runners quite forcefully: "So the next time he [the runner] come into the bag, he didn't get all the way into the bag. Flat put the stop on him. Sometimes they had to help him [the runner] off the field." Milburn, who was interviewing her brother, added, "Is that what you call 'taking him out'?" He replied with a laugh, "He took them out all the time." Harding added, "But we only played according to what the referees and umpires made us play," suggesting that the physicality of their play was a response to unfair officiating. Reflecting on that years later, it is significant that Harding remembered this, and admired the way Chase defied and challenged umpires treating him unfairly.

Terrell made a similar point about Washington, describing the way he defended himself against incoming runners heading into home. He said, "Talk about guys coming into home plate, he [Washington] wasn't a rough guy, but nobody tried to rough him up, because he stood his ground."[30] He "stood his ground," refusing to let people push him around—something he could do on the baseball diamond, if not always in everyday life. Indeed, Terrell suggested Washington carried this confidence that came from a sense of who he was, saying "And he let everybody know, wherever we played baseball, that he was our catcher." That he remembered the confidence and strength that he saw in Donise Washington and wanted to share it suggests both the social and emotional power of sport, as well as the way the former All-Stars told their stories, highlighting and emphasizing what they felt was important about their experiences.

Both King Terrell's and Boomer Harding's memories of Flat Chase and Donise Washington also reflect models of heterosexual Black masculinity, exuding competence, confidence, and respectability in a racist society that denigrated Black people. Harding and Terrell's admiration for players who "stood their ground" was echoed by members of the second generation, children and younger relatives of the players. Blake Harding, for example, described the way sport gave his father a chance to demand respect. He claimed, "when he went on the field he didn't have to be subservient to anybody, and he wouldn't be. And I think that shaped all of their lives, as much as it could."[31] Harding argued that his father took that confidence into his daily life, insisting on respect both as a city mail carrier, and as an umpire and referee in community sports. Likewise, Douglas Talbot, speaking about his uncle Ross Talbot, said, "I recall as a young boy that my uncle—everywhere he went, he had an air about him that I'm either superior to you or equal to you. Which actually helped me."[32] Donald Tabron Jr. as well admired his father's persistence in getting into the electrician apprenticeship program at Ford Motor Company's River Rouge plant at a time when few Black people were accepted.[33] Not only do these anecdotes reveal a more complex picture of the Chatham Coloured All-Stars as "baseball heroes," they also suggest how stories of resistance and respect were part of family memories of these men.

Finally, the oral histories and newspaper interviews with the former Chatham Coloured All-Stars players also reveal the memories of the camaraderie and close relationships among the players, as well as the joy they got from baseball itself. While many people have fond memories of playing sports, for Black people living in a racist society, these memories have a different significance. As the editors of *Remembering Jim Crow* note, memories shared among Black Americans often featured stories of pride and resilience and community connections in the face of continued marginalization. King Terrell's 1980 oral history interview described in great detail his sense of pride and identity he got from playing baseball, and his relationships with his teammates.[34] As his session with interviewer Wanda

Milburn was ending, he told her he wanted to share his three favourite moments in his time playing baseball. Notably, none of the moments were about winning a particular championship or title, but all revealed what baseball gave him. He began by describing the very last baseball game he played, at the age of forty-two. Terrell recalled he and his teammates were playing in Buxton against a team from Detroit and people were teasing him about his age, saying "he's too old to play baseball." Defying the doubters, Terrell claimed he hit the ball deep into centre field. Flat Chase followed him, hitting a home run. Describing Chase's home run, Terrell remarked, "And they said it was one of the longest balls that was ever hit out there." Besides displaying the pride he felt about his own performance, this memory also focused on the joy he got from watching Chase, and the way other people acknowledged and celebrated his skills. Indeed, Chase's record-breaking home run in Welland during the OBAA playoffs, described earlier, was Terrell's second favourite baseball moment. His final story was about getting a home run from a pitch from Art Fidler, the former professional minor league pitcher who played for Strathroy when the All-Stars were part of the WCBA Big Six in 1935 and 1936. Although Strathroy was a more experienced team, Terrell proudly claimed, "I don't think Strathroy ever beat Chatham at any time we ever played them," noting the team was "a big bunch of guys." Terrell was also clearly proud of hitting a home run from a ball pitched by the former professional player, saying it was "the kind of a ball that I liked to hit and I connected." He claimed that when he hit it, the ball cleared a big, black barn at the back of Stirling Park. He concluded his stories, and the interview, by saying, "That's three incidents in my life, I never will forget."[35] Cherished memories, Terrell's stories also remind us of the way sports were part of the larger quest for agency, self-expression, and community relationships.

Besides freely sharing their memories, the former members of the Chatham Coloured All-Stars also got together at various times to commemorate the team. The first known such reunion was the baseball game against the Chatham Shermans in 1947, and it is possible there were other informal games after that. The first known formal, public event happened in 1967 during the "Fergie Jenkins Day" held in Chatham to celebrate the young Chathamite's success with the Chicago Cubs. According to a *London Free Press* article, Orville Wright, chair of the Fergie Jenkins Day committee, planned to recognize the All-Stars during a community dinner held in Jenkins's honour.[36] Although the next day's newspaper coverage focused on Jenkins, it is significant that Wright, who was emcee for the event, wanted to remind the crowd that the major league pitcher came from a community with a rich history of Black baseball teams.[37]

Another public celebration for the All-Stars took place in 1984, when the Chatham City Council presented plaques and medals to the former team members to mark the fiftieth anniversary of their 1934 Intermediate B championship win.[38] All six members of the 1934 championship team still alive in 1984 attended—Boomer Harding, Donald Tabron, Donise Washington, Sagasta Harding, Hyle Robbins, and Cliff Olbey—along with Ben Talbot and Orville Wright, suggesting the continued bond among them. Four of them came from their homes in Michigan to take part. In fact, Tabron would occasionally drive up from Detroit to Chatham to visit, often taking his youngest son with him.[39] Donald Tabron Jr. recalled, "My dad would get bored and say, 'hey son, it's a nice day let's take a drive to Chatham and see who we can find. You know I haven't talked to the guys up there in a while. I wonder who's still around?'"[40] Before and after the event, some of the team members spoke with *Chatham Daily News* sports columnist Bill Reddick, who produced three articles featuring their memories and stories.[41] Conversations ranged from discussions of who might have been good enough to play professional baseball, to personal recollections of the racism they experienced as Black men in sports, to the details and insights about their championship run. Their enthusiasm in sharing those memories with the reporter reflected the way their time as Chatham Coloured All-Stars remained with them many decades later.

The last two surviving members of the team, Donald Tabron and Sagasta Harding, got together for the last time when the Toronto Blue Jays invited them to throw the first pitch at a July 2002 game, in recognition of MLB's tribute to the "Negro Leagues." The newspaper interviews conducted with both men suggested they were surprised, but pleased, by the interest. Tabron exclaimed, "At no time in my life did I think something like this might happen."[42] Harding, who was ninety-four at the time, said he never expected it, "But I wouldn't have missed it for the world."[43] Horace Chase, son of Earl "Flat" Chase, also took part in the ceremonies. The game was attended by about 300 friends and family members of the former players who came by bus from Chatham. That was the last "reunion" of the members of the Chatham Coloured All-Stars. A few months after the Blue Jays event, Sagasta Harding passed away in Michigan.[44] Donald Tabron Sr., one of the youngest of the original players, lived until December 2008.[45]

Conclusion: "Had a lot of fun together, a lot of trouble too"

In a single sentence, Wanda Milburn captured the essence of the Chatham Coloured All-Stars' history when she said: "The All-Stars were a coloured ball team who played in the Depression years, and who made history, who had a lot of fun together, and a lot of trouble together too."[46] As the younger sister of three members of the team, Milburn witnessed many of the events discussed in this book. She celebrated that the team "made history," but she also knew the price they paid to do it. She saw first-hand the challenges the Black men faced in the 1930s as they navigated their way through the years in the white amateur baseball leagues. She herself had experienced the racialized and class-based society that limited her own opportunities for recreation and after-school jobs. Milburn, who was involved in sports herself in those years, was aware of both the "fun" and the "trouble" that were part of the experiences, and the history, of this team.

Indeed, this team endured a lot of "trouble," but they also grew as a team, gaining confidence as they moved into the more competitive baseball circuits of southwestern Ontario after their 1934 championship win. That confidence also made it easier for them to speak out—first, perhaps by proxy, when the author of the "A colored fan" letter to the editor appealed for understanding and "Canadian sporting justice" in the wake of overt racism. It also helped Len Harding when he challenged the OBA in 1939 over unfair treatment, defying the provincial amateur baseball body in a very public way. There was a powerful symbolism in a Black baseball team refusing to accept unfair terms demanded of them, saying they wanted "a fair break" like everyone else. Later, former members of the All-Stars helped integrate amateur baseball in Chatham. They also continued to support younger players by forming a new team, the Taylor AC, when they were not finding spots on white city teams.

While this history of Chatham Coloured All-Stars focuses on the 1930s, the team's origins are much deeper, connected to a Black, intercommunity, transborder diasporic network. The All-Stars owed much to the earlier team, the Colored Giants, which was part of a wider Black baseball network that stretched from Chatham, North Buxton, London, and across the river to Detroit. Through their frequent exhibition games in Chatham, and the annual "Michigan-Ontario" Black championships in the mid-1920s, the Colored Giants carved out a space for Black baseball in the community. Intergenerational family and community ties connected the Colored Giants (and the Black teams that preceded them), the Chatham Coloured All-Stars, and the Taylor AC/Panthers. Indeed, the genealogies of these teams displayed the family relationships, the siblings, in-laws, cousins, and friends, at the core of the baseball world. Those relationships suggest something of what helped keep the teams together and the connective thread of baseball in the wider Black community.

Perhaps the most powerful reminder of the significance of baseball in Chatham, North Buxton, Windsor, and London in the first half of the twentieth century is the way that the history of this team and other Black teams in the community was revisited and shared through scrapbooks, oral histories, newspaper interviews, and commemorative acts. Besides these acts of memory, the way people spoke about and described the teams and the players offers insights into how they processed and reflected the larger experience of living in a racist world. That included the discussions about lost opportunities in sport which recognized the systemic racism that affected their lives. It also included the former players and community members describing what they valued and admired in the team, whether it was players who "stood their ground" against unfair or rough treatment on the diamond, or a model of heterosexual, Black masculinity embodying competence, respectability, and community-mindedness. More than just fond memories of a well-loved baseball team, the way the former players, family, and community members memorialized and spoke about these Black baseball teams hints at the way baseball heroes offered hope in hard times. It also suggests the deeper values that also led Black people in the region to organize for greater civil and economic rights, in the years when the Chatham Coloured All-Stars were playing and in the decades after. For the players themselves, being part of the All-Stars, a team that gained stature and recognition over the years, gave them a space to seek "Canadian sporting justice." They did not always get it, and a fully equitable, inclusive sporting environment remains elusive in Canada today. The history of Black baseball in southwestern Ontario, however, offers a window into how ordinary people, playing and watching baseball, envisioned a different world.

NOTES

Chapter 1: Introduction

1 Newspapers from the 1930s spelled the team's name "Colored," without the 'u.' In recent years, however, the team's name has been spelled as "Coloured" (including in a public history project I co-directed, "Breaking the Colour Barrier: Wilfred 'Boomer' Harding and the Chatham Coloured All-Stars"). To be consistent with current usage, the "our" spelling is used in this book.

2 "All-Stars Take Shermans, 8-6, in Ball Tilt," *Chatham Daily News*, August 25, 1947, 10.

3 Wilfred Harding, interviewed by Wanda Milburn and Vivian Chavis, August 27, 1980, Dresden, Ontario. Multicultural History Society of Ontario.

4 Ernie Miller, "Boomer Harding—one great guy," *London Free Press*, September 8, 1978, B1 (Evening/Regional Edition).

5 Alan Metcalfe, "The Anatomy of Power in Amateur Sport in Ontario, 1918–1936," *Canadian Journal of the History of Sport* 22, 2 (December 1991): 47–67. Founded in 1918, the OBAA was the largest amateur baseball organization in the province. Metcalfe notes that in 1925, the Eastern Ontario Baseball Association broke away from the OBAA, effectively creating two provincial amateur baseball organizations.

6 For a study of the team the year they won the OBAA championship, see Heidi L.M. Jacobs, *1934: The Chatham Coloured All-Stars' Barrier-Breaking Year* (Windsor, Ontario: Biblioasis, 2023).

7 There is some variation in the spelling of this team's name. In the early 1940s, the *Chatham Daily News* referred to it as "Sherman's" and it was known as "Sherman's-Arcades" in 1942 and 1943. In the later 1940s, however, the apostrophe was dropped and it was known as "Shermans." For consistency, this book will refer to them as "Shermans" throughout, except when making direct citations from the newspaper.

8 "All-Stars Take Shermans, 8-6, in Ball Tilt," *Chatham Daily News*, August 25, 1947, 10.

9 Earl Chase was known widely in the community by his nickname, "Flat," apparently a reference to his flat-flooted running style. The press also referred to him as "Flat," as did his former teammates in oral history interviews. Since his nickname was so widely used, in most cases, he is referred to as "Flat" in this book.

10 For an overview of Chase's life, see John Phair, "Residents Recall Legend Earl 'Flat' Chase," *North Kent Leader*, February 15, 2006, 6, and his Chatham Sports Hall of Fame profile: https://chathamsportshalloffame.com/portfolio_page/earl-flat-chase/.

11 Wilfred Harding interview. MHSO. In this interview, he explained that he earned his nickname not through sports, but from his older sisters. Harding explained he had been trying to read the comics in the newspaper under a dim light, and misread the comic, "Boob McNutt" as "Booming Nut." His sisters, amused by his

mistake, started calling him "Booming," eventually evolving to "Boomer." The nickname stayed with him throughout his life. As most people, including his family members, called him by that nickname, he is referred to as "Boomer" throughout this book.

12 Mark Malone, "Boomer knew how to win," *Chatham Daily News,* September 10, 2003, 11. Also see his Chatham Sports Hall of Fame profile: https://chathamsportshalloffame.com/portfolio_page/wifred-boomer-harding/.

13 The newspaper did not give a first name or initial for the player named Crosby, but it was most likely William (Bill) Crosby, who played with the Taylor Athletic Club in the 1940s. Two other Crosbys, Clarence and Wilfred, played occasionally with the Chatham Coloured All-Stars in the 1930s, so it is also possible that the Crosby at the game was one of those two men.

14 See Barrington Walker, "Introduction: From a Property Right to Citizenship Rights—the African-Canadian Legal Odyssey," in *The African-Canadian Legal Odyssey: Historical Essays,* edited by Barrington Walker (Toronto: University of Toronto Press, 2012), 3–46.

15 Howell, *Northern Sandlots: A Social History of Maritime Baseball* (Toronto: University of Toronto Press, 1995), 179.

16 Howell, *Northern Sandlots,* 180.

17 Rob Ruck, *Sandlot Seasons: Sport in Black Pittsburgh* (Urbana and Chicago: University of Illinois Press, 1987), 3.

18 Ruck, *Sandlot Seasons,* 3.

19 Ruck, *Sandlot Seasons,* 3.

20 Ornella Nzindukiyimana and Kevin Wamsley, "'We Played Ball Just the Same,': Selected Recollections of Black Women's Sport Experiences in Southern Ontario (1920–1940s)," *International Journal of the History of Sport,* 36 (13–14) (September 2019): 1289–1310.

21 Nzindukiyimana and Wamsley, "'We Played Ball,'" 1302–3.

22 http://cdigs.uwindsor.ca/BreakingColourBarrier/.

23 Victoria Paraschak, "Aboriginal Peoples and the Construction of Canadian Sport Policy," in *Aboriginal Peoples and Sport in Canada: Historical Foundations and Contemporary Issues,* edited by Janice Forsyth and Audrey R. Giles (Vancouver: University of British Columbia Press, 2013), 110.

24 Paraschak, "Aboriginal Peoples," 110.

25 Paul Gilroy, *The Black Atlantic: Modernity and Double Consciousness* (Boston: Harvard University Press, 1993); Rinaldo Walcott, "'Who Is She and What Is She to You?': Mary Ann Shadd Cary and the (Im)possibility of Black/Canadian Studies," *Atlantis* 24, 2 (Spring/Summer 2000): 137–46.

26 Gamal Abdel-Shehid, *Who Da Man? Black Masculinities and Sporting Cultures* (Toronto: Canadian Scholars Press, 2005); Janelle Joseph, *Sport in the Black Atlantic: Cricket, Canada and the Caribbean Diaspora* (Manchester: Manchester University Press, 2017).

27 Howell, *Blood, Sweat, and Cheers: Sport and the Making of Modern Canada* (Toronto: University of Toronto Press, 2001), 51–82.

28 For a discussion of the commodification of the labour of Black athletes, see Harry Edwards, *The Revolt of the Black Athlete: 50th Anniversary Edition* (Chicago: University of Illinois Press, 2017).

29 Ruck, *Sandlot Seasons*, 3.

30 Ruck, *Sandlot Seasons*, 3.

31 Howell, *Northern Sandlots*, 195.

32 Howell, *Northern Sandlots*, 195.

33 Nzindukiyimana and Wamsley, "'We Played Ball,'" 1303.

34 Shakeia Taylor, "The Civil War, Civil Rights, and Black Baseball," *Hardball Times*, July 6, 2018. https://tht.fangraphs.com/the-civil-war-civil-rights-and-black-baseball/.

35 Katharine Hodgkin and Susannah Radstone, "Introduction: Contested Pasts," in *Contested Pasts: The Politics of Memory*, edited by Katharine Hodgkin and Susannah Radstone (London and New York: Routledge, 2003), 1–21.

36 Hodgkin and Radstone, "Introduction," 5.

37 William H. Chafe, Raymond Gavins, and Robert Korstad, eds., *Remembering Jim Crow: African Americans Talk About Life in the Segregated South* (New York: The New Press, 2001).

38 See Janelle Joseph, "An Intersectional Analysis of Black Sporting Masculinities," in *Race and Sport in Canada: Intersecting Inequalities*, edited by Simon C. Darnell, Yuka Nakamura, and Janelle Joseph (Toronto: Canadian Scholars' Press, 2012), 237–63; Janelle Joseph, *Sport in the Black Atlantic*; Martin Summers, *Manliness and its Discontents: The Black Middle Class and the Transformation of Masculinity, 1900–1930* (Chapel Hill, N.C.: University of North Carolina Press, 2004).

39 John Olbey, interviewed by Deirdre McCorkindale, July 6, 2016, Chatham, Ontario. "Breaking the Colour Barrier: Wilfred 'Boomer' Harding and the Chatham Coloured All-Stars" website. http://cdigs.uwindsor.ca/cdigs-ohms-ccas/viewer.php?cachefile=00013.xml.

40 http://cdigs.uwindsor.ca/BreakingColourBarrier/. See Heidi L.M. Jacobs, "Invisible in Plain View: Libraries, Archives, Digitization, Memory, and the 1934 Chatham Coloured All-Stars, in *Archives and Special Collections as Sites of Contestation*, edited by Mary Kandiuk (Sacramento, CA: Library Juice Press, 2020), 223–48.

41 Howell, *Blood, Sweat, and Cheers*, 66; 91–96.

42 Don Morrow and Kevin B. Wamsley, *Sport in Canada: A History, 3rd ed.* (Don Mills, Ontario: Oxford University Press, 2013), 154–77.

43 See Glen Bleske and Chris Lamb, "Covering the Integration of Baseball—A Look Back," *Editor and Publisher*, 130 (January 27, 1996): 48–50; Brian Carroll, "'Praising My People,' Newspaper Sports Coverage of the Integration of Baseball in Wichita, Kansas," *Kansas: A Journal of the Central Plains*, 33 (Winter 2010-2011): 245–55.

44 "Telling the Stories of Race and Sport in Canada: A Symposium." http://cdigs.uwindsor.ca/omeka-s/s/rsc/page/home. Thanks to Marsaydees Farrell and Ron Leary who worked on the oral histories for this project.

45 Joan Sangster, "Reflections on the Politics and Praxis of Working-Class Oral Histories," in *The Canadian Oral History Reader*, edited by Kristina R. Llewellyn,

Alexander Freund, and Nolan Reilly (Montreal and Kingston: McGill-Queen's University Press, 2015), 121–22.

46 For example, the Buxton National Historic Site and Museum was opened in 1967. In Chatham, Gwendolyn Robinson and Blanche Pryor, among others, were researching local Black history.

47 Sangster, "Reflections on the Politics and Praxis," 119–40.

48 Sangster, "Reflections on the Politics and Praxis," 132.

49 Wilfred Harding interview. MHSO.

50 See Nzindukiyimana and Wamsley, "'We Played Ball,'" 1294–95.

51 Kingsley Terrell, interviewed by Wanda Milburn, August 6, 1980, Chatham, Ontario. Multicultural History Society of Ontario.

52 Chafe et al., *Remembering Jim Crow*, 56.

53 Wanda Milburn, interviewed by Wilson Brooks, September 28, 1980, Chatham, Ontario. Multicultural History Society of Ontario.

54 Wilfred Harding interview. MHSO; Kingsley Terrell interview. MHSO; Ferguson Jenkins Sr., interviewed by Vivian Chavis and Wanda Milburn, n.d., c. 1980, Chatham, Ontario. Multicultural History Society of Ontario.

Chapter 2: Living in a Racialized World

1 Black population of Chatham compiled from Census of Canada, 1921, manuscript census, Kent District 93, Chatham City, Subdistricts 74, 75, 80, 81, and 82. These subdistricts cover roughly the neighbourhood known as the East End: Murray St. to the north, the railway tracks to the south, William St. in the east and Duke St. in the west. Black people were defined as "African" or "Negro." For the population of Chatham in 1921, see Canada, Dominion Bureau of Statistics, *Sixth Census of Canada, 1921, Volume 1, Population* (Ottawa: King's Printer, 1924), "Table 10, Area and Density of Cities and Towns, 1921, 1911, 1901," 220.

2 Carmen Poole, "Conspicuous Peripheries: Black Identity, Memory, and Community in Chatham, Ontario, 1860–1980," PhD diss. (University of Toronto, 2015), 187.

3 Barrington Walker, *Race on Trial: Black Defendants in Ontario's Criminal Courts, 1858–1958* (Toronto: University of Toronto Press, 2010), 68–69.

4 Constance Backhouse, *Colour Coded: A Legal History of Racism in Canada 1900–1950* (Toronto: University of Toronto Press, 1999); Robin Maynard, *Policing Black Lives: State Violence in Canada from Slavery to the Present* (Halifax and Winnipeg: Fernwood Publishing, 2017); Graham Reynolds with Wanda Robson, *Viola Desmond's Canada: A History of Blacks and Racial Segregation in the Promised Land* (Halifax and Winnipeg: Fernwood Publishing, 2016); Walker, *Race on Trial*; Barrington Walker, ed. *The African Canadian Legal Odyssey*; James St. G. Walker, *'Race,' Rights and the Law in the Supreme Court of Canada: Historical Case Studies* (Waterloo, Ontario: Wilfrid Laurier University Press, 1997).

5 James W. St. G. Walker, "The Law's Confirmation of Racial Inequality: *Christie vs. York*," in *The African Canadian Legal Odyssey*, 46.

6 Walker, "Introduction," 28.

7 Walker, "Introduction," 27.

8 Poole, "Conspicuous Peripheries," 181.

9 Colin Howell, *Northern Sandlots*, 171–95; Ornella Nzindukiyimana and Kevin Wamsley, "'We Played Ball'"; Rob Ruck, *Sandlot Seasons*.

10 Natasha Henry, "'Where Oh Where, Is Bet?' Locating Enslaved Black Women on the Ontario Landscape," in *Unsettling the Great White North: Black Canadian History*, edited by Funké Aladejebi and Michele Johnson (Toronto: University of Toronto Press, 2022), 95.

11 For history of Black people in Chatham and what is now southwestern Ontario in the nineteenth century, see Karolyn Smardz Frost, Veta Smith Tucker, eds., *A Fluid Frontier: Slavery, Resistance, and the Underground Railroad in the Detroit River Borderland* (Detroit: Wayne State University Press, 2016); Joyce Shadd Middleton, Bryan Prince, Karen Shadd-Evelyn, *Something to Hope For: The Story of the Fugitive Slave Settlement, Buxton, Canada West* (Chatham: Buxton National Historic Site and Museum, 1999); A.C. (Arlie) Robbins, *Legacy to Buxton* (Chatham: Ideal Printing, 1983); Gwendolyn Robinson and John W. Robinson, *Seek the Truth* (Chatham: 1989); Michael Wayne, "The Black Population of Canada West on the Eve of the American Civil War: A Reassessment Based on the Manuscript Census of 1861," *Social History/histoire sociale* 28, 56 (1995): 465–85.

12 Poole, "Conspicuous Peripheries," 178.

13 Poole, "Conspicuous Peripheries," 58, 74–77.

14 On Mary Ann Shadd, see Rosemary Sadlier, *Mary Ann Shadd: Publisher, Educator, Teacher, Lawyer, Suffragette* (Toronto: Umbrella Press, 1995); Walcott, "'Who Is She and What Is She to You?'"

15 Poole, "Conspicuous Peripheries, 178.

16 Poole, "Conspicuous Peripheries, 178.

17 See Cheryl Thompson, "Cultural Narratives of Race, Faith, and Community: The *Dawn of Tomorrow*, 1923–1971," *Canadian Journal of History* 50, 1 (2015): 30–61. *Dawn of Tomorrow* Issues from 1923–1925 can be found on Canadiana Online: https://www.canadiana.ca/.

18 Poole, "Conspicuous Peripheries," 181–203.

19 For the history of Africville, see Amanda Carvery-Taylor, *A Love Letter to Africville* (Halifax and Winnipeg: Fernwood Publishing, 2021); Donald H. Clairmont and Dennis William Magill, *Africville: The Life and Death of a Canadian Black Community* (Toronto: Canadian Scholars Press, 1999). See Willow Key, "In the Name of Progress: Postwar Urban Renewal and the Razing of Black Spaces in Windsor, Ontario," MA Major Paper (University of Windsor, 2023) for a history of the McDougall Street Corridor.

20 Tracey Adams, "Making a Living: African Canadian Workers in London, Ontario, 1861-1901," *Labour/Le Travail* 67 (Spring 2011): 9–43.

21 Census of Canada, 1921. Data collected from manuscript census, Kent District 93, Chatham City, Subdistricts 74, 75, 80, 81, and 82.

22 Census of Canada, 1921. Data collected from manuscript census, Kent District 93, Chatham City, Subdistricts 74, 75, 80, 81, and 82. Data on Canadian women

workers in 1921 from Ceta Ramkhalawansingh, "Women During the Great War," in *Women at Work: Ontario, 1850–1930*, edited by Janice Acton, Penny Goldsmith, Bonnie Shepherd (Toronto: Women's Educational Press, 1974), 268, Table C, The Canadian Population and Labour Force.

23 Peggy Bristow, "'Whatever you raise in the ground you can sell it in Chatham': Black Women in Buxton and Chatham, 1850–65," in *'We're Rooted Here and They Can't Pull Us Up': Essays in African Canadian Women's History*, edited by Peggy Bristow et al. (Toronto: University of Toronto Press, 1994), 69–142.

24 Census of Canada, 1921. Data collected from manuscript census, Kent District 93, Chatham City, Subdistricts 74, 75, 80, 81, and 82. Also, see Adams, "Making a Living," 39, for information on Black women workers in London.

25 Dionne Brand, "'We weren't allowed to go into factory work until Hitler started the war': The 1920s to the 1940s," in *'We're Rooted Here and They Can't Pull Us Up,'* 78–79. Also see Dionne Brand, *No Burden to Carry: Narratives of Black Working Women in Ontario 1920s to 1950s* (Toronto: Women's Press, 1991).

26 Kenneth Milburn, interviewed by Wilson Brooks, September 28, 1980, Chatham, Ontario. Multicultural History Society of Ontario.

27 Kingsley Terrell interview. MHSO.

28 Wanda Milburn interview. MHSO.

29 For a well-documented case of racial discrimination in nearby Dresden, Ontario in the 1950s, see the film *Dresden Story*, dir. Julian Biggs, National Film Board of Canada, 1954. Available online: https://www.nfb.ca/film/dresden_story/.

30 Pauline Parker Miller, interviewed by Miriam Wright, September 5, 2017, Chatham, Ontario. "Breaking the Colour Barrier: Wilfred 'Boomer' Harding and the Chatham Coloured All-Stars" website. http://cdigs.uwindsor.ca/cdigs-ohms-ccas/viewer.php?cachefile=00018.xml.

31 Kenneth Milburn interview. MHSO.

32 Beulah Cuzzens, interviewed by Vivian Chavis, November 3, 5, 1980, Windsor, Ontario. Multicultural History Society of Ontario.

33 Beulah Cuzzens interview, November 3, 5, 1980. MHSO.

34 Pauline Parker Miller interview, Breaking the Colour Barrier.

35 Beulah Cuzzens interview, November 3, 5, 1980. MHSO.

36 Beulah Cuzzens interview, November 3, 5, 1980. MHSO.

37 Wanda Milburn interview. MHSO.

38 Census of Canada, 1921, Ontario, 1921, District 93, Chatham City, Subdistrict 75. Florence Harding died as a young child.

39 Census of Canada, 1871, Ontario, District No. 2 Kent, Subdistrict C, Raleigh Division. According to the 1871 Census, the couple's oldest child, Julia, was born in Ontario in 1865 or 1866, suggesting the couple had arrived sometime before that time. The death record for Andrew Harding's sister, Julia (Province of Ontario, Death Record, Julia Ann Prather, February 13, 1934) indicates that their parents were born in Kentucky.

40 For background on interracial marriages in Chatham, see Marsaydees Ferrell, "Interracial Marriage in North America: A Case Study of Interracial Relationships in Chatham Ontario, 1901-1921," MA Major Paper (University of Windsor, 2021).

41 Wanda Milburn interview. MHSO. Also, Census of Canada, Ontario, Kent District 76, Subdistrict 3, Tilbury East.

42 Beulah Cuzzens, interviewed by Vivian Chavis, September 23, 1980. Multicultural History Society of Ontario; Wanda Milburn interview. MHSO. Also, Andrew and Sarah were married in Detroit, possibly because of family opposition at home (Michigan, US, Marriage records 1867-1952, Wayne County, Andrew Harding and Sarah Holmes, December 2, 1904).

43 Beulah Cuzzens interview, September 23, 1980. MHSO.

44 Census of Canada, 1921, Ontario, Kent District 93, Chatham City, Subdistrict 75.

45 Blake and Patricia Harding, interviewed by Miriam Wright, May 25, 2016, Chatham Ontario, "Breaking the Colour Barrier: Wilfred 'Boomer' Harding and the Chatham Coloured All-Stars" website. http://cdigs.uwindsor.ca/cdigs-ohms-ccas/viewer.php?cachefile=00001.xml#segment60.

46 Beulah Cuzzens interview, September 23, 1980; November 3, 5, 1980. MHSO.

47 "Chatham Notes," *Dawn of Tomorrow,* July 21, 1923, 4. Davis was the son of Delos Rogest Davis, who was among the first Black lawyers to practice in Canada, and the first Black lawyer appointed "King's Council" in the British Empire. See Davis family file, Amherstburg Freedom Museum website: https://amherstburgfreedom.org/family-histories/davis-family/.

48 Beulah Cuzzens interview, September 23, 1980. MHSO. Cuzzens claimed her sister worked for the law firm Roxborough, Taliaferro, and Jones. The 1931 Detroit City Directory has a listing for the Roxborough-Taliaferro-Jones firm, led by Charles A. Roxborough (US City Directories, 1822-1995 – Michigan, Detroit, 1931, Detroit, Michigan City Directory). Georgina Harding was working as a legal secretary in Detroit in that period. According to the US Federal Census, 1930, Michigan, Enumeration District 82-83, Supervisor's District 21, Detroit City, Georgina Harding was living as a boarder with a white family, and was working as a stenographer in a law firm.

49 Beulah Cuzzens interview, September 23, 1980. MHSO. According to Beulah Cuzzens, Georgina got her new job through John Dancy, a Black activist who founded the Detroit Urban League, which helped Black people find employment.

50 Wilfred Harding interview; Wanda Milburn interview; Beulah Cuzzens interview, September 23, 1980. MHSO.

51 Wanda Milburn interview. MHSO.

52 Beulah Cuzzens interview, November 3, 5, 1980. MHSO.

53 Wanda Milburn interview. MHSO.

54 Wilfred Harding interview. MHSO.

55 Beulah Cuzzens interview, November 3, 5, 1980. MHSO. She said her sister, Georgina, also sent her money when Beulah was at Normal School.

56 Census of Canada, 1901, Ontario, District 76 Kent, Subdistrict 13, Chatham City.

57 Census of Canada, 1921, Ontario, District 93, Subdistrict 81, Chatham City.

58 "Stirling-Imperial Ass'n Accomplish Fine Work in Interest of Chatham," *Chatham Daily News*, May 9, 1925, 3.

59 Besides Perkins, Albert Merrill, whose family owned the Merrill Hotel (Census of Canada, 1921, District 85 Kent, 85-44, subdistrict 6, No. 14 Chatham City) and Albert Tuck (Province of Ontario Death Record, Kent County, Chatham, Albert Tuck, August 13, 1944), an East End gas station owner, were identified.

60 Archie Stirling, Chatham Sports Hall of Fame. https://chathamsportshalloffame.com/portfolio_page/archie-stirling-1889-1975/. Also see "Stirling-Imperial Ass'n Accomplish Fine Work in Interest of Chatham," *Chatham Daily News,* May 9, 1925, 3, for a brief history of the origins of the park.

61 Leddy Library Archives and Special Collections, F0133 (Wilfred "Boomer" Harding Collection) Scrapbook 1, Archie Stirling, "A Brief History of Baseball in Chatham," in *Official Program —Chatham Victoria Day, May 22nd Baseball Games* (Chatham: Victoria Day Baseball Association, 1961).

62 For a discussion of such organizations in the Canadian context, see Craig Heron, "'Boys Will Be Boys': Working-Class Masculinities in the Age of Mass Production," *International Journal of Labor History* 69 (Spring 2006): 15–17; Howell, *Blood, Sweat, and Cheers,* 28-50.

63 "Stirling-Imperial Ass'n Accomplish Fine Work in Interest of Chatham," *Chatham Daily News,* May 9, 1925, 3.

64 "Boys' Pranks Are Dangerous," *Chatham Daily News,* May 9, 1925, 3.

65 "The Third Annual Community Gathering at Stirling Park," *Chatham Daily News,* June 27, 1924, 9; "Big Celebration Staged at Stirling-Imperial Park," *Chatham Daily News,* July 2, 1925, 3.

66 "The Third Annual Community Gathering at Stirling Park," *Chatham Daily News,* June 27, 1924, 9; Province of Ontario, Marriage Record. Clifford Olbey and Ethel Freeman, November 9, 1933.

67 "The Third Annual Community Gathering at Stirling Park," *Chatham Daily News,* June 27, 1924, 9.

68 "The Third Annual Community Gathering at Stirling Park," *Chatham Daily News,* June 27, 1924, 9.

69 Ernie Miller, "Boomer Harding—one great guy," *London Free Press*, September 7, 1978, B1 (Evening/regional edition).

70 Bill Reddick, "From the Bullpen," *Chatham Daily News,* October 4, 1984, 9.

71 Bill Reddick, "From the Bullpen," *Chatham Daily News,* October 4, 1984, 9.

72 John Olbey interview. "Breaking the Colour Barrier."

73 Beulah Cuzzens, interview, September 23, 1980. MHSO.

74 Bill Reddick, "From the Bullpen," *Chatham Daily News,* October 4, 1984, 9.

75 "Chatham's first champs played the game for fun," *London Free Press,* [most likely, October 20, 1967, no page number available]. This article is one of the newspaper clippings in the Harding Family Scrapbook. On the bottom of the clipping, someone had written "LFP, October 20, 1967" in pen. I and several other people searched the microfilmed collection of the *London Free Press* but we did not find the article. The *London Free Press* published several editions a day in that period, and it is possible that the article appeared in an edition that was not saved or microfilmed. The date October 20, 1967 makes sense, as the article

referred to an event occurring "tonight" that was reported on in the *Free Press* on October 21. The original clipping may be viewed at: Leddy Library Archives and Special Collections, F1033 (Wilfred "Boomer" Harding Collection), Scrapbook 1.

76 For background on the popularity of women's softball in this period, see Carly Adams, "'I Just Felt Like I Belonged to Them,': Women's Industrial Softball, London, Ontario, 1923–1935," *International Journal of the History of Sport* 38, 1 (September 2011): 75–94.

77 Wilfred Harding interview. MHSO.

78 For background on the North Buxton softball team, see Nzindukiyimana and Wamsley, "'We Played Ball'," 1296–97; Robbins, *Legacy*, 138–39.

79 "Abolition of Slavery Celebrated," *Chatham Daily News*, August 2, 1927, 1.

80 Beulah Cuzzens interview, September 23, 1980. MHSO. Evelyn Wright was the daughter of Duncan Williams, the Chatham Coloured All-Stars' manager in 1933. She was married to Orville Wright, who was a Secretary-scorekeeper for the All-Stars for several years in the 1930s. Evelyn and Orville Wright became leaders in community recreation, running programs for children and youth at the Taylor Community Centre in the 1940s and 1950s. Orville Wright also led the move to get a new public swimming pool built (the Orville Wright Community Pool). Also see Nzindukiyimana and Wamsley, "'We Played Ball'," 1293–94.

81 Brand, *No Burden to Carry*, 144.

82 Robinson and Robinson, *Seek the Truth*, 124.

83 Ernie Miller, "Boomer Harding—one great guy," *London Free Press*, September 7, 1978, B1 (Evening/regional edition).

Chapter 3: Origins

1 Wilfred Harding, interviewed by Daniel Kelly, n.d. (c. late 1970s), Chatham, Ontario. "Breaking the Colour Barrier: Wilfred "Boomer" Harding and the Chatham Coloured All-Stars" website. http://cdigs.uwindsor.ca/cdigs-ohms-ccas/viewer.php?cachefile=00004.xml.

2 Metcalfe, *Canada Learns to Play*, 87.

3 William Humber, *Diamonds of the North: A Concise History of Baseball in Canada* (Toronto: Oxford University Press, 1995), 139–49.

4 Humber, *Diamonds of the North*, 142. Humber argues that most Black people playing baseball in nineteenth-century Canada likely learned the game north of the border, as most Black migrants from the United States left before the game was well-established there.

5 Howell, *Northern Sandlots*, 179.

6 Ian Kennedy, "Sixty Three Years Before the Chatham All-Stars the Town's First All-Black Team Took the Field," *Chatham-Kent Sports Network*, August 1, 2021 https://www.cksn.ca/2021/08/sixty-three-years-before-the-chatham-all-stars-the-towns-first-all-black-team-took-the-field/.

7 Metcalfe, *Canada Learns to Play*, 88–89.

8 Metcalfe, *Canada Learns to Play*, 89–90; Howell, *Northern Sandlots*, 174–79.

9 Howell, *Northern Sandlots*, 173.

10 "Crack Ball Team Coming," *London Advertiser*, April 16, 1895, 2.

11 "Leamington," *Amherstburg Echo,* June 9, 1905, 2.

12 For background on the "Negro Leagues," see Neil Lanctot, *Negro League Baseball: The Rise and Ruin of a Black Institution* (Philadelphia: University of Pennsylvania Press, 2004); Larry Lester, et. al, *Black Baseball in Detroit* (Charleston, SC: Arcadia Publishing, 2000); Jerry Molloy, ed., *Sol White's History of Colored Base Ball* (Lincoln, Nebraska: University of Nebraska Press, 1995).

13 See James N. Gregory, *The Southern Diaspora: How the Great Migrations of Black and White Southerners Transformed America* (Chapel Hill: University of North Carolina Press, 2005).

14 Gerald L. Early, *A Level Playing Field: African American Athletes and the Republic of Sports* (Cambridge, Mass.: Harvard University Press, 2011), 217; Susan Koprince, "Baseball as History and Myth in August Wilson's 'Fences,'" *African American Review* 40, 2 (Summer 2006): 349–58.

15 Quoted in Gary Joyce, "Fitting Tribute," *Sportsnet*, n.d. https://www.sportsnet.ca/baseball/mlb/meet-researcher-shedding-light-baseballs-overlooked-heroes/.

16 "Crowd of 2000 Watch Colored Stars" *Border Cities Star,* August 4, 1931, Second Section, 3. The team roster reported in the article closely matched the players shown in a 1930 photograph of the Detroit Stars, as seen in Lester et al., *Black Baseball in Detroit,* 62.

17 Lanctot, Negro League Baseball, 5–6; 13.

18 Lanctot, Negro League Baseball, 9.

19 "Powerful Team is Selected to Meet Colored Aggregation," *Border Cities Star,* June 7, 1930, Second Section, 2; "Colored Giants Meet Riverside," *Border Cities Star,* June 20, 1930, Second Section, 2; "Two Games at Wigle Park Saturday," *Border Cities Star,* May 8, 1931, Second Section, 3; "Marigolds in Twilight Tilt Here Thursday," *Border Cities Star,* July 17, 1935, Section Section, 5; "Detroit Nine Meet Emery," *Windsor Daily Star,* June 25, 1936, Second Section, 5.

20 See Natasha Henry, *Emancipation Day: Celebrating Freedom in Canada* (Toronto: National Heritage Books, 2010).

21 "Successful Celebration" *Chatham Daily Planet*, August 4, 1903, 1.

22 "Local," *Chatham Daily Planet*, July 31, 1906, 5.

23 For background on the Colored Giants, see Fred Osmon, *The History of Baseball in Chatham 'N Kent: Over 100 Years* (Chatham: 2015), 16–17, 21–22; Robbins, *Legacy,* 142–44; Robinson and Robinson, *Seek the Truth*, 121.

24 "Colored Team Hurls Challenge at Regt," *Chatham Daily News*, August 30, 1915, 5.

25 Census of Canada, 1911, Ontario, District 85, Subdistrict 54. Chatham City Province of Ontario. Parker was born after his father, Frank, had died. Parker's mother, Mary Ann (Franklin) Parker, worked as a domestic servant.

26 Province of Ontario, Birth Record, Kent County, Duncan Williams, June 18, 1885. Province of Ontario, Marriage Record, Kent County, Duncan Williams and Henrietta Vandusen, December 24, 1906. Joseph Parker was married to May Vandusen, sister of Williams's wife, Henrietta. Also, see Province of Ontario,

Certificate of Marriage, Kent County, Orville Wright and Evelyn Williams, September 27, 1937.

27 Province of Ontario, Marriage Record, Kent County, Percy Parker and Bertha Rhody, September 10, 1923; Census of Canada, 1911, Ontario, District 85, Subdistrict 44, Chatham City.

28 "Reach Ball was Maltreated," *Chatham Daily Planet*, June 15, 1915, 5; "Locals Win Again," *Chatham Daily News*, August 24, 1915, 5.

29 Robbins, *Legacy*, 137.

30 Robbins, *Legacy*, 138.

31 Robbins, *Legacy*, 236 (notes). Robbins cited information obtained from two former ball players, William Rhue and Stanley Prince, about early ball players in the community. The players they identified included George Scott, Lytle Riddle, Charles Robbins, Duncan Vincent, and Ben and Robert Harding who had all played for the North Buxton team in 1915.

32 Middleton et al., *Something to Hope For*, 69. The Buxton Homecoming games were held at the farm of James and Elizabeth Robbins in the 1920s.

33 Howell, *Blood, Northern Sandlots*, 174. For discussions of newspaper coverage of Black baseball see Brian Carroll, "'Praising My People', 245–46; Pat Washburn, *The African-American Record Journal* (Evanston, Ill.: Northwestern University Press, 2008); David K. Wiggins, "Wendell Smith, the *Pittsburgh Courier Journal* and the Campaign to Include Blacks in Organized Baseball, 1933-1945," *Journal of Sport History* 10, 2 (Summer 1983): 5-29.

34 "Big Game Thursday," *Chatham Daily Planet*, June 2, 1915, 5.

35 "Reach Ball Was Maltreated," *Chatham Daily Planet*, June 15, 1915, 5.

36 "Reach Ball Was Maltreated," *Chatham Daily Planet*, June 15, 1915, 5.

37 "Reach Ball Was Maltreated," *Chatham Daily Planet*, June 15, 1915, 5.

38 For example, see "Chatham Was Baseball Mad Yesterday," *Chatham Daily Planet*, June 25, 1915, 8, when the city league teams played a fund-raising game and gave themselves joke team names including the Barber Clerks, and the Married Men.

39 Joseph, "An Intersectional Analysis," 258.

40 Joseph, "An Intersectional Analysis," 258.

41 Janice Forsyth, "Bodies of Memory: Sports and Games at Canada's Residential Schools," in *Aboriginal Peoples and Sport in Canada: Historical Foundations and Contemporary Issues,* edited by Janice Forsyth and Audrey R. Giles (Vancouver: University of British Columbia Press, 2013), 15–34.

42 Forsyth, "Bodies of Memory," 32.

43 Forsyth, "Bodies of Memory," 32.

44 Janice Forsyth, *Reclaiming Tom Longboat: Indigenous Self-Determination in Canadian Sport* (Regina: University of Regina Press, 2020), 181.

45 For histories of some southwestern Ontario Indigenous athletes in the twentieth century, see Ian Kennedy, *On Account of Darkness: Shining Light on Race and Sport* (New Westminster, BC: Tidewater Press, 2022), 21–39; 85-93; 188–202.

46 For background on the Delaware Nation at Moraviantown (Eelünaapéewi Lahkéewiit), see Darryl Stonefish, *History of the Delaware Nation at Moraviantown* (Thamesville, Ontario: Moraviantown Research Office, 1995).

47 "Colored Giants Are Winners," *Chatham Daily Planet*, July 21, 1915, 3.

48 Ornella Nzindukiyimana, "'That's Jean Lowe': On Being a Black Canadian Female Athlete in 1940s Ontario," *International Journal of the History of Sport* 37, 14 (2020), 1372.

49 "Colored Team Hurls Challenge at Regt," *Chatham Daily News,* August 30, 1915, 5.

50 Canadian Overseas Expeditionary Forces, Attestation Paper, No. 2 Construction Battalion, Ray Ward, December 27, 1916; Canadian Overseas Expeditionary Forces, Attestation Paper, No. 2 Construction Battalion, Herbert Crosby, December 28, 1916. For insights into the creation of this battalion, see Melissa N. Shaw, "'Most Anxious to Serve Their King and Country': Black Canadians' Fight to Enlist in WWI and Emerging Race Consciousness in Ontario, 1914–1919," *Histoire sociale/ Social history* 49, 100 (November 2016): 543–80.

51 See team rosters: "Colored Giants Beat Stirlings by One Run," *Chatham Daily News*, July 24, 1925, 3; "The Stirlings Win Game," *Chatham Daily News*, July 21, 1926, 5.

52 "Locals – The Big Game," *Chatham Daily News*, September 18, 1925, 3.

53 "Locals – Colored Giants Won," *Chatham Daily News*, August 17, 1925, 3.

54 Census of Canada, 1911, Ontario, District 85, Subdistrict 54 (Lewis family, showing John had a sister named Hazel); Province of Ontario, Marriage Record, Kent County, Herbert Crosby and Hazel Lewis, September 28, 1915.

55 "Locals – Colored Giants Won," *Chatham Daily News*, August 17, 1925, 3.

56 "Locals – Colored Giants Won," *Chatham Daily News*, August 17, 1925, 3; "The Stirlings Win Game," *Chatham Daily News*, July 21, 1926, 5.

57 "Chatham's first champs played the game for fun," *London Free Press*, [likely October 20, 1967, no page number available].

58 "London Colored Stars," (team photo and caption), *London Free Press*, October 1, 1923, 14.

59 London-based players who played for both Chatham and London included Harry Coursey, Herbert Wilson, Harry (Hank) Anderson.

60 "London Notes," *Dawn of Tomorrow*, July 14, 1923, 3. As well, Chatham's Ray Ward played for the London team at least twice ("Colored Stars are Again Victorious," *Dawn of Tomorrow*, September 8, 1923, 1; "London Notes," *Dawn of Tomorrow*, July 14, 1923, 3).

61 Census of Canada, 1911, Ontario, District 94, Subdistrict 5, London City. "Harry Coursey Wins Three Track Events," *Dawn of Tomorrow*, May 10, 1924, 1; Picture of Harry Coursey, *Dawn of Tomorrow*, August 2, 1924, 1; "Sensation of M.A.A. Meet, London," *Dawn of Tomorrow*, September 20, 1924, 1. Coursey apparently qualified to compete in the 1924 Olympics but did not attend. His coaches claimed he needed to train more before he would be ready for major competitions.

62 "East A.C. and West Greys Win," *London Evening Free Press*, May 27, 1924, 12; "Scott-McHales Defeat Perrins," *London Evening Free Press*, July 19, 1924, 12.

63 Picture and caption of Harry Coursey, *Dawn of Tomorrow*, May 2, 1925, 1. McCormick's was a biscuit factory in London. Coursey participated in races at a 1924 McCormick's company picnic, so he may have been an employee or a family member of an employee. See "Great Time at Annual Picnic," *London Evening Free Press*, July 24, 1924, 3.

64 For insights into the *Dawn of Tomorrow* and the Black press in that period, see Cheryl Thompson, "Cultural Narratives of Race, Faith, and Community."

65 "Chatham Giants Beat Windsor," *Chatham Daily News*, September 3, 1926, 3. The London Braves were later renamed the London Majors.

66 Province of Ontario, Marriage Record, Middlesex County, Herbert Roy Wilson and Gladys Noris, June 19, 1912.

67 Wilfred Harding interview. MHSO.

68 Another London player recalled by Boomer Harding and Beulah Cuzzens was Fred Kelly. Kelly was born and raised in Ingersoll, Ontario, less than twenty-five miles away from London. As an adult, he moved to London where he found work as a chauffeur. Kelly had a brother, Charles (Charlie), a World War I veteran, who played with the London Colored Stars ("Ingersoll Notes," *Dawn of Tomorrow*, August 25, 1923, 4) as well as on a white, OBAA-affiliated team in Ingersoll ("Ingersoll Wins from McCormick's," *London Evening Free Press*, July 6, 1925, 8. In the game described in this article, pitcher Charlie Kelly, faced Harry Coursey who was pitching for the McCormick's).

69 For example, see "Locals – Stirlings Lost," *Chatham Daily News*, June 19, 1925; "The Foresters Defeat Giants," *Chatham Daily News*, July 20, 1925, 3; "Colored Giants Beat Stirlings by One Run," *Chatham Daily News*, July 24, 1925, 3; "County Leaguers Win," *Chatham Daily News*, July 29, 1925, 3; "Locals – Colored Giants Won," *Chatham Daily News*, August 17, 1925, 3.

70 For example, see "Colored Giants Beat Stirlings by One Run," *Chatham Daily News*, July 24, 1925, 3; "Title Game to Be Played Here," *Chatham Daily News*, September 9, 1925, 3.

71 "Title Game to Be Played Here," *Chatham Daily News*, September 9, 1925, 3.

72 "Chatham and Detroit Teams in Title Series," *Chatham Daily News*, September 18, 1925, 9.

73 "Championship Game on Local Lot Saturday," *Chatham Daily News*, September 17, 1926, 13.

74 Robbins, *Legacy*, 143–44. Arlie Robbins claims that the Taylor's Stars' manager, Walt Taylor, had Buxton connections, which was how the Colored Giants came to play them.

75 "Title Game to Be Played Here," *Chatham Daily News*, September 9, 1925, 3; "Championship Game on Local Lot Saturday," *Chatham Daily News*, September 17, 1926, 13.

76 "Title Game to Be Played Here," *Chatham Daily News*, September 9, 1925, 3; "Locals – Interest in Game," *Chatham Daily News*, September 16, 1925, 3.

77 "Locals – The Big Game," *Chatham Daily News*, September 18, 1925, 3.

78 "Visitors Lose to the Giants," *Chatham Daily News*, August 3, 1926, 3.

79 Thompson, "Cultural Narratives of Race, Faith, and Community," 57–58.

80 "London Notes," *Dawn of Tomorrow*, February 2, 1924, 3. This concert was a fund-raiser for one of the Colored Stars players, George Chandler, who was ill.

81 "London Notes," *Dawn of Tomorrow*, August 11, 1923, 5; "Colored Stars Are Again Victorious," *Dawn of Tomorrow*, September 8, 1923, 1.

82 "London Notes," *Dawn of Tomorrow*, August 25, 1923, 5. Although the *Dawn of Tomorrow* referred to the "Elites" as a baseball team, they could have been a soft-ball team, as the game was popular among young women in London in the 1920s (see Adams, "I Just Felt Like I Belonged").

83 Advertisement – London Colored Stars vs. Arkona Giants, *Watford Guide-Advocate*, July 20, 1923, 4.

84 "London Notes," *Dawn of Tomorrow*, August 11, 1923, 5.

85 Thompson, "Cultural Narratives of Race, Faith, and Community," 57. Her article notes that a London-based choral group, performing in 1931, advertised their program as including "old-time spirituals, popular songs, old-time favourites."

86 See Cheryl Thompson, *Uncle: Race, Nostalgia, and the Politics of Loyalty* (Toronto: Coach House Books, 2021).

Chapter 4: A New Black Baseball Team in Chatham, 1933

1 Leddy Library Archives and Special Collections, F0133 (Wilfred "Boomer" Harding Collection) Scrapbook 1, Archie Stirling, "A Brief History of Baseball in Chatham," in *Official Program – Chatham Victoria Day, May 22nd Baseball Games* (Chatham: Victoria Day Baseball Association, 1961).

2 "Walpole, Chatham Baseball Teams Meet Here Friday," *Chatham Daily News*, June 21, 1932, 8. This was an exhibition game between an Indigenous team from Bkejwanong, and an "all-star" team comprised of members of Chatham's Junior team and Intermediate-age players from Chatham who were playing in other communities.

3 "Blenheim Defeated the Burg in a Kent League Game" *Chatham Daily News*, June 17, 1932, 12.

4 Metcalfe, *Canada Learns to Play*, 86–87.

5 Metcalfe, "The Anatomy of Power," 52. An Ontario provincial softball association was created in 1923.

6 Alan Metcalfe, "The Anatomy of Power," 56.

7 "Women's Soft Ball League May Be Organized in Near Future," *Chatham Daily News*, June 14, 1924, 9; "City Softball League," *Chatham Daily News*, May 16, 1925, 5. Chatham had a ten-team men's softball league and a women's softball league. With perhaps a couple of exceptions, organized softball was overwhelming white in Chatham in the 1920s and 1930s.

8 "City Softball League Season Will Open Monday Night," *Chatham Daily News*, May 6, 1933, 11; "Chatham Church Softball League Opens Season May 9," *Chatham Daily News*, April 24, 1933, 8. Softball was also very popular in nearby Windsor. See "Softball," *Border Cities Star*, July 22, 1933, Second Section, 2.

9 Advertisement for Wanless Trophy (baseball) game, *Chatham Daily News*, September 20, 1933, 11. Admission was ten cents, fifteen cents for cushioned seats. In the same period, admission to city softball games was by donation.

10 "Chatham City Baseball League Will Open May 18," *Chatham Daily News*, May 6, 1933, 11.

11 "Chatham City Baseball League Will Open May 18," *Chatham Daily News*, May 6, 1933, 11.

12 "Tuxis Boys Lose to the Stirling Boys," *Chatham Daily News*, June 28, 1924, 9. Carl Harding was in the lineup. King Terrell began playing for the Stirling-Imperials in 1926. See "Locals Beat Blenheim's Jr. Baseball Nine," *Chatham Daily News*, May 21, 1926, 9. That same season, Stirling also tried to bring a Black player from Ingersoll, Ontario, R. (nicknamed "Rabbit") Marshall to play with the Stirling-Imperials, but the OBAA eligibility rules would not allow it. See "Locals Can't Use Marshall," *Chatham Daily News*, May 20, 1926, 13. Marshall also occasionally played with the Chatham Colored Giants. There may have been one or two other Black people on the Stirling-Imperial Juniors, as a couple of the players had surnames (Simms, Jackson) also found in the Chatham-area Black community. First names, or even first initials were rarely included in baseball game write-ups (unless there were two players with the same surname), making it harder to identify people.

13 Kingsley Terrell interview. MHSO.

14 Kingsley Terrell interview. MHSO; Edward Wright, interviewed by Marsaydees Ferrell, July 6, 2018. "Telling the Stories of Race and Sport in Canada" website. http://cdigs.uwindsor.ca/omeka-s/s/rsc/page/interview-with-ed-wright.

15 Kingsley Terrell interview. MHSO.

16 For a discussion on white allies in Black sports, see Louis Moore, *We Will Win the Day: The Civil Rights Movement, the Black Athlete, and the Quest for Equality* (Santa Barbara, California: Prager, 2017), Chapter 2, 21–49.

17 "May Hold Kent Public Schools Athletics Meet," *Chatham Daily News*, October 2, 1925, 9.

18 Robinson and Robinson, *Seek the Truth*, 57. Gwen and John W. Robinson claim Charles Lynn used to advocate for rights for Black people, and once protested a "whites only" sign in a local restaurant.

19 Kingsley Terrell interview. MHSO.

20 Wilfred Harding interview. MHSO.

21 Sometime in 1933, Clarence Crosby moved to London and became involved with Black baseball teams there. See "London Notes," *Dawn of Tomorrow*, December 1933, 4.

22 Wilfred Harding, interviewed by Daniel Kelly. "Breaking the Colour Barrier."

23 "Chatham Notes," *Dawn of Tomorrow*, November 10, 1923, 5; Kingsley Terrell interview. MHSO; "Chatham's first champs played the game for fun," *London Free Press*, [likely October 20, 1967].

24 "Chatham's first champs played the game for fun," *London Free Press*, [likely October 20, 1967].

25 Wilfred Harding interview. MHSO.

26 "Wilfred Harding is Senior Champion of Secondary Schools," *Chatham Daily News*, October 6, 1933, 10.

27 "Harding Out of the Game for Rest of Season," *Chatham Daily News*, March 6, 1934, 1.

28 Wilfred Harding interview. MHSO.

29 "Blenheim Defeated the Burg in a Kent League Game," *Chatham Daily News*, June 17, 1932, 12; Wilfred Harding interview. MHSO

30 Jennifer Miss, interviewed by Alastair Staffen, October 5, 2016, by telephone. "Breaking the Colour Barrier: "Wilfred 'Boomer' Harding and the Chatham Coloured All-Stars" website. http://cdigs.uwindsor.ca/cdigs-ohms-ccas/viewer.php?cachefile=00017.xml.

31 Douglas Talbot Jr. interviewed by Heidi Jacobs, October 29, 2016, Grosse Pointe Shores, Michigan. "Breaking the Colour Barrier: Wilfred 'Boomer' Harding and the Chatham Coloured All-Stars website. http://cdigs.uwindsor.ca/cdigs-ohms-ccas/viewer.php?cachefile=00007.xml. Also see Census of Canada, 1911, Ontario, District 85, Subdistrict 64, Chatham City. Their other brother, Douglas, had moved to Michigan for work and did not play with the All-Stars in the 1930s.

32 Their mother was a Terrell, sister of former Colored Giants player Charles Terrell.

33 Census of Canada, 1921. Ontario, District 93, Subdistrict 81, Chatham City.

34 John Olbey interview. "Breaking the Colour Barrier."

35 Kingsley Terrell interview. MHSO.

36 Wilfred Harding, interviewed by Daniel Kelly. "Breaking the Colour Barrier."

37 Province of Ontario, Marriage Record, Kent County, Gouy Ladd and Elizabeth Steer, December 19, 1938; Dominion of Canada, Voter's List, 1935, Chatham.

38 Wilfred Harding interview. MHSO; Kingsley Terrell interview. MHSO.

39 Kingsley Terrell interview. MHSO.

40 "Reach Ball was Maltreated, *Chatham Daily Planet*, June 15, 1935, 5.

41 Census of Canada, 1921, Ontario, District 77, Subdistrict 45, Windsor City; Ferguson Jenkins, Sr., interview. MHSO.

42 Ferguson Jenkins, Sr., interview. MHSO. George Harding also played at least one game for the Chatham Colored Giants: "The Stirlings Win Game," *Chatham Daily News*, July 21, 1926, 5.

43 Kingsley Terrell interview. MHSO; Wilfred Harding interview. MHSO.

44 Kingsley Terrell interview. MHSO.

45 Wilfred Harding, interviewed by Daniel Kelly. "Breaking the Colour Barrier."

46 Wilfred Harding, interview. MHSO.

47 Wilfred Harding, interviewed by Daniel Kelly. "Breaking the Colour Barrier."

48 Morrow and Wamsley. *Sport in Canada*, 155.

49 Stacy L. Lorenz and Jay Scherer, "The Sports-Media Complex and Canadian Culture," in *Sport and Recreation in Canadian History*, edited by Carly Adams (Champaign, Illinois: Human Kinetics, 2021), 253.

50 Howell, *Blood, Sweat, and Cheers*, 95.

51 Lorenz and Scherer, "The Sport-Media Complex," 261.

52 Nzindukiyimana, "'That's Jean Lowe'," 1372.

53 "Team Standings" *Chatham Daily News*, July 26, 1933, 8; "Chatham Juniors Will Play in Tilbury on Thursday," *Chatham Daily News*, July 26, 1933, 8. The Stars ended up in third place, behind the Duns and the Merchants, with a record of four wins and ten losses. The Juniors, who had been playing in the Chatham City Baseball League, left competition before the end of the season to compete in the Kent Junior OBAA playoffs. The Merchants and Duns went on to the city league playoffs.

54 "Duns Won Last Night, Leading City Baseball League," *Chatham Daily News*, June 6, 1933, 9.

55 "R.G. Duns Beat Chatham Stars in City Baseball Game," *Chatham Daily News*, June 26, 1933, 9.

56 "Merchants Winners of Last Night's Baseball Game," *Chatham Daily News*, July 5, 1933, 9.

57 Miller, "Muscular Assimilationism," 146–82.

58 "Chatham Boys Win in London," *Chatham Daily News*, July 14, 1933, 9. One exception—this newspaper article, provided by a wire service, about a game between the Stars and a Black team from London included an attempt to mimic southern US Black dialect, using the phrase "hot-diggety-dog." The *Chatham Daily News* still printed this, but for the most part, they did not make overt references to race in 1933.

59 Wilfred Harding interview. MHSO.

60 Wilfred Harding, interviewed by Daniel Kelly. "Breaking the Colour Barrier."

61 "City Baseball League Game Ends in Score of 5-5," *Chatham Daily News*, May 30, 1933, 9.

62 "Stars Win Wanless Trophy in Two Straight Games," *Chatham Daily News*, October 10, 1933, 8.

63 Ernie Miller, "Boomer Harding—one great guy," *London Free Press*, September 7, 1978, Evening/regional edition, B1.

64 "London Notes," *Dawn of Tomorrow*, June 30, 1933, 5; "Chatham Boys Win in London," *Chatham Daily News*, July 14, 1933, 9.

65 "Casual Comment on Current Sport," *Chatham Daily News*, August 28, 1933, 8.

66 Bill Reddick, "From the Bullpen," *Chatham Daily News*, October 4, 1984, 9.

67 Howell, *Northern Sandlots*, 173.

68 Wilfred Harding, interviewed by Daniel Kelly. "Breaking the Colour Barrier."

69 Bill Reddick, "From the Bullpen," *Chatham Daily News*, October 4, 1984, 9.

70 Kingsley Terrell interview. MHSO.

71 For background on the Hotel London team, see Vanessa Brown, *The Grand Old Lady: A History of Hotel London* (London, Ontario: London and Middlesex Historical Society, 2015), 23–26, 105–6.

72 "London Hotel Ball Team Scores Again," *Dawn of Tomorrow*, July 8, 1933, 1.

73 Roy and Harry Anderson had played with the London Colored Stars.

74 Brown, *The Grand Old Lady*, 105–6.

75 "Chatham Notes," *Dawn of Tomorrow*, May 22, 1933, 5.

76 "Chatham Boys Win in London," *Chatham Daily News*, July 14, 1933, 9.

77 "London Notes," *Dawn of Tomorrow*, June 30, 1933, 5.

78 "London Hotel Ball Team Scores Again," *Dawn of Tomorrow*, July 8, 1933, 1.

79 Duncan Williams Jr. sometimes played with the Chatham Stars, so it is not clear if the Williams listed on the roster, playing right field, was father or son.

80 "Casual Comment on Current Sport," *Chatham Daily News*, October 2, 1933, 8. The London city league was not affiliated with the OBAA.

81 "Hotel London Question," *Dawn of Tomorrow*, April 6, 1934, 1; "Editorial – Hotel London Discharges Colored Help and Replaces Them with White Ex-Service Men," *Dawn of Tomorrow*, June 1934, 2; Brown, *The Grand Old Lady*, 23–26.

82 "London Notes," *Dawn of Tomorrow*, April 6, 1934, 5. According to the *Dawn of Tomorrow*, Flat Chase and a white ball player from Chatham, Dutch Scott, joined the Harlem Aces for a game.

83 Census of Canada, 1921, Ontario, District 93, Subdistrict 52, Raleigh Township.

84 Earl Chase Jr. and Shyla Chase, interviewed by Alastair Staffen, July 11, 2016, Chatham, Ontario. "Breaking the Colour Barrier: Wilfred 'Boomer' Harding and the Chatham Coloured All-Stars" website. http://cdigs.uwindsor.ca/cdigs-ohms-ccas/viewer.php?cachefile=00008.xml.

85 Earl Chase Jr. interview. "Breaking the Colour Barrier."

86 Ferguson Jenkins, Sr. interview. MHSO.

87 "North Essex Baseball," *Amherstburg Echo*, August 18, 1933, 7.

88 "With Border Softball," and "Softball," *Border Cities Star*, June 14, 1934, Second Section, 4. Windsor had two adult men's softball leagues and one girls' league.

89 "Three Games are Scheduled," *Border Cities Star*, June 17, 1933, Second Section, 3. Also, see "Stars, LaSalle Bid for Lead," *Border Cities Star*, May 20, 1933, Second Section, 2; North Essex Baseball," *Amherstburg Echo*, August 11, 1933, 7; "County Sports" *Amherstburg Echo*, August 25, 1933, 7; "Stars Play Moose Nine," *Windsor Daily Star*, May 22, 1937, Second Section, 4.

90 "New Club for Border Loop," *Border Cities Star*, July 4, 1935, Second Section, 3.

91 "Colored Nine in 1936 Bow," *Windsor Daily Star*, May 22, 1936, Second Section, 5; "Dr. Dix Meets Colored Giants," *Windsor Daily Star*, June 5, 1936, Second Section, 3. The Windsor Colored Stars were also active exhibition game players. In fact, in 1936, when the Windsor baseball league was not operating, the Stars recruited a few American players and renamed themselves the Michigan-Ontario Colored Giants.

92 "Stars Defeat Belle River," *Border Cities Star*, August 14, 1933, Second Section, 2; "Belle River is in Top Berth," Border Cities Star, July 10, 1933, Second Section, 2.

93 For example, see his mid-July batting record for 1934: "City Baseball League Records," *Chatham Daily News*, July 23, 1934, 11. Chase was the top batter, with a .525 record—meaning he hit the ball half the times he went to bat, which is considered high.

94 Bruce Kidd, *The Struggle for Canadian Sport* (Toronto: University of Toronto Press, 1996), 5.

95 Joseph, "An Intersectional Analysis," 258.

96 Karl Linholm, "Bat lefty – it's a big deal," *Addison County Independent,* August 26, 2021. https://www.addisonindependent.com/2021/08/26/karl-lindholm-bat-lefty-its-a-big-deal/. The article cited a study published in the October, 2017 *New England Journal of Medicine* which examined batting records in major league baseball players from 1871 to 2016. Although right handers who batted left represented just twelve percent of all players, they comprised thirty-two percent of those considered top batters (Ty Cobb and Ted Williams among the most notable). The study also asserts that convention and tradition, not physical reasons, lead most right-handers to stand to the left of home plate when batting.

97 Kingsley Terrell interview. MHSO.

98 Kingsley Terrell interview. MHSO.

99 Wilfred Harding, interviewed by Daniel Kelly. "Breaking the Colour Barrier."

100 Art Cartier, "Sport Talk," *Chatham Daily News,* September 28, 1939, Second Section, 2.

101 The term "pull hitter" is used to describe someone who can hit to the same side from which they bat. While most left-handed batters would hit into right field, a left-handed pull hitter could hit strongly into left field.

102 "Chatham's first champs played the game for fun," *London Free Press*, [likely October 20, 1967].

103 For example, see Simon Sharkey-Gotlieb, "Rizzo Becomes First Left-handed Throwing Third Baseman Since 1997," *The Score*, n.d. https://www.thescore.com/mlb/news/1356687.

104 Kingsley Terrell interview. MHSO.

105 Wilfred Harding interview. MHSO.

106 Kingsley Terrell interview. MHSO.

107 Wilfred Harding, interviewed by Daniel Kelly. "Breaking the Colour Barrier."

108 Kingsley Terrell interview. MHSO. Wanda Milburn made these comments while interviewing Terrell.

109 "Wanless Trophy Series to Get Underway Saturday," *Chatham Daily News*, August 24, 1933, 13.

110 "Two Baseball Games at Stirling Park on Saturday," *Chatham Daily News*, September 22, 1933, 10.

111 "Stars, Juniors Win Wanless Trophy Game Saturday," *Chatham Daily News*, September 25, 1933, 8.

112 "Stars Win Wanless Trophy in Two Straight Games," *Chatham Daily News*, October 10, 1933, 8.

113 "Chatham Stars, Juniors in Wanless Trophy Finals," *Chatham Daily News*, Oct 2, 1933, 8.

114 "Stars Win Wanless Trophy in Two Straight Games," *Chatham Daily News*, Oct 10, 1933, 8.

Chapter 5: Playing in Racialized Spaces

1 "Sport in Short," *Chatham Daily News,* August 15, 1934, 11.

2 "Chatham Stars Beat Penetang in First O.B.A.A. Final," *Chatham Daily News*, October 16, 1934, 11.

3 Leddy Library Archives and Special Collections, F1033 (Wilfred "Boomer" Harding Collection), Scrapbook 1, "Ontario Baseball Association – Championships" n.d., but the names on the list suggest it was for the 1939 OBA playoff season. Also, the organization's name was changed from "Ontario Baseball Amateur Association" to "Ontario Baseball Association" in 1939. On this form, the team was called "Chatham All-Stars."

4 Doug Scurr, "Chatham Colored Stars Return Under New Name," *Chatham Daily News*, June 12, 1946 [no page number]. This article is one of the news clippings in the Harding Collection (Leddy Library Archives and Special Collections, F1033 (Wilfred "Boomer" Harding Collection), Scrapbook 1). The page number could not be verified as this issue is missing from the *Chatham Daily News* microfilm collection.

5 Pauline Parker Miller interview. "Breaking the Colour Barrier." Mrs. Miller said that someone from Detroit named Johnson owned the building where her father had his barber shop.

6 The *Chatham Daily News* sports columns regularly referred to him as "Happy," as did former members of the Chatham Coloured All-Stars. In 1915, however, a newspaper article referred to him by the nickname "Sleepy": "Colored Giants the Winners," *Chatham Daily Planet*, July 21, 1915, 3.

7 Census of Canada, 1911, Ontario, District 85, Subdistrict 54, Chatham City; Province of Ontario, Marriage Record, Kent County, Louis Pryor and Blanche Braxton, June 13, 1917; "Chatham Notes," *Dawn of Tomorrow*, May 17, 1924, 4; US Federal Census, 1930, Michigan, Enumeration District 82-319, Supervisor's District 22; Province of Ontario, Certificate of Death, Thomas Pryor, May 1, 1933. Louis Pryor's father, Thomas, was born in Kentucky, but came to Chatham as a child with his parents. Before Louis was born, Thomas and his wife Maggie moved to Michigan, but they returned to Chatham when their children were young. Sometime in the 1920s, Thomas and Maggie moved back to Detroit, and their son Louis lived with them and worked in a factory.

8 Pauline Williams and Cleata Morris interview. "Breaking the Colour Barrier."

9 Wilfred Harding interview. MHSO.

10 Pauline Williams and Cleata Morris interview. "Breaking the Colour Barrier."

11 The local press in the 1930s almost always referred to him as "Don" Washington, but in the oral history interviews and several newspaper interviews, his former teammates usually referred to him by his full name, Donise. As well, Pauline Parker Miller, daughter of All-Stars manager Joseph Parker, referred to him as "Donise" in the oral history interview she did in 2017.

12 Bill Reddick, "From the Bullpen," *Chatham Daily News*, October 5, 1984, 9.

13 Bill Reddick, "From the Bullpen," *Chatham Daily News*, October 5, 1984, 9.

14 Donald Tabron Jr. interviewed by Miriam Wright, November 21, 2019, Detroit, Michigan. "Breaking the Colour Barrier: Wilfred "Boomer" Harding and the Chatham Coloured All-Stars" website; US WWII Draft Registration Card, Serial No. 4584, Order No. 436, Donald Tabron; US Federal Census, 1920, Indiana, Gibson County, Patoka Township, Princeton City, Supervisor's District 1, Enumeration District 21.

15 US WWII Draft Registration Card, Serial No. 4584, Order No. 436, Donald Tabron.

16 See *Encyclopedia Britannica,* s.v. "Tri-State Tornado of 1925." https://www.britannica.com/event/Tri-State-Tornado-of-1925; "Southern Railway Shop, Princeton, Indiana, Tri-State Tornado Damage, March 18, 1925," postcard, Flickr site: https://www.flickr.com/photos/82856031@N04/28941628081.

17 US WWII Draft Registration Card, Serial No. 1515, Order No. 2420, Donise Washington. His draft card indicated he was born in 1907, but all other records of his birth (e.g., Social Security data) indicates he was born in 1908.

18 US Federal Census, 1930, Michigan, Wayne County, Enumeration District 82-269, Supervisor's District 21. The census record gives his birthplace as Arkansas, but this is most likely a mistake, as all other records of his birth indicate Memphis. His wife and her parents were also migrants, having been born in southern US states. It is not known if the couple had separated at the time he came to Chatham—they did not formally divorce until some years later. Washington later remarried, was divorced, and remarried again.

19 "Sweet memories for '34 All-Star," *Chatham Daily News*, July 16, 2001, 9. Washington spent three years in Chatham and another two in Strathroy, Ontario.

20 "Stars Win Two Straight in City Baseball," *Chatham Daily News*, May 22, 1934, Second Section, 7. "Two-bagger" refers to a batter making it to second base after hitting the ball.

21 Dave Feschuk, "Those All-Star seasons," *National Post*, July 13, 2002, S3.

22 Beulah Cuzzens interview, September 23, 1980. MHSO.

23 Wilfred Harding interview. MHSO.

24 Kingsley Terrell interview. MHSO.

25 Kingsley Terrell interview. MHSO.

26 Pauline Parker Miller interview. "Breaking the Colour Barrier."

27 Wilfred Harding interview. MHSO.

28 Kingsley Terrell interview. MHSO.

29 Donald Tabron Jr. interview. "Breaking the Colour Barrier."

30 Jack Calder, "Analyzing Sport," *Chatham Daily News*, September 5, 1934, 11.

31 Kingsley Terrell interview. MHSO.

32 "City Baseball League Record," *Chatham Daily News*, July 23, 1934, 11.

33 Kingsley Terrell interview. MHSO.

34 Kingsley Terrell interview. MHSO.

35 John Olbey interview. "Breaking the Colour Barrier."

36 "City Baseball League Statistics," *Chatham Daily News*, June 21, 1934, Second Section, 5.

37 "City Baseball League Record," *Chatham Daily News*, July 23, 1934, 11. Chase # 1, Olbey # 4, L. Harding # 7, Washington # 8, W. Harding # 9.

38 Gare Joyce, "Fitting Tribute," Sportsnet, n.d. https://www.sportsnet.ca/baseball/mlb/meet-researcher-shedding-light-baseballs-overlooked-heroes/.

39 City Baseball League Record, *Chatham Daily News*, July 23, 1934, 11.

40 Kingsley Terrell interview. MHSO; Wilfred Harding interview. MHSO.

41 "Good Program for Local Baseball Fans This Week," *Chatham Daily News*, July 31, 1933, 8; "Chatham Team Divides Double Header with Detroit," *Chatham Daily News*, August 2, 1934, Second Section, 5; "Stars Win Thrilling Game from Detroit," *Chatham Daily News*, September 4, 1934, 11. The Detroit team also came to Chatham for Emancipation Day in 1935. "Chatham Stars Lose First Game of Double Header," *Chatham Daily News*, August 1, 1935, First Section, 9.

42 For information on Lawrence Terrell's career, see Seamheads Negro League Database (https://www.seamheads.com/NegroLgs/player.php?playerID=terre01law). Another member of Taylor's Stars who played in Chatham (in 1935), Charles "Red" House, later played with the Detroit Stars (1937) as well as the Detroit Wolves. See Lester et al., *Black Baseball in Detroit*, 89.

43 Michigan, Wayne County, Marriage Licence, Lawrence Terrell and Edna Cummins, August 5, 1934. The two Terrells were not known to be related. Lawrence Terrell was born in Missouri. King Terrell's great-great-grandfather, Tolliver Terrell, was born in Virginia. See Province of Ontario, Death Record, Chatham City, Tolliver Terrell, April 12, 1899.

44 The rosters for Taylor's Detroit Stars were different in 1934 and 1935, suggesting the team was a loose collection of players. Three of the Taylor's team members from 1935 also played on another touring team, the Detroit Cubs. See Lester et al., *Black Baseball in Detroit*, 80. The players were William Love, William Friday, and either Barney or D. Jenkins.

45 Bill Reddick, "Out of the Bullpen," *Chatham Daily News*, October 4, 1984, 9.

46 Wilfred Harding, interviewed by Daniel Kelly. "Breaking the Colour Barrier."

47 "Chatham Team Divides Double Header with Detroit," *Chatham Daily News*, August 2, 1934, Second Section, 5.

48 Wilfred Harding interview. MHSO.

49 Wilfred Harding interview. MHSO.

50 "Kent Bridge and Stars to Replay Game," *Chatham Daily News*, June 5, 1934, 11. Kent Bridge was a small community outside Chatham that often had a team in the Chatham City Baseball League.

51 Wilfred Harding, interviewed by Daniel Kelly. "Breaking the Colour Barrier."

52 Ruck, *Sandlot Seasons*, 206.

53 Wilfred Harding, interviewed by Daniel Kelly. "Breaking the Colour Barrier."

54 Ferguson Jenkins Sr. interview. MHSO.

55 "Kent Bridge and Stars to Replay Game," *Chatham Daily News*, June 5, 1934, 11.

56 "Kent Bridge and Stars to Replay Game," *Chatham Daily News*, June 5, 1934, 11.

57 "Stars Defeat Kent Bridge in League Game," *Chatham Daily News*, June 16, 1934, Second Section, 7. They played again a week later, and the All-Stars won by a score of 11-5.
58 "Duns Hand Stars First Defeat of Present Campaign," *Chatham Daily News*, June 8, 1934, Second Section, 5.
59 Wilfred Harding, interviewed by Daniel Kelly. "Breaking the Colour Barrier." Kelly drew Harding's attention to that particular article, and Harding identified one of the people involved.
60 Nzindukiyimana and Wamsley, "'We Played Ball'," 1302.
61 Kingsley Terrell interview. MHSO.
62 Nell Irvin Painter, *The History of White People* (New York and London: W.W. Norton and Company, 2010).
63 Craig Heron, "Boys Will Be Boys," 11–12.
64 Morrow and Wamsley, *Sport in Canada*, 155–77.
65 Such was his stature that after Marsh died suddenly in 1936, an award for Canada's top athlete was created in his honour. After concerns were raised about the racism in his columns, in 2022, the award was renamed the Northern Star Award. See Janice Forsyth, "The Lou Marsh Trophy builds on a racist legacy, tainting the award's image," *The Conversation*, February 7, 2021. https://theconversation.com/the-lou-marsh-trophy-builds-on-a-racist-legacy-tainting-the-awards-meaning-154322.
66 For example, during the 1935 baseball season, Calder engaged in a mock "feud" with a sports editor and columnist, Chick Appel, who worked for the *Stratford Beacon-Herald*. See "Analyzing Sport" columns, August 14, 1935, Second Section, 1, and September 9, 1935, Second Section, 1.
67 For example, see Jack Calder, "Analyzing Sport," *Chatham Daily News*, May 25, 1934, Second Section, 7; Jack Calder, "Analyzing Sport," *Chatham Daily News*, August 2, 1934, Second Section, 5.
68 Jack Calder, "Analyzing Sport," *Chatham Daily News*, August 9, 1934, First Section, 5.
69 Jack Calder, "Analyzing Sport," *Chatham Daily News*, August 9, 1934, First Section, 5.
70 For example, see the Jack Calder, "Analyzing Sport" columns from 1934 in the *Chatham Daily News* for June 8, July 9, July 20, July 23, July 24, among others.
71 Jack Calder, "Analyzing Sport," *Chatham Daily News*, July 31, 1934, 11.
72 Jack Calder, "Analyzing Sport," *Chatham Daily News*, August 20, 1934, 8.
73 Jack Calder, "Analyzing Sport," *Chatham Daily News*, September 12, 1934, 11.
74 Jack Calder, "Analyzing Sport," *Chatham Daily News*, September 27, 1934, Second Section, 7.
75 Census of Canada, 1921, Ontario, District 93, Subdistrict 71, Chatham City. Jack Calder was born in Saskatchewan, but he moved to Chatham with his family before he was six years old, when the 1921 census was taken.
76 Jack Calder, "Analyzing Sport," *Chatham Daily News*, July 31, 1934, 11.
77 Jack Calder, "Analyzing Sport," *Chatham Daily News*, July 31, 1934, 11.
78 Jack Calder, "Analyzing Sport," *Chatham Daily News*, September 5, 1934, 11.
79 Jack Calder, "Analyzing Sport," *Chatham Daily News*, August 8, 1934, 11.

80 Jack Calder, "Analyzing Sport," *Chatham Daily News*, August 17, 1934, 11.
81 "Stars Begin O.B.A.A. Playdowns Thursday," *Chatham Daily News*, September 5, 1934, 11.
82 Jack Calder, "Analyzing Sport," *Chatham Daily News*, September 5, 1934, 11.
83 See especially Jack Calder, "Analyzing Sport," *Chatham Daily News*, October 15, 1934, 11.
84 Joseph, "An Intersectional Analysis," 258.
85 Jack Calder, "Analyzing Sport," *Chatham Daily News*, September 10, 1934, 8.
86 Jack Calder, "Analyzing Sport," *Chatham Daily News*, July 23, 1934, 11.
87 Jack Calder, "Chatham Stars Win First Game of Playdowns," *Chatham Daily News*, September 10, 1934, 8.
88 Jack Calder, "City Team Progresses in O.B.A.A. 11-7 Victory over Welland," *Chatham Daily News*, September 27, 1934, Second Section, 7.
89 Jack Calder, "Analyzing Sport," *Chatham Daily News*, July 20, 1934, 11. Calder used the term "fighting" a few times, in describing the Merchants' attempts to make the Essex County Baseball League playoffs, but he did not talk about the Merchants players' bodies the way he did the All-Stars.
90 For example, see "Stars Go to Island," *Border Cities Star*, July 19, 1935, Second Section, 5. This article described the Windsor Colored Stars as a "peppery and aggressive aggregation." Also see, "New Club for Border Loop," *Border Cities Star*, July 4, 1935, Second Section, 3, which said this of the Colored Stars: "like all colored nines, the Stars have plenty of pep."
91 Jack Calder, "Analyzing Sport," *Chatham Daily News*, September 12, 1934, 11. Specifically, Calder suggested it be set to Ferde Grofe's Grand Canyon Suite, which was composed in the early 1930s.
92 Wilfred Harding, interviewed by Daniel Kelly. "Breaking the Colour Barrier."
93 Jack Calder, "Analyzing Sport," *Chatham Daily News*, September 12, 1934, 11. Calder also talked about Parker in another column on September 10.
94 Bill Reddick, "From the Bullpen," *Chatham Daily News*, October 4, 1984, 9.
95 Leddy Library Archives and Special Collections, F1033 (Wilfred "Boomer" Harding Collection), Scrapbook 1.

Chapter 6: Becoming the All-Stars

1 See Walker, *Race on Trial*, 3; Brand, *No Burden to Carry*, 151, 153. This source features an oral history from June Robbins (sister of Chatham Coloured All-Stars players Hyle and Stanton) who identified several communities in Kent County where Black people were not welcome after sundown.
2 The RG Duns, for example, playing in the city league, were sponsored by a local cigar maker.
3 Wilfred Harding interview. MHSO.
4 Wilfred Harding, interviewed by Daniel Kelly. "Breaking the Colour Barrier."
5 Ernie Miller, "Boomer Harding—one great guy," *London Free Press*, September 7, 1978, B1 (Evening/regional edition).

6 Kingsley Terrell interview. MHSO.
7 "Stars Begin O.B.A.A. Playdowns Thursday," *Chatham Daily News*, September 5, 1934, 11. Although Sarnia is in Lambton County, they were playing in a Middlesex County league.
8 "Stars Win First Game of Playdowns," *Chatham Daily News*, September 10, 1934, 8.
9 "Chathamites Advance Through Default," *Chatham Daily News*, September 14, 1934, 11.
10 "Two Chatham Teams Defeated in Dual Playoffs," *Chatham Daily News*, September 21, 1934, 11.
11 "Welland Beaten in Playoffs," *Chatham Daily News*, September 24, 1934, 8. This article appeared to be from a wire service.
12 Ernie Miller, "Boomer Harding—one great guy," *London Free Press*, September 7, 1978, B1 (Evening/regional edition).
13 "Welland Beaten in Playoffs," *Chatham Daily News*, September 24, 1934, 8. The newspaper account of the game indicates that Terrell was the pitcher that day.
14 Ernie Miller, "Boomer Harding—one great guy," *London Free Press*, September 7, 1978, B1 (Evening/regional edition).
15 Kingsley Terrell interview. MHSO.
16 Ernie Miller, "Boomer Harding—one great guy," *London Free Press*, September 7, 1978, B1 (Evening/regional edition).
17 Bill Reddick, "From the Bullpen," *Chatham Daily News*, October 5, 1984, 9.
18 "At London," *Border Cities Star*, September 25, 1934, Second Section, 2.
19 "City Team Progresses in O.B.A.A.," *Chatham Daily News*, September 27, 1934, Second Section, 7.
20 Jack Calder, "Analyzing Sport," *Chatham Daily News*, September 27, 1934, Second Section, 7.
21 "Chatham Stars Will Go East," *Chatham Daily News*, October 1, 1934, 11.
22 Jack Calder, "Analyzing Sport," *Chatham Daily News*, September 27, 1934, Second Section, 7.
23 "Chatham Stars Will Go East," *Chatham Daily News*, October 1, 1934, 11.
24 "Stars Meet Milton in O.B.A.A. Playoffs Thursday," *Chatham Daily News*, October 2, 1934, 11.
25 "Penetang Wins," *Chatham Daily News*, October 9, 1934, 12. Penetanguishene was in the North Simcoe League, and Meaford was in the Grey County League.
26 "Stars Meet Milton in O.B.A.A. Playoffs Thursday," *Chatham Daily News*, October 2, 1934, 11.
27 "Chatham Stars Will Go East," *Chatham Daily News*, October 1, 1934, 11.
28 Wilfred Harding interview. MHSO; Ferguson Jenkins Sr. interview. MHSO. Kingsley Terrell interview. MHSO.
29 Wilfred Harding interviewed by Daniel Kelly. "Breaking the Colour Barrier."
30 Wilfred Harding interviewed by Daniel Kelly. "Breaking the Colour Barrier." The story about the coat also appeared in Ralph Heckler, "The Mighty Flattener," *Chatham Daily News*, May 7, 1954, 13.
31 Kingsley Terrell interview. MHSO.

32 "Chatham Stars Win First Game of O.B.A.A. Semi-Finals," *Chatham Daily News*, October 5, 1934, Second Section, 4.

33 "Stars Badly Beaten in Semi-Final Game," *Chatham Daily News*, October 9, 1934, 12.

34 Jack Calder, "Analyzing Sport," *Chatham Daily News*, October 15, 1934, 11.

35 The article on the Milton-Chatham game had been provided by a wire service, and Calder's column indicated he was in Chatham covering a rugby game the day the All-Stars were playing in Milton.

36 "Chatham Stars Enter O.B.A.A. Final," *Chatham Daily News*, October 12, 1934, 11.

37 Wilfred Harding interviewed by Daniel Kelly. "Breaking the Colour Barrier."

38 Wilfred Harding, interviewed by Daniel Kelly. "Breaking the Colour Barrier."

39 Although the *Chatham Daily News* referred to the team as the "Shipbuilders," the official name was Foundry Rangers.

40 "Chatham Stars Home, Ready for Thursday Game," *Chatham Daily News*, October 16, 1934, 11.

41 Ernie Miller, "Boomer Harding—one great guy," *London Free Press*, September 7, 1978, B1 (Evening/regional edition).

42 Kingsley Terrell interview. MHSO.

43 Bill Reddick, "From the Bullpen," October 4, 1984, 9; MHSO Kingsley Terrell.

44 Bill Reddick, "From the Bullpen," *Chatham Daily News*, October 4, 1984, 9.

45 Blake and Pat Harding interview, May 25, 2016. "Breaking the Colour Barrier."

46 Kingsley Terrell interview. MHSO.

47 Wilfred Harding interview. MHSO.

48 Bill Reddick, "From the Bullpen," *Chatham Daily News*, October 4, 1984, 9.

49 Kingsley Terrell interview. MHSO.

50 "Analyzing Sport," *Chatham Daily News*, October 13, 1934, Second Section, 5.

51 "Chatham Stars Beat Penetang in First O.B.A.A. Final," *Chatham Daily News*, October 16, 1934, 11.

52 For background on Marchildon's career, see Phil Marchildon and Brian Kendall, *Ace: Canada's Pitching Sensation and Wartime Hero* (Toronto: Viking Press, 1993).

53 Canadian Baseball Hall of Fame website. https://baseballhalloffame.ca/hall-of-famer/phil-marchildon/.

54 Marchildon and Kendall, *Ace*, 14.

55 "Penetang Evens Final Series with Stars," *Chatham Daily News*, October 19, 1934, 11.

56 Jack Calder, "Analyzing Sport," *Chatham Daily News*, October 19, 1934, 11.

57 "Dispute Delays Title Contest," *Border Cities Star*, October 19, 1934, Second Section, 4.

58 "Penetang Evens Final Series with Stars," *Chatham Daily News*, October 19, 1934, 11.

59 "Chatham Stars Ready for Big Game Monday," *Chatham Daily News*, October 20, 1934, Second Section, 5.

60 "Stars and Penetang Play to Eleven Inning 2-2 Tie," *Chatham Daily News*, October 23, 1934, Second Section, 5.

61 "Stars and Penetang Play to Eleven Inning 2-2 Tie," *Chatham Daily News*, October 23, 1934, Second Section, 5.

62 "Stars and Penetang Play to Eleven Inning 2-2 Tie," *Chatham Daily News,* October 23, 1934, Second Section, 5. The posted game time was 2:09. In "Chatham Stars Ready for Big Game Monday," *Chatham Daily News,* October 20, 1934, Second Section, 5, it said the third game of the series would start at 2:15 pm. If the game started on time, it would have been 4:30 pm when the game ended.

63 "Penetang, Chatham Tie," *Border Cities Star,* October 23, 1934, Second Section, 2.

64 Ernie Miller, "Boomer Harding—one great guy," *London Free Press*, September 7, 1978, B1 (Evening/regional edition).

65 Wilfred Harding, interviewed by Daniel Kelly. "Breaking the Colour Barrier."

66 Ernie Miller, "Boomer Harding—one great guy," *London Free Press*, September 7, 1978, B1 (Evening/regional edition).

67 Bill "Reddick, From the Bullpen," *Chatham Daily News,* October 5, 1984, 9.

68 Wilfred Harding interview. MHSO. Stirling would have been speaking to OBAA Secretary W.J. Snyder, who lived in Hamilton, not Toronto.

69 Kingsley Terrell interview. MHSO.

70 Metcalfe, "The Anatomy of Power," 57–60.

71 "Chatham 'Stars' Trounce Penetang in Final Game to Win Provincial Intermediate Baseball Championship," *Chatham Daily News*, October 24, 1934, Second Section, 5.

72 "Penetang Evens Final Series with Stars," *Chatham Daily News*, October 19, 1934, 11.

73 Bill Reddick, "From the Bullpen," *Chatham Daily News*, October 5, 1984, 9.

74 "Crowds Acclaim Victorious Chatham Team," *Chatham Daily News*, October 24, 1934, 1.

75 Kidd, *The Struggle for Canadian Sport*, 5; Russell Field, "'There's more people here tonight than at a first night of the Metropolitan': Professional Hockey Spectatorship in the 1920s and 1930s in New York and Toronto," in *Canada's Game: Hockey and Identity*, edited by Andrew Holman (Montreal and Kingston: McGill-Queen's University Press, 2009): 127–50.

76 Kingsley Terrell interview. MHSO.

77 Pauline Parker Miller interview. "Breaking the Colour Barrier."

78 John Olbey interview. "Breaking the Colour Barrier."

79 See Ethan Michaeli, *The Defender: How the Legendary Black Newspaper Changed America*. (Boston: Houghton-Mifflin Harcourt, 2016).

80 Dorothy L. Binga, "Chatham, Ont.," *Chicago Defender*, April 14, 1934, 23 and June 9, 1934, 30. Dorothy Binga's father, Bethune Binga Sr., was the son of Jesse C. Binga, founder of the first Black American-owned bank in the United States. See Don Hayner, *Binga: The Rise and Fall of Chicago's First Black Banker* (Evanston, Illinois: Northwestern University Press, 2019). Also, see Robinson and Robinson, *Seek the Truth*, 49–51 for a history of the Binga family in Chatham.

81 "Chatham, Ont.," *Chicago Defender*, November 3, 1934, 23. This article may have been written by Dorothy Binga's father, Bethune Binga Sr. A short note in this column indicated Dorothy Binga was ill and staying with friends in Toledo. Bethune Binga Sr. wrote the Chatham news columns for the *Chicago Defender* between 1935 and 1938.

82 For a discussion of white newspaper coverage of Black athletic achievements in the US, see Brian Carroll, "'Praising My People,'" 245–46.
83 John Olbey interview. "Breaking the Colour Barrier."
84 Pauline Williams and Cleata Morris interview. "Breaking the Colour Barrier."
85 Blake and Pat Harding interview, May 25, 2016. "Breaking the Colour Barrier."
86 Jack Calder, "Analyzing Sport," *Chatham Daily News*, October 24, 1934, Second Section, 5.
87 "Crowds Acclaim Victorious Chatham Team," *Chatham Daily News*, October 24, 1934, 1.
88 "Crowds Acclaim Victorious Chatham Team," *Chatham Daily News*, October 24, 1934, 1.
89 Wilfred Harding, interviewed by Daniel Kelly. "Breaking the Colour Barrier."
90 Mike Bennett, "All-Stars shine again," *London Free Press*, July 13, 2002, E1.
91 Wilfred Harding, interviewed by Daniel Kelly. "Breaking the Colour Barrier."
92 Wilfred Harding interview. MHSO.
93 Bill Reddick, "From the Bullpen," *Chatham Daily News*, October 5, 1984, 9.

Chapter 7: New Opportunities and Continued Racial Conflict in the 1935 Season

1 Art Cartier, "Sport Talk," *Chatham Daily News*, April 26, 1940, Second Section, 1. Cartier outlined the history of the WCBA, noting it was formed in 1931, but underwent a big expansion in 1935, more than doubling its affiliated clubs from twenty to forty-eight.
2 Jack Calder, "Analyzing Sport," *Chatham Daily News*, March 25, 1935, Second Section, 1.
3 Jack Calder, "Analyzing Sport," *Chatham Daily News*, April 18, 1935, Second Section, 1.
4 Jack Calder, "Analyzing Sport," *Chatham Daily News*, April 5, 1935, Second Section, 1.
5 Jack Calder, "Analyzing Sport," *Chatham Daily News*, March 25, 1935, Second Section, 1.
6 Jack Calder, "Analyzing Sport," *Chatham Daily News*, April 18, 1935, Second Section, 1.
7 Metcalfe, "Anatomy of Power," 57–60.
8 Wilfred Harding interview. MHSO; Ferguson Jenkins Sr. interview. MHSO; Kingsley Terrell interview. MHSO.
9 Kingsley Terrell interview. MHSO.
10 Wilfred Harding interview. MHSO; Wilfred Harding, interviewed by Daniel Kelly. "Breaking the Colour Barrier."
11 Wilfred Harding interview. MHSO.
12 Jack Calder, "Analyzing Sport," *Chatham Daily News*, April 18, 1935, Second Section, 1.
13 Canadian Baseball Hall of Fame and Museum, St. Mary's Ontario, "Ontario Baseball Amateur Association Constitution and By-Laws 1934," 50.

14 Jack Calder, "Analyzing Sport," *Chatham Daily News*, April 18, 1935, Second Section, 1.

15 Jack Calder, "Analyzing Sport," *Chatham Daily News*, April 18, 1935, Second Section, 1.

16 Jack Calder, "Analyzing Sport," *Chatham Daily News*, April 25, 1935, Second Section, 1.

17 "Stars Open Fire in League Finals," *Chatham Daily News*, August 27, 1935, Second Section, 1.

18 Pauline Williams and Cleata Morris interview. "Breaking the Colour Barrier;" Mark Malone, "Chatham Colored All-Stars honoured," *Chatham Daily News*, July 15, 2002, 1.

19 John Olbey interview. "Breaking the Colour Barrier."

20 Jenkins played a few games with the All-Stars in 1934, but did not play regularly until 1935.

21 Province of Ontario, Birth Record, Essex County, Ferguson Jenkins, August 25, 1909; Census of Canada, 1921, Ontario, District 77, Subdistrict 45, Windsor City; Ferguson Jenkins Sr. interview. MHSO.

22 "North Essex Baseball," *Amherstburg Echo*, August 18, 1933, 7.

23 Kingsley Terrell interview. MHSO.

24 "Stars Open Fire in League Finals," *Chatham Daily News*, August 27, 1935, Second Section, 1.

25 Jack Calder, "Analyzing Sport," *Chatham Daily News*, April 5, 1935, Second Section, 1. The *Chatham Daily News* usually spelled his name incorrectly, using "Shaugnosh" or some variation.

26 Jeffrey Powers-Beck, "Chief: The American Indian Integration of Baseball, 1897–1945," *American Indian Quarterly* 25, 4 (Fall 2001): 508–38. For another work on baseball and residential schools, see David J. Laliberte, "Natives, Neighbours, and the National Game: Baseball and the Pipestone Indian Training School," *Minnesota History*, 62, 2 (Summer 2010): 60–69.

27 Robert Kiyoshk, interviewed by Burton Jacobs and Gladys Tooshkenig, Walpole Island, April 1, 1979. Archives of Ontario, Tape #IH-oA.005.

28 Frances Miskokomon, interviewed by Gladys Tooshkenig and Burton Jacobs, December 7, 1978, Walpole Island. Archives of Ontario, Tape #IH-OA.006.

29 "Pay Tribute to the Work of Rev. C. Draper," *Chatham Daily News*, August 28, 1934, 12. Rev. Draper was an Anglican priest who organized baseball at the Walpole Island First Nation for many years, suggesting the role of the church in promoting the sport.

30 Frances Miskokomon interview. Archives of Ontario.

31 Census of Canada, 1921, Ontario, District 96, Subdistrict 45, Walpole Island. For background on Bkejwanong, see Dean M. Jacobs, "Bkejwanong, 'The place where the waters divide': A perspective on earth, water, air and fire," in *Earth, water, air and fire: Studies in Canadian Ethnohistory*, edited by David T. McNab (Waterloo: Wilfrid Laurier University Press, 1998), 9–19.

32 "Chatham Juniors Beat Walpole Lads in League Game," *Chatham Daily News*, June 13, 1932, 8. In 1932, Elijah Edward Pinnance was the president of the Walpole Island Juniors. He came with the team to Chatham for at least one game and took part in the opening ceremonies.

33 "Walpole Lads Defeated by Maple City Lads Saturday," *Chatham Daily News*, July 11, 1932, 8.

34 "Casual Comment on Current Sport," *Chatham Daily News*, July 20, 1932, 8.

35 "Walpole, Chatham Baseball Teams Meet Here Friday," *Chatham Daily News*, June 21, 1932, 8; "All Stars Win from Duns, 9-4," *Chatham Daily News*, July 14, 1933, 9.

36 "Walpole Island Team Drops Game to Chatham Stars," *Chatham Daily News*, June 1, 1934, 11; "Advertisement, Baseball Tournament at Kent Bridge," *Chatham Daily News*, August 13, 1934, 8; "Sport in Short," *Chatham Daily News*, August 15, 1934, 11; "Three Ball Games at Walpole Fair," *Chatham Daily News*, August 28, 1934, 12. The All-Stars also played against a team from the Delaware First Nation at Moraviantown (Eelünaapéewi Lahkéewiit). "Stars Beat Moraviantown," *Chatham Daily News*, August 29, 1934, 11.

37 Jack Calder, "Analyzing Sport," *Chatham Daily News*, April 5, 1935, Second Section, 1.

38 Jack Calder, "Analyzing Sport," *Chatham Daily News*, July 19, 1935, Second Section, 1.

39 Jack Calder, "Analyzing Sport," *Chatham Daily News*, August 29, 1935, Second Section, 1.

40 Jack Calder, "Analyzing Sport," *Chatham Daily News*, August 6, 1935, Second Section, 1.

41 For background on racist portrayals of Indigenous athletes in the media, see Janice Forsyth, *Reclaiming Tom Longboat*, 2-4: Bruce Kidd, "In Defence of Tom Longboat," *Sport in Society 16*, 4 (May 2013): 515–32; Jeffrey Powers-Beck, "Chief," 509–10.

42 "Walpole Seniors, Chatham Stars Play Here Thursday," *Chatham Daily News*, May 30, 1934, Second Section, 5.

43 Jack Calder, "Analyzing Sport," *Chatham Daily News*, July 19, 1935, Second Section, 1; "Colored All-Stars Eliminated from O.B.A.A. Race," *Chatham Daily News*, September 20, 1935, Second Section, 1; Jack Calder, "Analyzing Sport," *Chatham Daily News*, August 26, 1935, Second Section, 1.

44 Art Cartier, "Sport Talk," *Chatham Daily News*, August 10, 1937, Second Section, 1.

45 Shognosh played with the Chatham Coloured All-Stars in 1935, 1938, and 1939. In 1937, he played for the Walpole Island Intermediate B team which was playing in the Kent County Baseball League.

46 Ferguson Jenkins Sr. interview. MHSO.

47 Wilfred Harding interview. MHSO.

48 Wilfred Harding interview. MHSO; Kingsley Terrell interview. MHSO.

49 Bill Reddick, "From the Bullpen," *Chatham Daily News*, October 4, 1984, 9. Note: the racial slur was spelled out in full in the original text.

50 Ferguson Jenkins Sr. interview. MHSO.

51 Wilfred Harding, interviewed by Daniel Kelly. "Breaking the Colour Barrier."

52 "Baseball Crowd Sees Smart Game," *Strathroy Age Dispatch*, June 20, 1935 [page number missing].

53 Nzindukiyimana and Wamsley, "'We Played Ball,'" 1300–1.

54 Sheldon Gillis, "Putting It On Ice: A Social History of Hockey in the Maritimes, 1880–1914," MA thesis (Saint Mary's University, 1994), 77–78.

55 "Baseball Crowd See Smart Game," *Strathroy Age Dispatch*, June 20, 1935 [page number missing].

56 "Strathroy Loses Game at Chatham Park," *Strathroy Age Dispatch*, June 27, 1935 [page number missing].

57 Jack Calder, "Analyzing Sport," *Chatham Daily News*, June 22, 1935, Second Section, 1.

58 A colored fan, "Stars Are Sportsmen," letter to the editor, *Chatham Daily News*, June 26, 1935, 4. This is not the only example of readers challenging racist sports coverage. See William Humber, *Cheering for the Home Team: The Story of Baseball in Canada* (Erin, Ontario: Boston Mills Press, 1983), 105 for a discussion of an 1887 incident where a member of the Black community in Hamilton, Ontario asked the *Hamilton Spectator* for an apology over racist sports coverage.

59 I expect the letter was at least partially a collective effort, written with the team's input. Several people could have been involved, including Len Harding, who later became the All-Stars manager; he would speak out about unfair treatment the team received in 1939. Another possible author or co-author is the All-Stars' team Secretary and scorekeeper, Orville Wright, who was active in other Black-led community organizations in Chatham in the 1930s and later in the 1940s. Len and Wilfred Harding's sisters, Georgina and Beulah, although not living in Chatham at the time, may also have offered advice. Georgina was working as a legal secretary at a Black law firm in Detroit, and Beulah was a teacher; both were aware of civil rights issues. Another family associated with advocacy for Black people were the Bingas—Bethune Sr. and Dorothy, who were local correspondents for the *Chicago Defender*, one of the United States' most prominent Black-owned newspapers. Bethune Binga Sr. was the All-Stars' Secretary-Treasurer in 1936 and 1937 (see "Chatham Colored Baseballers Organize," *Chatham Daily News*, April 14, 1937). In 1940, he was manager for a Junior-age Black boys' baseball team.

60 A colored fan, "Stars Are Sportsmen," letter to the editor, *Chatham Daily News*, June 26, 1935, 4.

61 A colored fan, "Stars Are Sportsmen," letter to the editor, *Chatham Daily News*, June 26, 1935, 4.

62 A colored fan, "Stars Are Sportsmen," letter to the editor, *Chatham Daily News*, June 26, 1935, 4.

63 A colored fan, "Stars Are Sportsmen," letter to the editor, *Chatham Daily News*, June 26, 1935, 4.

64 Shaw, "'Most Anxious to Serve,'" 555. Also see 551–52; 554–61.

65 See Carla Marano, "'Rising Strongly and Rapidly': The United Negro Improvement Association in Canada, 1919-1940," *Canadian Historical Review* 91, 2 (June 2010): 233-59.

66 Thompson, "Cultivating Narratives of Race, Faith, and Community," 30 (citing the abstract).

67 "Chatham Notes," *Dawn of Tomorrow*, July 21, 1923, 4. The item included a short note: "Give her [Beulah Harding] your subscription for a Canadian enterprise fostered by colored people."

68 "Celebrate Ninety Second Anniversary of Freedom," *Chatham Daily News*, August 2, 1932, 1; "Emancipation Day Celebrated Here," *Chatham Daily News*, August 1, 1933, 1.

69 Irene Moore Davis, "The Central Citizens Association's Unique Approach to the Elimination of Racial Discrimination," address given to the Essex County Black Historical Research Society, Windsor, Ontario, March 21, 2019.

70 "London Beat Chatham "All Stars" in O.B.A.A. Game," *Chatham Daily News*, June 7, 1935, Second Section, 1. Chatham and London were tied for second place in the standings.

71 "Value of a Smile," *Chatham Daily News*, July 6, 1935, 4.

72 "Value of a Smile," *Chatham Daily News*, July 6, 1935, 4.

73 Ferguson Jenkins Sr. interview. MHSO.

74 Wilfred Harding, interviewed by Daniel Kelly. "Breaking the Colour Barrier."

75 Bill Reddick, "From the Bullpen," *Chatham Daily News*, October 4, 1984, 9.

76 Bill Reddick, "From the Bullpen," *Chatham Daily News*, October 4, 1984, 9.

77 Wilfred Harding interview. MHSO.

78 Ferguson Jenkins Sr. interview. MHSO.

79 For background on Black baseball players' experiences in Canada, see John Holway, *Black Diamonds: Life in the Negro League from the Men Who Lived It* (Wesport, CT: Meckler Books, 1989).

80 "Stars Hurler Gets Better with Every New Mound Job," *Chatham Daily News*, July 12, 1935, Second Section, 1.

81 Kingsley Terrell interview. MHSO; Bill Reddick, *Chatham Daily News*, "From the Bullpen," October 4, 1984, 9.

82 Jack Calder, "Analyzing Sport," *Chatham Daily News*, August 31, 1935, Second Section, 1.

83 "Stars Clash with Rivals From County," *Chatham Daily News*, August 3, 1935, Second Section, 1.

84 Jack Calder, "Analyzing Sport," *Chatham Daily News*, August 26, 1935, Second Section, 1.

85 "Chatham Colored All-Stars Gain Final Round of Western Counties League," *Chatham Daily News*, August 26, 1935, Second Section, 1.

86 Jack Calder, "Analyzing Sport," *Chatham Daily News*, August 26, 1935, Second Section, 1. Also, Calder described him as a "brainy right-hander" in Jack Calder, "Analyzing Sport," *Chatham Daily News*, August 31, 1935, Second Section, 1.

87 "Chatham Eliminates Wallaceburg in Intercounty Playoffs," *Windsor Daily Star*, August 26, 1935, Second Section, 4.

88 "Chatham Stars Tie Wallaceburg Series," *Chatham Daily News*, August 23, 1935, Second Section, 1; "Chatham Colored All-Stars Gain Final Round of Western Counties League," *Chatham Daily News*, August 26, 1935, Second Section, 1.

89 "Chatham Colored All-Stars Gain Final Round of Western Counties League," *Chatham Daily News*, August 26, 1935, Second Section, 1.

90 Jack Calder, "Chase Bats and Hurls Stars to Playoff Win," *Chatham Daily News*, August 29, 1935, Second Section, 1.

91 Jack Calder, "Analyzing Sport," *Chatham Daily News*, August 29, 1935, Second Section, 1.

92 Jack Calder, "Chase Bats and Hurls Stars to Playoff Win," *Chatham Daily News*, August 29, 1935, Second Section, 1.

93 "Second Western Counties League Championship Won by Chatham as Stars Whip Strathroy in Two Games," *Chatham Daily News*, September 3, 1935, Second Section, 1.

94 Fidler had played minor league professional baseball for several years in the United States before returning to his hometown of Strathroy. See "Art Fidler," *Baseball Reference* https://www.baseball-reference.com/register/player.fcgi?id=fidler003---.

95 "Stars, Playing As in 1934, Lose First Game to Sandwich," *Chatham Daily News*, September 13, 1935, Second Section, 1. Calder's "Analyzing Sport" column for the same date, September 13, 1935, Second Section, 1-2, suggests he had seen the game, so he likely wrote the article on the game with Sandwich as well.

96 "Stars, Playing As in 1934, Lose First Game to Sandwich," *Chatham Daily News*, September 13, 1935, Second Section, 1.

97 Art Cartier, "Sport Talk," *Chatham Daily News*, September 5, 1939, Second Section, 1.

98 Jack Calder, "Analyzing Sport," *Chatham Daily News*, September 13, 1935, Second Section, 1-2; "Stars, Playing As in 1934, Lose First Game to Sandwich" *Chatham Daily News*, September 13, 1935, Second Section, 1; Jack Calder, "Still Errorful, Stars Lose Tilt," *Chatham Daily News*, September 16, 1935, Second Section, 1; "Colored All-Stars Eliminated from O.B.A.A. Race," *Chatham Daily News*, September 20, 1935, Second Section, 1.

99 Jack Calder, "Still Errorful, Stars Lose Tilt," *Chatham Daily News*, September 16, 1935, Second Section, 1.

100 "Colored All-Stars Eliminated from O.B.A.A. Run," *Chatham Daily News*, September 20, 1935, Second Section, 1.

101 Ferguson Jenkins Sr. interview. MHSO.

102 Jack Calder, "Analyzing Sport," *Chatham Daily News*, September 16, 1935, Second Section, 1–2; Jack Calder, "Analyzing Sport," *Chatham Daily News*, September 18, 1935, Second Section, 1.

103 Kingsley Terrell interview. MHSO.

104 Wilfred Harding interview. MHSO.

105 Jack Calder, "Analyzing Sport," *Chatham Daily News*, September 16, 1935, Second Section, 1–2.

106 Jack Calder, "Analyzing Sport," *Chatham Daily News*, September 18, 1935, Second Section, 1–2.

107 Howell, *Blood, Sweat, and Cheers*, 51–82.

Chapter 8: "All we ask is a fair break"

1 Art Cartier, "Sport Talk," *Chatham Daily News*, September 5, 1939, Second Section, 1 provides an overview of the All-Stars' post-1934 history.

2 "Chatham Colored Baseballers Organize," *Chatham Daily News*, April 14, 1937, Second Section 1.

3 Art Cartier, "Analyzing Sport," *Chatham Daily News*, April 24, 1937, Second Section, 1.

4 Art Cartier, "Sport Talk," *Chatham Daily News*, September 5, 1939, Second Section, 1.

5 Art Cartier, "Sport Talk," *Chatham Daily News*, June 12, 1939, Second Section, 1.

6 "Amateur Baseball," *Chatham Daily News*, June 19, 1939, Second Section, 1. London, Sarnia, Strathroy, and Petrolia were playing in the Michigan-Ontario league with several teams from Michigan, including two from Port Huron.

7 "City Baseball Loop Meeting Friday Night," *Chatham Daily News*, May 2, 1939, 8.

8 "Steel Upset All-Stars in Industrial Ball Thriller," *Chatham Daily News*, May 22, 1939, Second Section, 1.

9 Art Cartier, "Analyzing Sport," *Chatham Daily News*, May 4, 1937, Second Section, 1.

10 "Defeat Blenheim in 13 Thrilling Frames; Chase Cracks Homer," *Chatham Daily News*, August 13, 1937, Second Section, 1.

11 "Andrew Harding Captures Senior Boys' Championship," *Chatham Daily News*, June 11, 1935, Second Section, 1.

12 Blake and Pat Harding, June 22, 2016, "Breaking the Colour Barrier."

13 "C.Y.O. Trim Kinsmen," *Chatham Daily News*, June 27, 1939, Second Section, 1. Of the boys playing on the two youth teams, perhaps one may have been Black (surname Browning—there were several Browning brothers who played baseball in this period).

14 Art Cartier, "Sport Talk," *Chatham Daily News*, June 12, 1939, Second Section, 1.

15 "Colored Lads Celebrate on Big Holiday," *Chatham Daily News*, August 2, 1939, Second Section, 1. Gerald Browning had also been playing with the All-Stars since 1937. Bill Henson, who later played for Taylor AC, was the great-grandson of Josiah Henson, noted abolitionist from the area.

16 Art Cartier, "Sport Talk," *Chatham Daily News*, July 14, 1939, Second Section, 1.

17 Art Cartier, "Sport Talk," *Chatham Daily News*, June 19, 1939, Second Section, 1.

18 Wilfred Harding, interviewed by Daniel Kelly. "Breaking the Colour Barrier."

19 Wilfred Harding interview. MHSO.

20 "Wanless Trophy Series to Get Underway Saturday," *Chatham Daily News*, August 24, 1933, 13. Scott signed on to play with the Stars for the league championship series.

21 Wilfred Harding interview. MHSO; Ferguson Jenkins Sr., interview, MHSO.

22 Wilfred Harding, interviewed by Daniel Kelly. "Breaking the Colour Barrier."

23 Ferguson Jenkins Sr. interview. MHSO.

24 "Chatham Colored Baseballers Organize," *Chatham Daily News*, April 14, 1937, Second Section, 1.

25 "Managers Discuss Wild Ball Game," *Chatham Daily News*, August 8, Second Section, 1. Ross Talbot was absent from the All-Stars' lineup in mid-summer, so he may have been away or unable to play.

26 Kingsley Terrell interview. MHSO; Wilfred Harding interview. MHSO.

27 Wilfred Harding interview. MHSO.

28 Pauline Parker Miller interview. "Breaking the Colour Barrier."

29 Wilfred Harding interview. MHSO.

30 "Jack Calder Joins R.C.A.F.," *Chatham Daily News*, May 8, 1940, Second Section, 1. Calder started reporting with the Canadian Press in 1937. As this article notes, he joined the Royal Canadian Air Force in 1940. Calder, who served as a navigator, died in 1944 when his plane was shot down over Germany. For an account of his time with the air force, see Ralph Keefer, *Grounded in Eire: The Story of Two RAF Fliers Interned in Ireland During World War II* (Montreal and Kingston: McGill-Queen's University Press, 2001).

31 Census of Canada, 1921, Ontario, District 93, subdistrict 71, Chatham City.

32 Mike Bennett, "All-Stars shine again," *London Free Press*, July 13, 2002, E1.

33 "Stars Shatter Losing Streak with 9-4 Win," *Chatham Daily News*, July 4, 1939, Second Section, 1.

34 "Stars Battle Kent Bridge," *Chatham Daily News*, July 11, 1939, Second Section, 1.

35 "Large Crowd Expected at Athletic Park," *Chatham Daily News*, July 1, 1939, Second Section, 1.

36 "Industrial Batting Averages," *Chatham Daily News*, June 27, 1939, Second Section, 1.

37 "Stars Shatter Losing Streak with 9-4 Win," *Chatham Daily News*, July 4, 1939, Second Section, 1.

38 "Industrial Race Close in Stretch," *Chatham Daily News*, July 21, 1939, Second Section, 1.

39 "Ontario Steel and Stars Win Games in Industrial Loop," *Chatham Daily News*, August 8, 1939, Second Section, 2.

40 "Managers Discuss Wild Ball Game," *Chatham Daily News*, August 8, 1939, Second Section, 1.

41 "Ontario Steel and Stars Win Games in Industrial Loop," *Chatham Daily News*, August 8, 1939, Second Section, 2. The newspaper article on the game did not mention any Kent Bridge players getting hit during the ninth inning, but it mentioned a player getting his glasses broken in the eighth inning after the ball bounced off his bat and hit him in the face.

42 Wilfred Harding, interviewed by Daniel Kelly. "Breaking the Colour Barrier."

43 "Industrial League Officials Hold Session," *Chatham Daily News*, August 9, 1939, Second Section, 1. There was another incident during the playoffs where a fight

broke out after opposing team members directed verbal abuse at All-Stars players. See "The Chatham All-Stars Eliminate Leamington," *Chatham Daily News*, September 15, 1939, Second Section, 1.

44 "Steel, Stars Ball Winners in Industrial," *Chatham Daily News*, August 14, 1939, Second Section, 1.

45 "Withdrawal By All-Stars," *Chatham Daily News*, August 16, 1939, Second Section, 1.

46 Len Harding, "Colored All-Stars Outline Stand in Open Letter" (letter to the Sports Editor), *Chatham Daily News*, August 18, 1939, Second Section, 2.

47 "Industrial League Teams Will Play," *Chatham Daily News*, August 11, 1939, Second Section, 1. The paper did give the incorrect time for the All-Stars/Libbys game, announcing it would start later in the afternoon, not 1:45.

48 Ruck, *Sandlot Seasons*, 209.

49 "Colored Folk Hold Holiday," *Chatham Daily News*, August 2, 1939, 2.

50 "Colored Folk Hold Holiday," *Chatham Daily News*, August 2, 1939, 2. Stewart had been the business manager of the Black newspaper, *The Dawn of Tomorrow*. See "Dawn of Tomorrow," (publisher information) *Dawn of Tomorrow*, March 25, 1932, 2.

51 "Colored Folk Hold Holiday," *Chatham Daily News*, August 2, 1939, 2. For background on First Baptist Institutional Church in Hamtramck, see https://www.fbicdetroit.org/history. Biographical details on Wright: Michigan, US, Death Records, 1867–1952, Rev. Benjamin H. Wright, August 4, 1945.

52 Beulah Cuzzens, interview, September 23, 1980. MHSO.

53 The African Methodist Episcopalian Church is an American-based, predominantly Black protestant church founded in the late eighteenth century, with congregations throughout North America.

54 Beulah Cuzzens interview, September 23, 1980. MHSO.

55 Blake and Pat Harding interview, May 25, 2016. "Breaking the Colour Barrier."

56 Beulah Cuzzens, interview, September 23, 1980s. MHSO. At the firm where Georgina Harding reportedly worked, one of the partners, Charles A. Roxborough III, was elected to the Michigan State Senate in 1930, making him the first Black man elected to that body. Another partner, Charles W. Jones, later became the first Black judge in Michigan. Charles Roxborough's brother, John, was the long-time promoter and manager of boxer Joe Louis. Beulah Harding married Earle Cuzzens who was a business associate of John Roxborough.

57 "Tilbury-All Stars Play Here Tomorrow," *Chatham Daily News*, August 29, 1939, Second Section, 1.

58 "Chatham All-Stars are Kent Intermediate A Champs," *Chatham Daily News*, September 5, 1939, Second Section, 1.

59 "The Chatham All-Stars Meet Leamington Here," *Chatham Daily News*, September 13, 1939, Second Section, 1.

60 "The Chatham All-Stars Eliminate Leamington," *Chatham Daily News*, September 15, 1939, Second Section, 1; "Stars Shunt LaSalle in Intermediate Race," *Chatham Daily News*, September 22, 1939, Second Section, 1.

61 Art Cartier, "Sport Talk," *Chatham Daily News*, September 18, 1939, Second Section, 1.

62 "Chatham Stars-Aylmer Open O.B.A. Semi-Finals Here," *Chatham Daily News*, September 26, 1939, Second Section, 1.

63 "Chatham All-Stars Rally to Upset Aylmer Champions," *Chatham Daily News*, September 28, 1939, Section Section, 3.

64 "Last Year's Champions Bow on Home Diamond," *Chatham Daily News*, October 5, 1939, Second Section, 1.

65 Art Cartier, "Sport Talk," *Chatham Daily News*, October 9, 1939, Second Section, 1.

66 Art Cartier, "Sport Talk," *Chatham Daily News*, October 5, 1939, Second Section, 1.

67 "Chatham-Meaford Game Rained Out," *Chatham Daily News*, October 10, 1939, Second Section, 1.

68 Art Cartier, "Sport Talk," *Chatham Daily News*, October 12, 1939, Second Section, 1.

69 Ferguson Jenkins Sr. interview. MHSO.

70 Art Cartier, "Sport Talk," *Chatham Daily News*, October 12, 1939, Second Section, 1.

71 "Stars Trim Meaford in First of Finals," *Chatham Daily News*, October 13, 1939, Second Section, 1.

72 Art Cartier, "Elmer Goldsmith Hot on Mound for Meaford," *Chatham Daily News*, October 19, 1939, Second Section, 1.

73 Art Cartier, "Elmer Goldsmith Hot on Mound for Meaford," *Chatham Daily News*, October 19, 1939, Second Section, 1.

74 "Meafords Knot Up Chatham," *London Free Press*, October 19, 1939, 18. This article also ran in the *Windsor Daily Star* on the same date.

75 "Meafords Knot Up Chatham," *London Free Press*, October 19, 1939, 18.

76 "The Chatham All-Stars May Refuse to Play Deciding O.B.A. Final," *Chatham Daily News*, Oct 20, 1939, Second Section, 1. Teams did not get full compensation if games were rained out, as travel money often came from the admission fees collected from spectators.

77 Art Cartier, "Elmer Goldsmith Hot on Mound for Meaford," *Chatham Daily News*, October 19, 1939, Second Section, 1.

78 "Meaford-Chatham O.B.A. Final Opener Here Thursday," *Chatham Daily News*, October 11, 1939, Second Section, 1.

79 "All Stars Confident of Winning the Title," *Chatham Daily News*, October 11, 1939, Section Section, 1.

80 Art Cartier, "Stars Trim Meaford in First of Finals," *Chatham Daily News*, October 13, 1939, Second Section, 1.

81 Art Cartier, "Sport Talk," *Chatham Daily News*, October 13, 1939, Section Section, 1.

82 Art Cartier, "Sport Talk," *Chatham Daily News*, October 21, 1939, Second Section, 1.

83 Art Cartier, "Sport Talk," *Chatham Daily News*, October 19, 1939, Second Section, 1.

84 Art Cartier, "Sport Talk," *Chatham Daily News*, October 26, 1939, Second Section, 4.

85 "The Chatham All-Stars May Refuse to Play Deciding O.B.A. Final," *Chatham Daily News*, October 20, 1939, Second Section, 1; Art Cartier, "Sport Talk," *Chatham Daily News*, October 26, 1939, Second Section, 4.

86 Art Cartier, "Sport Talk," *Chatham Daily News*, October 21, 1939, Second Section, 1.

87 Census of Canada, 1911, Ontario, District 60, Subdistrict 53, Chesley Town; Bruce County Museum and Cultural Centre, Southampton, Ontario. Photograph collection, "Christmas 1902, Illustrated Number of the *Chesley Enterprise,*" Item # A958.034.001.

88 Art Cartier, "Sport Talk," *Chatham Daily News*, October 26, 1939, Second Section, 4.

89 "The Chatham All-Stars May Refuse to Play Deciding O.B.A. Final," *Chatham Daily News*, October 20, 1939, Second Section, 1; "Chatham All Stars Decide Against Going to Hanover," *Chatham Daily News*, October 21, 1939, Second Section, 1.

90 Wilfred Harding interview. MHSO.

91 Wilfred Harding, interviewed by Daniel Kelly. "Breaking the Colour Barrier."

92 A. Roustabouter, "Roustabouts," *Chatham Daily News*, October 26, 1939. Second Section, 4.

93 Dominion Elector's Act, List of Electors, 1935, Grey-Bruce, Polling Division 3, Town of Chesley; Dominion Elector's Act, 1938, Rural List of Electors, Grey Bruce, Polling Division 36, Chesley 3. According to the electoral lists, McDonald had been a "publisher," in 1935, suggesting he may have taken over the *Chesley Enterprise* from his father. By 1938, however, his occupation was listed as "agent."

94 Art Cartier, "Sport Talk," *Chatham Daily News*, October 26, 1939, Second Section, 4; also "Knight Discusses Family History," *Meaford Express*, September 26, 2012 https://www.simcoe.com/news-story/2071496-knight-discusses-family-history/.

95 "The Chatham All-Stars May Refuse to Play Deciding O.B.A. Final," *Chatham Daily News*, October 20, 1939, Second Section, 1.

96 "The Chatham All-Stars May Refuse to Play Deciding O.B.A. Final," *Chatham Daily News*, October 20, 1939, Second Section, 1.

97 "The Chatham All-Stars May Refuse to Play Deciding O.B.A. Final," *Chatham Daily News*, October 20, 1939, Section Section, 1.

98 "Chatham All Stars Decide Against Going to Hanover," *Chatham Daily News*, October 21, 1939, Second Section, 1.

99 "Chatham All Stars Decide Against Going to Hanover," *Chatham Daily News*, October 21, 1939, Second Section, 1.

100 Ruck, *Sandlot Seasons*, 3.

101 Art Cartier, "Sport Talk," *Chatham Daily News*, October 23, 1939, Second Section, 1.

102 "Meaford is Awarded O.B.A. Intermediate 'A' Title," *Owen Sound Daily Sun Times*, October 25, 1939, 10. The story was relayed to the Chatham audiences through Art Cartier, "Sport Talk," *Chatham Daily News*, October 26, 1939, Second Section, 4; A. Roustabouter, "Roustabouts," *Chatham Daily News*, October 26, 1939, Second Section, 4. Roustabouter noted that the *Owen Sound Daily Sun Times* article had been picked up by the Canadian Press.

103 Cited in "Sport Talk," *Chatham Daily News*, October 26, 1939, Second Section, 4.

104 Art Cartier, "Sport Talk," *Chatham Daily News*, October 26, 1939, Second Section, 4; A. Roustabouter, "Roustabouts," *Chatham Daily News*, October 26 1939, Second Section, 4.

105 Art Cartier, "Sport Talk," *Chatham Daily News*, October 26, 1939, Second Section, 4; A. Roustabouter, "Roustabouts," *Chatham Daily News*, October 26 1939, Second Section, 4.

106 Art Cartier, "Sport Talk," *Chatham Daily News*, October 27, 1939, Second Section, 1.

107 Cited in Art Cartier, "Sport Talk," *Chatham Daily News*, October 24, 1939, Second Section, 1.

108 Dick Payne, "Casual Comment on Sport," *Owen Sound Daily Sun Times*, October 26, 1939, 12. Also cited in Art Cartier, "Sport Talk," *Chatham Daily News*, October 27, 1939, Second Section, 1.

109 Red Taylor, "Sport Spice," *Woodstock Sentinel-Review*, October 31, 1939, 6.

110 "Chatham Nine Refuse to Play," *London Free Press*, October 21, 1939, 20.

111 Cited in Art Cartier, "Sport Talk," *Chatham Daily News*, October 24, 1939, Second Section, 1.

112 Art Cartier, "Sport Talk," *Chatham Daily News*, October 28, 1939, Second Section, 1.

113 "May Form New Baseball Group," *London Free Press*, October 26, 1939, 23; "Chatham Would Start New O.B.A.," *Brantford Expositor*, October 26, 1939, 12; "Another Threat to O.B.A.," *Windsor Daily Star*, October 26, 1939, Second Section, 2.

114 Reported in Art Cartier, "Sport Talk," *Chatham Daily News*, October 31, 1939, Second Section, 1.

115 Art Cartier, "Sport Talk," *Chatham Daily News*, October 31, 1939, Second Section, 1.

116 This includes sportswriters publishing in newspapers from Owen Sound, St. Thomas, Woodstock, London, Windsor, and Peterborough.

117 Art Cartier, "Sport Talk," *Chatham Daily News*, October 31, 1939, Second Section, 1.

118 Kidd, *The Struggle for Canadian Sport*, 11; Metcalfe, "The Anatomy of Power," 47.

119 Metcalfe, "The Anatomy of Power," 56–60.

120 Art Cartier, "Sport Talk," *Chatham Daily News*, October 28, 1939, Second Section, 1. Cartier had excerpted a column from Cec Perdue, of the *Peterborough Examiner*. Perdue claimed that the Peterborough team protested the OBA's playoff plan that would have had them playing against far distant regional winners, but not the Toronto winners, which were much closer to Peterborough. According to Perdue, the Peterborough team refused to attend a series against the Northern Ontario district winners because they could not afford it and felt it was "an injustice." After "harsh words were bandied about," the OBA relented and allowed them to compete in the finals.

121 For example, see "May Form New Baseball Group," *London Free Press*, October 26, 1939, 23; A. Roustabouter, "Roustabouts," *Chatham Daily News*, October 28, 1939, Second Section, 1; "Council Flays O.B.A. League," *Woodstock Sentinel-Review*, October 31, 1939, 6.

122 Art Cartier, "Sport Talk," *Chatham Daily News*, October 31, 1939, Second Section, 1.

123 Art Cartier, "Sport Talk," *Chatham Daily News*, November 2, 1939, Second Section, 2.

124 Art Cartier, "Sport Talk," *Chatham Daily News*, November 2, 1939, Second Section, 2.

125 "Meaford Knights Refuse to Play Chatham All-Stars," *Chatham Daily News*, November 3, 1939, Second Section, 1. The article indicated the phone call took place at the *Chatham Daily News* office, with Stirling, Harding, and Cartier present.

126 Art Cartier, "Sport Talk," *Chatham Daily News*, October 27, 1939, Second Section, 1.

127 "O.B.A. Supports Chatham Claim at Committee Meeting," *Chatham Daily News*, November 6, 1939, Second Section, 1; Art Cartier, "Sport Talk," *Chatham Daily News*, November 6, 1939, Second Section, 1.

128 "Chatham Nine Gets Civic Sympathy," *London Free Press*, October 27, 1939, 21; "Council Flays O.B.A. League," *Woodstock Sentinel-Review*, October 31, 1939, 6.

129 A. Roustabouter, "Roustabouts," *Chatham Daily News*, October 26, 1939, Second Section, 4. Also see Roustabouter's column on October 28, 1939, Second Section, 1.

130 Art Cartier, "Sport Talk," *Chatham Daily News*, October 12, 1940, Second Section, 1.

131 Wilfred Harding interview. MHSO.

132 Art Cartier, "Lenny Harding Laid to Rest," *Windsor Daily Star*, February 25, 1942 [page number unknown]. This article was saved in the Milburn family scrapbook, which Frances Dungey, daughter of Ken and Wanda Milburn, shared with us. While the date is correct (it appeared on the clipping itself), the article is not in the microfilmed version of the *Windsor Daily Star* for that date. Just one edition (the final edition) was microfilmed, and this article likely appeared in an earlier edition.

Chapter 9: After the All-Stars

1 Brand, "'We weren't allowed to go into factory work,'" 78–79.

2 For background on Burnett and the NUA, see Ross Lambertson, *Repression and Resistance: Canadian Human Rights Activists, 1930-1960* (Toronto: University of Toronto Press, 2005), 299-317. Also, see Buxton National Historic Site, National Unity Association files, 2000.6.181.

3 Gouy Ladd's father, Frederick, and Alvin's father, Edward, were brothers. See Census of Canada, 1901, Ontario, District 76, Subdistrict C, Polling Subdistrict 7, Dover Township for information on Frederick and Edward's family. Information about Edward's children can be found in Census of Canada, 1921, Ontario, District 93, Subdistrict 18, Dover Township.

4 "Chatham Stars Make Home Debut Thursday," *Chatham Daily News*, June 5, 1940, Second Section, 1; "Box Scores," *Chatham Daily News*, August 2, 1940, Second Section, 2.

5 Census of Canada, 1921, Ontario, District 93, Subdistrict 80, Chatham City.

6 See "Juniors Win at Kent Bridge," *Chatham Daily News*, May 16, 1925, 5; "Locals Best Blenheim's Jr Baseball Nine," *Chatham Daily News*, May 21, 1926, 9.

7 "Stars and Duns Winners of Holiday Baseball Games," *Chatham Daily News*, May 25, 1933, 13.

8 Art Cartier, "Sport Talk," *Chatham Daily News*, June 15, 1939, Second Section, 2. Both Wilfred and Leo Belanger were pitching for the Steels in the Chatham Industrial League that year.

9 Art Cartier, "Sport Talk," *Chatham Daily News*, August 20, 1940, Second Section, 1.

10 "Briscos Beat the Stirlings," *Chatham Daily News*, June 14, 1926, 13.

11 Art Cartier, "Sport Talk," *Chatham Daily News*, May 29, 1940, Second Section, 1.

12 Art Cartier, "Sport Talk," *Chatham Daily News*, August 12, 1940, Second Section, 1.

13 "Belanger Pitches One-Hitter," *Chatham Daily News*, August 9, 1940, Second Section, 1.

14 Art Cartier, "Sport Talk," *Chatham Daily News*, August 12, 1940, Second Section, 1.

15 Art Cartier, "Sport Talk," October 10, 1940, Second Section, 1.

16 "No Baseball in Chatham on Saturday," *Chatham Daily News*, September 27, 1940, Second Section, 1.

17 "Stars Default Senior Final to C.Y.O. Team," *Chatham Daily News*, October 12, 1940, Second Section, 1.

18 "Stars Default Senior Final to C.Y.O. Team," *Chatham Daily News*, October 12, 1940, Second Section, 1.

19 "Meeting Will Be Held in Wallaceburg," *Chatham Daily News*, May 11, 1941, Second Section, 1.

20 "Chatham Teams Defeated in Season's Openers," *Chatham Daily News*, May 26, 1941, Second Section, 1.

21 Earl Chase Jr. interview. "Breaking the Colour Barrier."

22 "Chatham Defeats London 9-1 to Annex Senior 'A' Title," *Chatham Daily News*, September 14, 1942, Second Section, 1.

23 A.E. Vanhorne, "To the Sherman [*sic*] Baseball Team," published in Charles Carney, "Sports Review," *Chatham Daily News*, September 15, 1942, Second Section, 1.

24 "Srigley Shines Again but Pettiford Stopped," *Windsor Daily Star*, August 15, 1938, Second Section, 2. Morgan's name is in the roster. After the war, Morgan returned to Windsor where he worked for the city (see Dominion Elections Act, Electoral District of Essex West, City of Windsor, 1949). He also continued to be active in sports, particularly softball, as a member of the Dayus Roofers and Cock Brothers softball teams.

25 Information about the McCurdy family can be found in the Provincial Archives of Ontario, Alvin McCurdy Collection. For a digital exhibit, see http://www.archives.gov.on.ca/en/explore/online/alvin_mccurdy/index.aspx. After the war, George McCurdy became involved in union leadership and later served as the director of the Nova Scotia Human Rights Commission.

26 Doug Scurr, "Sports Review," *Chatham Daily News*, September 9, 1943, Second Section, 2.

27 "Soldiers Lose Wild Game, 9-4," *Chatham Daily News*, July 16, 1943, Second Section 3.

28 "B.T.C. Take Exhibition Game Before Large Crowd," *Chatham Daily News*, July 27, 1943, Second Section, 2.

29 Doug Scurr. "Sports Review," *Chatham Daily News,* September 9, 1943, Second Section, 2.

30 "No. 12 Basic Training Centre Takes Kent Baseball Title," *Chatham Daily News*, September 10, 1943, Second Section, 2.

31 "Leamington's Bill Wagner Hurls Chatham Army to Western Counties Throne," *Windsor Daily Star*, October 12, 1943, Second Section, 2.

32 "Arcades Whip Toronto Baers and Take Intermediate Title," *Chatham Daily News*, October 10, 1944, 7. The WCBA had returned to the OBA in 1944, making the Chatham team eligible to compete at the provincial level.

33 Team picture, London Majors, *London Free Press*, August 12, 1944, 12. Harry Coursey, of the Chatham Colored Giants, had played on this same team, when it was called the Braves, in 1926.

34 "London, Kingston Meet for Title Here Tonight," *London Free Press*, August 12, 1944, 12. For background on the Kingston Ponies, see http://www.kingstonponies baseball.com/teams/default.asp?u=DGARRISON&s=baseball&p=about.

35 "Intermediate 'A' O.B.A. Champions," *Chatham Daily News*, October 27, 1947, 8.

36 Matt Dennis, "Sports Review," *Chatham Daily News*, October 24, 1947, 12. Two other Black men, Peter Browning and Charles Gibson, also played on the Legion soccer team. All three men—Harding, Browning, and Gibson, also played with the Taylor AC baseball team, which will be discussed later in this chapter.

37 "Chatham Hadleys Capture Intermediate 'A' O.B.A. Crown," *Chatham Daily News*, October 18, 1948, 10. Although the team name was different (different sponsor), many of the players from the 1948 Chatham Hadleys played on the 1947 Chatham Shermans. Throughout the 1940s, two white men, Lew Sadlier and Joe Cohen, were the managers and assistant managers for Chatham's Intermediate A teams.

38 Frances Dungey personal collection, 1948 Chatham Maple Leafs team photo.

39 Horace Chase interview. "Breaking the Colour Barrier."

40 "Art Sellers' Four-Hit Game a Shade 'Too Hot' for Libbys," *Chatham Daily News*, May 22, 1946, Second Section, 2; Matt Dennis, "Sports Review," *Chatham Daily News*, Sept 20, 1946, 10. Besides Boomer Harding, Andy Harding, as well as several players with the Taylor AC baseball team, were also playing softball, including Peter Browning, Charles Gibson, Chuck Cooper, and Ken Milburn.

41 Matt Dennis, "Sports Review—'Flat' Chase," *Chatham Daily News*, October 30, 1947, 16.

42 Brand, "'We weren't allowed to go into factory work,'" 178–79.

43 Blake and Pat Harding interview, May 25, 2016. "Breaking the Colour Barrier."

44 Tracey Harding, interviewed by Salma Abumueeiz, by telephone, August 15, 2016, "Breaking the Colour Barrier: Wilfred 'Boomer' Harding and the Chatham Coloured All-Stars" website. http://cdigs.uwindsor.ca/cdigs-ohms-ccas/viewer.php?cachefile=00016.xml.

45 Horace Chase interview. "Breaking the Colour Barrier."

46 Ken Milburn interview. MHSO.

47 Nzindukiyimana and Wamsley, "'We Played Ball,'" 1290.

48 "Tilbury Wins Over Chatham Junior Nine," *Chatham Daily News*, June 8, 1940, Second Section, 2.

49 Doug Scurr, "Chatham Colored Stars Return Under New Name," *Chatham Daily News*, June 12, 1946 [no page number available].

50 Poole, "Conspicuous Peripheries," 248; Robinson and Robinson, *Seek the Truth*, 92–98; 124–25.

51 Jean Simmons, interviewed by Marsaydees Ferrell, Chatham, Ontario, August 10, 2018. "Telling the Stories of Race and Sport in Canada" website. http://cdigs.uwindsor.ca/omeka-s/s/rsc/page/interview-with-jean-simmons.

52 Rosetta Alliet, interviewed by Marsaydees Ferrell, Chatham, Ontario, August 10, 2018. "Telling the Stories of Race and Sport in Canada" website. http://cdigs.uwindsor.ca/omeka-s/s/rsc/page/interview-with-rosetta-rosie-alliet.

53 Ken Milburn interview. MHSO.

54 Robinson and Robinson, *Seek the Truth*, 124–25.

55 See biographies of two Black men and professional hockey: Herbert Carnegie with Robert Payne, *A Fly in a Pail of Milk: The Herb Carnegie Story* (Oakville, Mosaic Press, 1997); Willie O'Ree with Michael McKinley, *Willie: The Game-Changing Story of the NHL's First Black Player* (Toronto: Viking Canada, 2020).

56 Blake and Pat Harding interview, May 25, 2016. "Breaking the Colour Barrier."

57 Blake and Pat Harding interview, June 22, 2016. "Breaking the Colour Barrier."

58 "Chatham man recognized for 55 years of athletic achievement and ability," *Mainly for Seniors, Kent*, February 26, 1988, 3.

59 "Army Takes First Game," *Windsor Daily Star*, March 3, 1943, Second Section, 2.

60 "Chatham man recognized for 55 years of athletic achievement and ability," *Mainly for Seniors, Kent*, February 26, 1988, 3.

61 Michael J. Rodden, "Sports Highways," *Kingston Whig-Standard*, November 23, 1944, 8.

62 "Sharpshooter Calles Leads Vimy to Victory Over Headquarters," *Kingston Whig-Standard*, January 9, 1945, 8.

63 "Barriefield's Flashy Forwards Pile Up Season's Record Score," *Kingston Whig-Standard*, November 28, 1944, 8. This is a write-up on two games—the game featuring the Barriefield Bears mentions team members Adam Brown (ex and future Detroit Red Wings), and Edgar Laprade (future New York Rangers), and Cliff Simpson (played briefly for Detroit Red Wings and spent most of his career in the minor leagues). Boomer Harding scored the winning goal in this game.

64 Harding spent the 1946-7 season playing for the Windsor Staffords, a farm team for the Detroit Red Wings which played in the International Hockey League. His signing with the team attracted the attention of the American Black press, including the *Michigan Chronicle* and the *Pittsburgh Courier*. See Will Robinson, "Boomer Harding Signed by Crack Ice Sextet," *The Pittsburgh Courier*, November 16, 1946 [page number not available, but the original clipping is in Leddy Library Special Collections and Archives, F1033 (Wilfred "Boomer" Harding Collection), Scrapbook 2]. Will Robinson, the author of the piece, was a Detroit coach and scout who later became the first Black basketball head coach in the NCAA. Another clipping saved in the Harding scrapbook is Bill Matney, "'Boomer' Harding Makes History at Olympia," *Michigan Chronicle*, November 16, 1946, 16. Matney later became the first Black correspondent for NBC news.

65 Leddy Library Special Collections and Archives, F1033 (Wilfred "Boomer" Harding Collection), Scrapbook 2, "Ice Hockey Match, December 14, 1945 at the Ice Rink, Paisley" (event program listing the names of the players on the hockey teams).

66 Leddy Library Special Collections and Archives, F1033 (Wilfred "Boomer" Harding Collection), Scrapbook 2, Wilfred Harding to Beulah Cuzzens, December 15, 1945.

67 Doug Scurr, "Chatham Colored Stars Return Under New Name," *Chatham Daily News*, June 12, 1946 [page number not available].

68 "Taylor A.C. Opens Season at Dresden," *Chatham Daily News*, May 16, 1946, Second Section, 2.

69 Doug Scurr, "Chatham Colored Stars Return Under New Name," *Chatham Daily News*, June 12, 1946 [page number not available].

70 "Tilbury Wins over Chatham Junior Nine," *Chatham Daily News*, June 8, 1940, Second Section, 2. An article about an organizational meeting for Junior teams in the region suggests that Bethune Binga Sr. was the manager for the Red Sox in 1940. See "Ten Teams in Ball Loop," *Chatham Daily News*, May 11, 1940, Second Section, 1.

71 Morley Reekie, "Sports Review - Harding's Nine," *Chatham Daily News*, May 18, 1946, Second Section, 2.

72 "Tilbury Wins over Chatham Junior Nine," *Chatham Daily News*, June 8, 1940, Second Section, 2.

73 Ken Milburn interview. MHSO.

74 Doug Scurr, "Chatham Colored Stars Return Under New Name," *Chatham Daily News*, June 12, 1946 [page number not available].

75 John Olbey interview. "Breaking the Colour Barrier."

76 "Tilbury Wins over Chatham Junior Nine," *Chatham Daily News*, June 8, 1940, Second Section, 2. Abie Scott and Ken Milburn were on the roster.

77 Ellwood Shreve, "Time heals, but also steals, memories from Chatham Second World War vet" *Chatham Daily News*, November 9, 2020. https://www.chathamdailynews.ca/news/local-news/time-heals-but-also-steals-memories-from-chatham-second-world-war-vet. Olbey was also featured in a 2021 documentary, directed and written by Adrian Callendar, "Black Liberators WWII."

78 He would have been entitled to free educational training through the Department of Veterans' Affairs. See Jack Granatstein and Peter Neary, eds. *The Veterans' Charter and Post-Word War II Canada* (Montreal and Kingston: McGill-Queen's University Press, 1998).

79 "Taylor A.C. Opens Season at Dresden," *Chatham Daily News*, May 16, 1946, Second Section, 2.

80 Doug Scurr, "Chatham Colored Stars Return Under New Name," *Chatham Daily News*, June 12, 1946 [page number not available].

81 Joseph, "An Intersectional Analysis," 258.

82 "Taylors Share Kent Loop Lead with Chatham Seniors," *Chatham Daily News*, July 9, 1946, Second Section, 2.

83 "Seniors Blank Taylors to Even Intermediate A Series," *Chatham Daily News*, September 13, 1946, Second Section, 2.

84 "Taylor A.C. Opens Season at Dresden," *Chatham Daily News*, May 16, 1946, Second Section, 2.

85 Morley Reekie, "Sports Review," *Chatham Daily News*, July 15, 1946, Second Section, 2.
86 "All Stars on Short End of 4-0 Tilt," *Chatham Daily News*, August 23, 1946, Second Section, 7.
87 Morley Reekie, "Sports Review," *Chatham Daily News*, August 12, 1946, Second Section, 2.
88 Wilfred Harding, interviewed by Daniel Kelly. "Breaking the Colour Barrier."
89 Morley Reekie, "Sports Review," *Chatham Daily News*, August 12, 1946, Second Section, 2.
90 "Boomer Tries Hurling Role and Sets His Club on Top," *Chatham Daily News*, July 17, 1946, Second Section, 2.
91 "Taylors Aim to Hold Lead in Kent Loop," *Chatham Daily News*, July 18, 1946, Second Section, 2.
92 "Taylor A.C. Whips Seniors in Abbreviated Game, 13-8," *Chatham Daily News*, September 16, 1946, Second Section, 2.
93 "Manager Lew Sadlier Centre of Taylor A.C. Protest," September 18, 1946, 10. The Taylor AC protested because the manager of the Chatham Seniors, Lew Sadlier, played for the Seniors (in street clothes) when the Seniors were short one player for the semi-final game against the Taylor AC. The Taylor AC claimed Sadlier should not have played, as he was not a signed member of the team. The Seniors defeated the Taylor AC in that game.
94 "Panthers Oust Ridgetown in WCBA 'C' Playoffs," *Chatham Daily News*, August 13, 1951, 12. A Black team called the Montreal Panthers played in the Quebec Provincial League in the 1930s. It is not known if the Ontario team was aware of this earlier team when they named themselves "Panthers."
95 Besides being a referee for soccer, over the years he was also a hockey referee and a baseball umpire. See "Chatham man recognized for 55 years of athletic achievement and ability," *Mostly for Seniors, Kent*, February 26, 1988, 3.
96 Blake and Pat Harding interview, May 25, 2016. "Breaking the Colour Barrier."
97 Bruce Huff, "Panthers left mark on Chatham," *London Free Press*, July 25, 1999, C7.
98 "Panthers After Second WCBA Championship," *Chatham Daily News*, September 16, 1958, 10.
99 Dorothy Wright Wallace, interviewed by Heidi Jacobs, November 18, 2016, Chatham, Ontario. "Breaking the Colour Barrier: Wilfred 'Boomer' Harding and the Chatham Coloured All-Stars" website. https://cdigs.uwindsor.ca/cdigs-ohms-ccas/viewer.php?cachefile=00005.xml.
100 Bruce Huff, "Panthers left mark on Chatham," *London Free Press*, July 25, 1999, C7.
101 "Chatham Panthers Trip Wheatley 6-3 in WCBA," *Chatham Daily News*, August 17, 1951, 10.
102 "Panthers After Second WCBA Championship" (team photo), *Chatham Daily News*, Sept 16, 1958, 10.
103 Foster also played softball with the Dayus Roofers/Cock Brothers in Windsor in this period.

104 "Panthers Host Strathroy; Minors Tackle Riverside," *Chatham Daily News*, August 2, 1958, 12.

105 Bruce Huff, "Panthers left mark on Chatham," *London Free Press*, July 25, 1999, C7. Bruce Huff became a sportswriter and editor, working for the *Toronto Sun* and the *London Free Press*, among others.

106 "Provost Pitches to Western Counties Title," *Chatham Daily News*, September 9, 1957, 10; "Panthers Slated to Meet Owen Sound in OBA Set," *Chatham Daily News*, September 10, 1957, 11.

107 Earl Chase Jr. interview. "Breaking the Colour Barrier."

108 Technically, the Panthers were a Senior team, but were given permission to play Intermediate Ball by the OBA.

109 "Chatham Panthers Trip Wheatley 6-3 in WCBA," *Chatham Daily News*, August 17, 1951, 10; "Panthers Lose to Corunna," *Chatham Daily News*, September 6, 1951, 17.

110 "Provost Pitches to Western Counties Title," *Chatham Daily News*, September 9, 1957, 10; "Sport in Short," *Chatham Daily News*, October 7, 1957, 18; Ernie Miller, "Stumping Around," *Chatham Daily News*, October 16, 1957, 14.

111 "Panthers Trip Sarnia, Host Giants Saturday," *Chatham Daily News*, Aug 27, 1958, 12.

112 Bruce Huff, "Panthers left mark on Chatham," *London Free Press*, July 25, 1999, C7.

113 Blake and Pat Harding interview, May 25, 2016. "Breaking the Colour Barrier."

114 Blake and Pat Harding interview, May 25, 2016. "Breaking the Colour Barrier."

115 Blake and Pat Harding interview, June 22, 2016. "Breaking the Colour Barrier."

116 Dorothy Wright Wallace interview. "Breaking the Colour Barrier."

117 See Martin Summers, *Manliness and its Discontents*.

118 Edward Wright interview. "Telling the Stories of Race and Sports in Canada" website.

119 Joseph, "An Intersectional Analysis," 258.

120 Edward Wright interview. "Telling the Stories of Race and Sports in Canada" website.

121 See "Shermans Defeat Batawa 6–1 in Opening Playoff Final," *Chatham Daily News*, October 20, 1947, 14; "Bob Grant Hurls 3-Hit Ball, Williams, Mahon, Scott Star in Well-Played WCBA Tilt," *Chatham Daily News*, August 20, 1947, 12.

122 Matt Dennis, "Sports Review," *Chatham Daily News*, July 31, 1948, 11; "Abie Scott Clouts Homer for Brantford," *Chatham Daily News*, September 9, 1949, 16.

123 Edward Wright interview. "Telling the Stories of Race and Sports in Canada" website.

124 Wright attended Boston University on a hockey scholarship, and he had a forty-plus year career in coaching at the State University of New York at Buffalo, where he became the first Black head coach in NCAA hockey. See his entry at the Chatham Sports Hall of Fame: www.chathamsportshalloffame.com/athlete-legend-new/wright%2C-ed-. Also, see Gwendolyn Robinson, *The Greater Journey* (Chatham: 2016), 249–67 on Wright's sports and coaching career, and Ian Kennedy, *On Account of Darkness*, 145–56.

125 Edward Wright interview. "Telling the Stories of Race and Sports in Canada" website.

126 Horace Chase interview. "Breaking the Colour Barrier."

127 Earl Chase Jr. interview. "Breaking the Colour Barrier."

128 Horace Chase interview. "Breaking the Colour Barrier."

129 Dorothy Wright Wallace interview. "Breaking the Colour Barrier."

130 Rosetta Alliet interview. "Telling the Stories of Race and Sport in Canada" website.
131 Howell, *Northern Sandlots*, 180.
132 Rosetta Alliet interview. "Telling the Stories of Race and Sport in Canada" website.
133 Edward Wright interview. "Telling the Stories of Race and Sports in Canada" website.
134 Jean Simmons interview. "Telling the Stories of Race and Sport in Canada" website.
135 "Golden memories for boys of '51," *Chatham Daily News*, October 10, 2001, 11.
136 Edward Wright interview. "Telling the Stories of Race and Sports in Canada" website.

Chapter 10: Conclusion

1 Chafe, Gavins, and Korstad, eds., *Remembering Jim Crow*, xxxi.
2 See Fergie Jenkins with Lew Freedman, *Fergie: My Life from the Cubs to Cooperstown* (Chicago: Triumph Books, 2009).
3 See Mike Bennett, "'70 Kent Concretes…team of a lifetime," *Chatham Daily News*, October 31, 1980, 8. Bennett had been a bat boy with the Kent Concretes, managed by Gouy Ladd, which won the 1970 OBA Senior A championship. Bennett spoke strongly about Ladd's leadership, saying "When things were too serious, Gouy was there to shed some light. When someone was in the dumps and needed a lift, they went to Gouy. When the team was falling apart, players at each other's throats, Gouy was their island in a stormy sea."
4 Earl Chase, Jr. interview. "Breaking the Colour Barrier."
5 Dorothy Wright Wallace interview. "Breaking the Colour Barrier."
6 Douglas Talbot interview. "Breaking the Colour Barrier."
7 Ferguson Jenkins Sr. interview. MHSO.
8 Ferguson Jenkins, Jr., interviewed by Heidi Jacobs, Windsor, Ontario, October 1, 2016, "Breaking the Colour Barrier: Wilfred 'Boomer' Harding and the Chatham Coloured All-Stars" website, https://cdigs.uwindsor.ca/cdigs-ohms-ccas/viewer.php?cachefile=00012.xml.
9 Pauline Williams and Cleata Morris interview. "Breaking the Colour Barrier."
10 John Olbey interview. "Breaking the Colour Barrier."
11 US Department of Veterans' Affairs BIRLS Death File, 1850-2010. Washington enlisted in 1942 and was discharged in September, 1945; 1950 Federal US Census, Michigan, Wayne County, Detroit, 85-592.
12 Wilfred Harding interview. MHSO.
13 Donald Tabron Jr. interview. "Breaking the Colour Barrier."
14 US World War II Draft Card, Serial No. 891, Order No. 1988, Hyle Robbins.
15 Pauline Williams and Cleata Morris interview. "Breaking the Colour Barrier."
16 "'Glad he had his day,'" *Chatham Daily News*, December 12, 2002, 11.
17 Pauline Williams and Cleata Morris interview. "Breaking the Colour Barrier."
18 "Earl Chase," *Chatham Daily News*, May 11, 1954, 3.
19 Bruce Huff, "Sport Slant," *Chatham Daily News*, May 8, 1954, 14.
20 Kingsley Terrell interview. MHSO.
21 "Chatham's first champs played the game for fun," *London Free Press* [likely October 20, 1967].

22 Ernie Miller "Boomer Harding—one great guy," *London Free Press*, September 7, 1978, E1 (Evening/regional edition).
23 "Chatham's first champs played the game for fun," *London Free Press* [likely October 20, 1967].
24 Ernie Miller, "Boomer Harding—one great guy," *London Free Press*, September 7, 1978, B1 (Evening/regional edition).
25 Dave Feschuk, "Those All-Stars seasons," *National Post*, July 13, 2002, S3.
26 Kingsley Terrell interview. MHSO.
27 "Chatham's first champs played the game for fun," *London Free Press*, October 20, 1967 [likely October 20, 1967].
28 Chafe et. al., *Remembering Jim Crow*, xxx.
29 Wilfred Harding interview. MHSO.
30 Kingsley Terrell interview. MHSO.
31 Blake and Pat Harding interview, May 25, 2016. "Breaking the Colour Barrier."
32 Douglas Talbot interview. "Breaking the Colour Barrier."
33 Donald Tabron Jr. interview. "Breaking the Colour Barrier."
34 Kingsley Terrell interview. MHSO.
35 Kingsley Terrell interview. MHSO.
36 "Chatham's first champs played the game for fun," *London Free Press* [likely October 20, 1967].
37 "650 Cheer Fergie in Grand Ovation," *Chatham Daily News*, October 21, 1967, 10.
38 Leddy Library Archives and Special Collections, F1033 (Wilfred "Boomer" Harding Collection), Scrapbook 1, Art Cartier to Mayor M.N. Archibald (Chatham), August 15, 1984. In this letter, Art Cartier suggested to the Chatham Mayor that the city consider holding a special event to commemorate the fiftieth anniversary of the Chatham Coloured All-Stars' 1934 championship. Cartier, who had moved to London years earlier to work for the *London Free Press*, was a member of the City of London's Board of Control. Cartier had sent a copy of his letter to Archibald to Boomer Harding, with a short note letting him know he had contacted the mayor.
39 Mike Bennett, "Sweet memories for '34 All-Star," *Chatham Daily News*, July 16, 2001, 9.
40 Donald Tabron Jr. interview. "Breaking the Colour Barrier."
41 Bill Reddick, "'34 champs denied opportunity in pro ball," *Chatham Daily News*, October 10, 1934, 9; Bill Reddick, "From the Bullpen," *Chatham Daily News*, October 4, 1984, 9; Bill Reddick, "From the Bullpen," *Chatham Daily News*, October 5, 1984, 9.
42 Mark Malone, "Chatham Colored All-Stars honoured," *Chatham Daily News*, July 15, 2002, 1.
43 Mark Malone, "Star treatment," *Chatham Daily News*, July 15, 2002, 9.
44 "'Glad he had his day,'" *Chatham Daily News*, December 12, 2002, 11.
45 Tom Hawthorne, "Ringer from Detroit was the last of the Chatham Colored All-Stars," *Globe and Mail*, February 2, 2009, S8.
46 Kingsley Terrell interview. MHSO.

SELECTED BIBLIOGRAPHY

PRIMARY SOURCES

Newspapers

Border Cities Star/Windsor Daily Star
Chatham Daily News
Chatham Daily Planet
Dawn of Tomorrow, The
London Free Press

Oral History Collections

"Breaking the Colour Barrier: Wilfred 'Boomer' Harding and the Chatham Coloured All-Stars" Oral History Collection (digital collection). http://cdigs.uwindsor.ca/BreakingColourBarrier/exhibits/show/oral-history/oral-histories.

Multicultural History Society of Ontario, Oral Testimonies, African-Canadian Collection.

"Telling the Stories of Race and Sport in Canada: A Symposium" Oral History Collection (digital collection). http://cdigs.uwindsor.ca/omeka-s/s/rsc/page/oral-histories.

Archival Sources/Online Sources

Ancestry.ca – Various digitized resources (online), including Province of Ontario birth, marriage, and death records; city directories. https://www.ancestry.ca/search/collections/catalog/?limitToCountry=1.

Government of Canada. Library and Archives Canada. Census of Canada, census returns, 1891, 1901, 1911, 1921 (online). https://www.bac-lac.gc.ca/eng/census/Pages/census.aspx.

University of Windsor, Leddy Library Archives and Special Collections, F1003 (Wilfred "Boomer" Harding Collection), Scrapbooks 1, 2, 3.

Secondary Sources

Abdel-Shehid, Gamal. *Who Da Man? Black Masculinities and Sporting Cultures.* Toronto: Canadian Scholars' Press Inc., 2005.

Adams, Carly. "'I Just Felt Like I Belonged to Them,': Women's Industrial Softball, London, Ontario, 1923–1935." *International Journal of the History of Sport* 38, 1 (September 2011): 75–94.

Adams, Carly, ed. *Sport and Recreation in Canadian History.* Champagne, Illinois: Human Kinetics, 2021.

Adams, Tracey. "Making a Living: African Canadian Workers in London, Ontario, 1861-1901." *Labour/Le Travail* 67 (Spring 2011): 9–43.

Backhouse, Constance. *Colour Coded: A Legal History of Racism in Canada 1900–1950.* Toronto: University of Toronto Press, 1999.

Bleske, Glen, and Chris Lamb. "Covering the Integration of Baseball – A Look Back." *Editor and Publisher* 130 (January 27, 1996): 48–50.

Brand, Dionne. *No Burden to Carry: Narratives of Black Working Women in Ontario 1920s to 1950s.* Toronto: Women's Press, 1991,

Brand, Dionne. "'We weren't allowed to go into factory work until Hitler started the war': The 1920s to the 1940s." In *'We're Rooted Here and They Can't Pull Us Up': Essays in African Canadian Women's History,* edited by Peggy Bristow, Dionne Brand, Linda Carty, Afua P. Cooper, Sylvia Hamilton, and Adrienne Shadd, 171–92. Toronto: University of Toronto Press, 1994.

Bristow, Peggy. "'Whatever you raise in the ground you can sell it in Chatham': Black Women in Buxton and Chatham, 1850-65." In *'We're Rooted Here and They Can't Pull Us Up': Essays in African Canadian Women's History,* edited by Peggy Bristow, Dionne Brand, Linda Carty, Afua P. Cooper, Sylvia Hamilton, and Adrienne Shadd, 69–142. Toronto: University of Toronto Press, 1994.

Brown, Vanessa. *The Grand Old Lady: A History of Hotel London.* London: London and Middlesex Historical Society, 2015.

Carnegie, Herbert with Robert Payne. *A Fly in a Pail of Milk: The Herb Carnegie Story.* Oakville: Mosaic Press, 1997.

Carroll, Brian. "'Praising My People': Newspaper Sports Coverage of the Integration of Baseball in Wichita, Kansas." *Kansas: A Journal of the Central Plains* 33 (Winter 2010–2011): 245-55.

Chafe, William H., Raymond Gavins, and Robert Korsted, eds. *Remembering Jim Crow: African Americans Tell About Life in the Segregated South.* New York: The New Press, 2001.

Early, Gerald L. *A Level Playing Field: African American Athletes and the Republic of Sports.* Cambridge, Massachusetts: Harvard University Press, 2011.

Ferrell, Marsaydees. "Interracial Marriage in North America: A Case Study of Interracial Relationships in Chatham Ontario, 1901-1921." MA Major Paper, University of Windsor, 2021.

Field, Russell. "'There's more people here tonight than at a first night of the Metropolitan': Professional Hockey Spectatorship in the 1920s and 1930s in

New York and Toronto." In *Canada's Game: Hockey and Identity,* edited by Andrew Holman, 127-50. Montreal and Kingston: McGill-Queen's Press, 2009.

Forsyth, Janice, "Bodies of Memory: Sports and Games at Canada's Residential Schools." In *Aboriginal Peoples and Sport in Canada: Historical Foundations and Contemporary Issues,* edited by Audrey R. Giles and Janice Forsyth, 15–34. Vancouver: University of British Columbia Press, 2013.

Forsyth, Janice. *Reclaiming Tom Longboat: Indigenous Self-Determination in Canadian Sport.* Regina: University of Regina Press, 2020.

Gilroy, Paul. *The Black Atlantic: Modernity and Double Consciousness.* Boston: Harvard University Press, 1993.

Henry, Natasha. *Emancipation Day: Celebrating Freedom in Canada.* Toronto: National Heritage Books, 2010.

Henry, Natasha. "Where Oh Where, Is Bet? Locating Enslaved Black Women on the Ontario Landscape." In *Unsettling the Great White North: Black Canadian History,* edited by Funké Aladejebi and Michele Johnson, 85-112. Toronto: University of Toronto Press, 2022.

Hodgkin, Katherine, and Susannah Radstone. "Introduction: Contested Pasts." In *Contested Pasts: The Politics of Memory,* edited by Katharine Hodgkin and Susannah Radstone, 1–21. London and New York: Routledge, 2003.

Howell, Colin D. *Blood, Sweat, and Cheers: Sport and the Making of Modern Canada.* Toronto: University of Toronto Press, 2001.

Howell, Colin D. *Northern Sandlots: A Social History of Maritime Baseball.* Toronto: University of Toronto Press, 1995.

Humber, William. *Cheering for the Home Team: The Story of Baseball in Canada.* Erin, Ontario: The Boston Mills Press, 1983.

Humber, William. *Diamonds of the North: A Concise History of Baseball in* Canada. Toronto: Oxford University Press, 1995.

Jacobs, Dean M. "Bkejwanong, 'The place where the waters divide': A perspective on earth, water, air and fire." In *Earth, water, air and fire: Studies in Canadian Ethnohistory,* edited by David T. McNab, 9–19. Waterloo: Wilfrid Laurier University Press, 1998.

Jacobs, Heidi L.M. "Invisible in Plain View: Libraries, Archives, Digitization, Memory, and the 1934 Chatham Coloured All-Stars." In *Archives and Special Collections as Sites of Contestation,* edited by Mary Kandiuk, 223–48. Sacramento, CA: Library Juice Press, 2020.

Jacobs, Heidi L.M. *1934: The Chatham Coloured All-Stars' Barrier-Breaking Year.* Windsor, Ontario: Biblioasis, 2023.

Jenkins Jr., Ferguson, with Lew Freedman. *Fergie: My Life from the Cubs to Cooperstown.* Chicago: Triumph Books, 2009.

Joseph, Janelle. "An Intersectional Analysis of Black Sporting Masculinities." In *Race and Sport in Canada: Intersecting Inequalities,* edited by Simon C. Darnell, Yuka Nakamura, and Janelle Joseph, 237–63. Toronto: Canadian Scholars' Press, 2012.

Joseph, Janelle. *Sport in the Black Atlantic: Cricket, Canada, and the Caribbean Diaspora.* Manchester: Manchester University Press, 2017.

Kennedy, Ian. *On Account of Darkness: Shining Light on Race and Sport*. New Westminster, BC: Tidewater Press, 2022.

Kidd, Bruce. "In Defence of Tom Longboat." *Sport in Society* 16, 4 (May 2013): 515–32.

Kidd, Bruce. *The Struggle for Canadian Sport*. Toronto: University of Toronto Press, 1996.

Koprince, Susan. "Baseball as History and Myth in August Wilson's 'Fences.'" *African American Review* 40, 2 (Summer 2006): 349–58.

Laliberte, David J. "Natives, Neighbours, and the National Game: Baseball and the Pipestone Indian Training School." *Minnesota History* 62, 2 (Summer 2010): 60–69.

Lambertson, Ross. *Repression and Resistance: Canadian Human Rights Activists, 1930-1960*. Toronto: University of Toronto Press, 2005.

Lanctot, Neil. *Negro League Baseball: The Rise and Ruin of a Black Institution*. Philadelphia: University of Pennsylvania Press, 2004.

Lester, Larry, Sammy J. Miller, and Dick Clark. *Black Baseball in Detroit*. Charleston, SC: Arcadia Publishing, 2000.

Lorenz, Stacy L. "'A Lively Interest on the Prairies': Western Canada, the Mass Media, and a 'World of Sport' 1870–1939." *Journal of Sport History* 27, 2 (Summer 2000): 195–227.

Lorenz, Stacy L. and Jay Scherer, "The Sports-Media Complex and Canadian Culture." In *Sport and Recreation in Canadian History*, edited by Carly Adams, 247–73. Champaign, Illinois: Human Kinetics, 2021.

Marchildon, Phil, and Brian Kendall. *Ace: Canada's Pitching Sensation and Wartime Hero*. Toronto: Viking Press, 1993.

Metcalfe, Alan. "The Anatomy of Power in Amateur Sport in Ontario, 1918–1936." *Canadian Journal of the History of Sport* 22, 2 (December 1991): 47–67.

Metcalfe, Alan. *Canada Learns to Play: The Emergence of Organized Sport, 1807–1914*. Toronto: McClelland and Stewart, 1987.

Michaeli, Ethan. *The Defender: How the Legendary Black Newspaper Changed America*. Boston: Houghton-Mifflin Harcourt, 2016.

Middleton, Joyce Shadd, Bryan Prince, and Karen Shadd-Evelyn. *Something to Hope for: The Story of the Fugitive Slave Settlement, Buxton, Canada West*. Chatham: Buxton National Historic Site and Museum, 1999.

Miller, Patrick B. "Muscular Assimilationism: Sport and the Paradoxes of Racial Reform." In *Race and Sport: The Struggle for Equality On and Off the Field*, edited by Scott Brooks, Charles Kenyatta Ross, and Porter L. Fortune, 146–82. Jackson, Mississippi: The University Press of Mississippi, 2004.

Morrow, Don, and Kevin Wamsley. *Sport in Canada: A History, 3rd Ed.* Don Mills, Ontario: Oxford University Press, 2013.

Mosher, Clayton James. *Discrimination and Denial: Systemic Racism in Ontario's Legal and Criminal Justice Systems, 1892–1961*. Toronto: University of Toronto Press, 1998.

Nzindukiyimana, Ornella. "'That's Jean Lowe': On Being a Black Canadian Track Athlete in 1940s Toronto." *The International Journal of the History of Sport* 37, 14 (2020): 1371–83.

Nzindukiyimana, Ornella, and Kevin Wamsley. "'We Played Ball Just The Same': Selected Recollections of Black Women's Sport Experiences in Southern Ontario (1920–1940s)." *International Journal of the History of Sport* 36, 13–14 (September 2019): 1289–310.

O'Ree, Willie, with Michael McKinley. *Willie: The Game-Changing Story of the NHL's First Black Player.* Toronto: Viking Canada, 2020.

Osmon, Fred. *The History of Baseball in Chatham 'N Kent: Over 100 Years.* Chatham, Ontario: 2015.

Painter, Nell Irvin. *The History of White People.* New York and London: W. W. Norton and Company, 2010.

Paraschak, Victoria. "Aboriginal Peoples and the Construction of Canadian Sport Policy." In *Aboriginal Peoples and Sport in Canada: Historical Foundations and Contemporary Issues,* edited by Janice Forsyth and Audrey R. Giles, 95–123. Vancouver: University of British Columbia Press, 2013.

Poole, Carmen. "Conspicuous Peripheries: Black Identity, Memory, and Community in Chatham, Ontario, 1860–1980." PhD diss., University of Toronto, 2015.

Powers-Beck, Jeffrey. "Chief: The American Indian Integration of Baseball, 1897–1945." *American Indian Quarterly* 25, 4 (Fall 2001): 508–38.

Ramkhalawansingh, Ceta. "Women During the Great War." In *Women at Work: Ontario, 1850–1930,* edited by Janice Acton, Penny Goldsmith, and Bonnie Shepherd, 261–307. Toronto: Women's Educational Press, 1974.

Reynolds, Graham, with Wanda Robson. *Viola Desmond's Canada: A History of Blacks and Racial Segregation in the Promised Land.* Halifax and Winnipeg: Fernwood Publishing, 2016.

Robbins, A. C. (Arlie). *Legacy to Buxton.* Chatham: Ideal Publishing, 1983.

Robinson, Gwendolyn. *The Greater Journey.* Chatham: 2016.

Robinson, Gwendolyn, and John W. Robinson. *Seek the Truth.* Chatham: 1989.

Ruck, Rob. *Sandlot Seasons: Sport in Black Pittsburgh.* Urbana and Chicago: University of Illinois Press, 1987.

Sadlier, Rosemary. *Mary Ann Shadd: Publisher, Educator, Teacher, Lawyer, Suffragette.* Toronto: Umbrella Press, 1995.

Sangster, Joan. "Reflections on the Politics and Praxis of Working Class Oral Histories." In *The Canadian Oral History Reader,* edited by Kristina R. Llewellyn, Alexander Freund, and Nolan Reilly, 119-40. Montreal and Kingston: McGill-Queen's University Press, 2015.

Shaw, Melissa N. "'Most Anxious to Serve Their King and Country': Black Canadians' Fight to Enlist in WWI and Emerging Race Consciousness in Ontario, 1914–1919." *Histoire sociale/Social history* 49, 100 (November 2016): 543–80.

Smardz Frost, Karolyn and Veta Smith Tucker, eds. *A Fluid Frontier: Slavery, Resistance, and the Underground Railroad in the Detroit River Borderland.* Detroit: Wayne State University Press, 2016.

Stonefish, Darryl. *History of the Delaware Nation at Moraviantown.* Thamesville, Ontario: Moraviantown Research Office, 1995.

Summers, Martin. *Manliness and Its Discontents: The Black Middle Class and the Transformation of Masculinity, 1900–1930.* Chapel Hill, NC: University of North Carolina Press, 2004.

Taylor, Shakeia. "The Civil War, Civil Rights, and Black Baseball." *Hardball Times,* July 6, 2018. https://tht.fangraphs.com/the-civil-war-civil-rights-and-black-baseball/.

Thompson, Cheryl. "Cultivating Narratives of Race, Faith, and Community: *The Dawn of Tomorrow,* 1923–1971." *Canadian Journal of History* 50, 1 (2015): 30–67.

Thompson, Cheryl. *Uncle: Race, Nostalgia, and the Politics of Loyalty.* Toronto: Coach House Books, 2021.

Walcott, Rinaldo. "'Who Is She and What is She to You?': Mary Ann Shadd Cary and the (Im)Possibility of Black Canadian Studies." *Atlantis* 24, 2 (2000): 137–46.

Walker, Barrington. "Introduction: From a Property Right to Citizenship Rights – the African-Canadian Legal Odyssey." In *The African-Canadian Legal Odyssey: Historical Essays,* edited by Barrington Walker, 3–46. Toronto: University of Toronto Press, 2012.

Walker, Barrington. *Race on Trial: Black Defendants in Ontario's Criminal Courts, 1858–1958.* Toronto: University of Toronto Press, 2010.

Walker, James St. G. *"Race," Rights and the Law in the Supreme Court of Canada: Historical Case Studies.* Waterloo, Ontario: Wilfrid Laurier University Press, 1997.

Washburn, Pat. *The African-American Record Journal.* Evanston, Illinois: Northwestern University Press, 2008.

Wayne, Michael. "The Black Population of Canada West on the Eve of the American Civil War: A Reassessment Based on the Manuscript Census of 1861." *Social History/histoire sociale* 28, 56 (1995): 465–85.

White, Sol. *Sol White's History of Colored Base Ball,* edited by Jerry Molloy. Lincoln, Nebraska: University of Nebraska Press, 1995.

Wiggins, David K. "Wendell Smith, the *Pittsburgh Courier Journal* and the Campaign to Include Blacks in Organized Baseball, 1933-1945." *Journal of Sport History* 10, 2 (Summer 1983): 5–29.

INDEX

Panthers

Panthers